IRS Tax Preparer Course & RTRP Exam Study Guide

1040 Series Exam

The comprehensive guide to passing the IRS Registered Tax Return Preparer Examination

Rain Hughes, CFP® EA

FASTFORWARD ACADEMY

Published by Fast Forward Academy, LLC
http://fastforwardacademy.com
(888) 798-PASS (7277)

ISBN 10 0983279454
ISBN 13 978-0-9832794-5-7

Printed in the United States of America

About Us

Fast Forward Academy, LLC provides companies and individuals around the world with the tools to manage their professional education needs efficiently. Our principal focus is to supply rapid training and streamlined continuing education to professionals in the fields of taxation, securities, and insurance. The name "Fast Forward Academy" reflects the scope of our mission—helping students and professionals accomplish more in less time. To realize this goal, we make every effort to provide the most useful and efficient exam prep material in the marketplace, all designed to help our students *Learn Fast and Pass*.

FREE Online Question Bank

Register online at **fastforwardacademy.com** and gain access to a number of free resources that will help you prepare for your exam. In addition to our free online question bank, we have a variety of tools to help you measure your performance and overall readiness to sit for the exam:

- The ***momentum indicator*** displays your overall performance trend.
- Discover how you measure up against other users with our ***Community vs. You*** feature.
- Track your ***study time***, including time per question.
- Our ***section analysis*** report and ***opportunities filter*** help you understand your weak areas.
- The ***answers report*** tracks each question, answer, and rationale that you see.

Practice Exams

How will you know when it is time to take the exam? Take a practice exam! Using our advanced testing platform, you can create simulated exams. Once you complete an exam, you can access numerous analytics and reports to measure your performance.

- **We Provide Feedback**. See how you measure up against the community, and track your progress with detailed analytics. Every answer is tracked to measure your progress.
- Move from question to question as needed—forward, backward, or jump to a specific question.
- An exact timer keeps track of the total test time to measure how fast you answer each question.
- Reports provide performance results, rationale, correct answers, and all the important metrics you need to *Learn Fast and Pass*:

  1) **Exam Analysis Report**: View your performance and compare yourself to the community for each section of the test. This report includes performance details specific to subjects covered on the exam. Areas of weakness are highlighted so you know where to focus your time efficiently.
  2) **Exam Answers Report**: View completed exams and dive into specific questions, answers, and rationale.
  3) **Exam Time Report**: View overall time and other metrics for each exam you take. The community is also measured so you can see how your time per question compares to others taking practice exams.

Preface

The use of the singular male pronoun throughout this text is not intended to suggest any gender bias. It is used to make the text easier to read. In every instance, the word "he" should be understood to refer equally to "he or she." Likewise, all references to singular taxpayers should be understood to refer to plural taxpayers, such as joint filers or married persons filing separately, except where it is specified or clear from the context that only the singular reference is appropriate.

Introduction

Thank you for choosing our ***IRS Tax Preparer Course and RTRP Exam Study Guide***. This course, along with our **FREE** online question bank, will provide you with everything you need to pass the IRS Exam. We designed our course to save you time, utilizing the experience of Enrolled Agents, CPAs, and former IRS employees. It provides only the *essential* material you need to pass the test and leaves out unnecessary information that would only bog you down. Our course is half the size ... on purpose!

Outline Format for Study-Efficiency

The IRS has approximately 100 separate forms, form instructions, and publications that "provide much of the basic information to assist you in preparing for the examination." There are thousands of pages within these documents, yet not one is designed to help you prepare for the exam. While the rules within these publications may appear overwhelming, you do not need to remember them all to pass.

In the field of taxation, there are often exceptions, additional details, or extenuating circumstances that could affect a situation. While this course is comprehensive, it does not include every rule (or variation of a rule) that "could" appear on the exam. This is intentional. Spending time on rules that do not show up on the exam will not help you pass. In this course, we cover the relevant information you must know to pass. If you stray too far from the path, you risk losing focus on the important details needed for success. The chapters within our study guide contain comprehensive outlines whenever possible. This format helps you better *visualize* and *retain* the important points of each section, resulting in maximum study efficiency and reduced study time. Each chapter is followed by a practice quiz (and detailed explanation) to help you fully comprehend the subject matter.

Understanding the Symbols Used in this Book

A "Key Concept" you should master. This information is very important in your review.

Practical information you might want to remember.

An example to demonstrate a point or concept.

A quick quiz question on important concepts. Answers appear in the back of the book.

Your Best Strategy to Pass

At Fast Forward Academy, we believe that in order to pass the IRS exam a student must have a solid strategy which reviews the material, provides access to drill questions with answers and explanations, and then allows for exam simulation to test readiness.

The best way to *Learn Fast and Pass* is to use the Fast Forward Academy tools as follows:

- Begin by reading the study guide, one chapter at a time. Take the chapter quiz at the end of each chapter.
- Before continuing to the next chapter, access our **FREE Test Bank** – available online at fastforwardacademy.com (students with the upgrade will proceed to the **Enhanced Test Bank**)
- Use the ***Chapter filter*** to select questions based on the specific chapter you are studying. Use the ***Repeat filter*** to select only new questions, questions you got wrong, or any question.
- After answering each question, review the correct answer and explanation to confirm you are on the right track. Be sure to read the explanation, even for questions you answer correctly, as each explanation may contain additional test tips. The explanations include chapter references where you can further review the concept being questioned. The subjects in certain "bonus" questions are either covered in multiple chapters or do not appear in the book.
- Repeat the steps above until all chapters have been reviewed.
- Your goal should be to score around 80% in the test bank prior to moving on to practice exams*

*You may choose to take an exam *before* you start studying. Benefits of taking a practice exam first include allowing seasoned professionals to pinpoint study time to specific areas of weakness, as well as providing the ability to watch scores improve while studying the material. Taking a practice exam first is not a requirement.

Now it is time to take a Practice Exam:

- Proceed to the Practice Exam dashboard. Click Create Exam and then click RTRP Exam and Yes. To begin the exam, click Start Exam
- Practice exams simulate the real test and provide options to search Publication 17 and the 1040 Return Form. You can also Mark a question for later review.
- Practice Exams can be completed in one sitting, or you can save and exit, returning to the exam at a later time to complete all the questions. Questions not answered when the time runs out will be counted as incorrect.
- Upon completion, you must mark the exam as Finished and return to the Practice Exam dashboard to receive your grade.
- Now you can use the Reports button to see a comprehensive breakdown of the subjects needing the most attention. Items in pink indicate scores of less than 25%

Time to study more...Test Bank – Step 2

- Following a Practice Exam, you now have additional tools to aid you with your studies. Return to the **Test Bank** and click the **Go To Step 2*** link (located just above the question filters)

- From this step you can interact directly with the questions from your practice exams. By clicking the ***Opportunities filter*** you have access to all of the topics tested, listed in order of weakest to strongest performance.
- Select a topic from the ***Opportunities*** list (items in pink indicate less than 25%) and set the ***Repeat filter*** to "Yes, give me any question."
- You may also use the ***Practice Exam filter*** to select a specific exam and interact with the questions from that test. In this instance, setting the ***Repeat filter*** to "Only questions I got wrong" allows you to focus on the most challenging exam questions.

*You can return to Step 1 at any time by clicking the Go back to Step 1 link

The Fast Forward Academy Best Strategy to Pass is a proven study method which garners excellent results. While the steps above can be executed in various manners, following this prescribed method will help facilitate successful completion of the IRS Registered Tax Return Preparer competency exam.

About the IRS Registered Tax Return Preparer Exam

The RTRP Exam, also known as the IRS Registered Tax Return Preparer Competency Exam, is single exam administered by Prometric on behalf of the Internal Revenue Service. The test is on basic preparer competency. As such, the test will focus on the ethical responsibilities of federal tax return preparers and the completion of Form 1040 series along with the basic related schedules and forms. Tax preparers are required to pass this competency test in order to achieve the title of Registered Tax Return Preparer. The test will have approximately 120 questions in a combination of multiple-choice and true/false format. The time limit for the test is expected to be between two and three hours.

RTPR Exam Topics	Percent of Exam
Domain 1: Preliminary Work and Taxpayer Data	15%
Domain 2: Treatment of Income and Assets	22%
Domain 3: Deductions and Credits	22%
Domain 4: Other Taxes	11%
Domain 5: Completion of the Filing Process	10%
Domain 6: Practices and Procedures	5%
Domain 7: Ethics	15%
TOTAL	**100%**

Exclusive Offer for Owners of the Study Guide:

If you did not purchase the book from our website and would like to receive a substantial discount on additional Course Materials, Practice Exams, Test Bank upgrades and other products please send us your proof of purchase for this book.

Send by fax: (407) 792-2695
E-mail to: bestproducts@fastforwardacademy.com
Or call us: (888) 798-PASS (7277)

TABLE OF CONTENTS

RTRP

TAX PREPARER COMPETENCY EXAM

FORM 1040 SERIES

1 Filing Information

General Requirements · Accounting Periods and Methods · Filing Requirements · Tax Withholding and Estimated Tax · Filing Status · Personal Exemptions and Dependents

This chapter summarizes some of the general rules and requirements contained in IRS Publication 17 and Form 1040 instructions regarding the preparation of U.S. Federal Income Tax Returns.

General Requirements

Social Security Number

Enter a valid *Social Security number* (SSN) for all parties on the return, including each dependent claimed. If no SSN is available, list the *individual taxpayer identification number* (ITIN) or *adoption taxpayer identification number* (ATIN) when applicable. If a child was born and died in the same year and a taxpayer does not have an SSN for the child, he may attach a copy of the child's birth certificate, death certificate, or hospital records instead. The document must show the child was born alive.

Individual Taxpayer Identification Number

An *Individual Taxpayer Identification Number (ITIN)* is a tax processing number issued by the IRS upon receipt of ***Form W-7***. The IRS issues ITINs to individuals required to have a U.S. taxpayer identification number who are not eligible for a Social Security Number (SSN) from the Social Security Administration. ITINs issue regardless of immigration status because both resident and nonresident aliens may have a U.S. filing or reporting requirement under the Internal Revenue Code. Individuals must have a filing requirement and file a valid federal income tax return to receive an ITIN, unless an exception applies. Each ITIN is a nine-digit number that always begins with the number nine.

Filing Deadlines

The income tax return is due by the 15th day of the 4th month after the close of the tax year. Usually, this falls on April 15. If the due date falls on a Saturday, Sunday or legal holiday, the due date is delayed until the next business day. The IRS considers a paper return "on time" when it arrives with a proper address and sufficient postage and bears a postmark on or before the due date. A return sent using IRS e-file is on time if the *authorized electronic return transmitter* postmarks the transmission by the due date.

Tax Payments

A non-business taxpayer with tax due on their return can pay by check, money order, or credit or debit card. Checks should be made payable to the "United States Treasury." The IRS instructs taxpayers to write identifying information on the check, including the first SSN used on the return. A payment by mail should include a ***Form 1040-V Payment Voucher***, although it is not a requirement.

Installments

A taxpayer may request a monthly installment plan if he is unable to pay the full amount of tax owed. Installment agreements generally provide up to 60 months to pay the tax. In certain circumstances, the payment period could be longer or the amount agreed to could be less than the amount of tax owed. An installment plan is not valid unless accepted by the IRS. However, if a taxpayer owes $10,000 or less and meets certain other criteria, the IRS must accept the request. Those requirements are:

- During the past five tax years, the taxpayer (and spouse if filing jointly) has timely filed all income tax returns and paid any tax due, and has not entered into an installment agreement for payment of income tax.
- The IRS determines that the taxpayer cannot pay the tax owed in full when it is due and the taxpayer gives the IRS any information needed to make that determination.
- The taxpayer agrees to pay the full amount within three years and to comply with the tax laws while the agreement is in effect.

An ***Installment agreement*** generally requires equal monthly payments, and the taxpayer must fully pay all of the tax owed within the time left in the 10-year period during which the IRS can collect the tax. If a taxpayer cannot pay in full by the end of the collection period, but can pay some of the tax owed, he may qualify for a partial payment installment agreement. To request an installment agreement a taxpayer can attach ***Form 9465*** to the front of his tax return, or–in cases where the return is already filed–mail it directly to the IRS. If the IRS approves a request, they send a notice detailing the terms of the agreement and request a fee of $105 ($52 if payments are by electronic funds withdrawal). Lower income taxpayers may qualify to pay a reduced fee of $43. Once approved, a taxpayer may submit a request to modify or terminate the installment agreement. This request will not suspend the statute of limitations on collection. While the IRS considers a request to modify or terminate the installment agreement, the taxpayer must comply with the existing agreement.

If a taxpayer is able to pay the full amount owed within 120 days, he should not request an installment agreement on Form 9465. Instead, he can call or apply online to establish a request to pay in full. A taxpayer who can pay within the 120-day period can avoid paying the fee to set up the agreement.

Refund Deposits

A taxpayer who is due a refund due to an overpayment of tax may apply his refund to his estimated tax liability for the following tax year, or request a repayment. The IRS can mail a check; however, the fastest way to receive a refund is through direct deposit. ***Form 8888*** is necessary when the taxpayer wants the refund to go into more than one account or he wants to buy up to $5,000 in paper series I savings bonds. Otherwise, a taxpayer may enter routing and account information for his financial institution or bank directly on his tax return. The taxpayer can have his refund (or part of it) deposited directly to a traditional IRA, Roth IRA, or SEP-IRA, but not a SIMPLE IRA. He must establish the IRA at a bank or other financial institution before requesting the direct deposit. The IRS can also send a deposit to a TreasuryDirect® online account to buy U.S. Treasury marketable securities and savings bonds.

Filing a Claim for Refund

The normal deadline for filing a claim for refund or credit is three years from date for filing the original return or two years after paying the tax, whichever is later. The IRS treats payments or returns made before the due date–without regard to extensions–as received on the due date.

The return of a taxpayer filed on March 1 is considered filed on the due date of April 15. However, if he had an extension to file (for example, until October 15) but files earlier and the IRS receives it July 1, the return is considered filed on July 1.

If a claim is filed within three years after the date of filing the return, the credit or refund cannot be more than the part of the tax paid within the three-year period–plus any extension of time for filing the return–immediately before the claim was filed. If a claim is filed after the 3-year period, but within two years from the time the tax is paid, the credit or refund cannot be more than the tax paid within the two years immediately before filing the claim.

You made estimated tax payments of $1,000 and got an automatic extension of time from April 15, 2011, to October 15, 2011, to file your 2010 income tax return. When filing your return on that date, you pay an additional $200 tax. Three years later, on October 15, 2014, you file an amended return and claim a refund of $700. Because you filed within 3 years after filing your return, you could get a refund of any tax paid after April 15, 2011.

The situation is the same as in the prior example, except that you file your return on October 31, 2011, after the extension period ends. You paid an additional $200 on that date. Three years later, on October 27, 2014, you file an amended return and claim a refund of $700. Although you filed your claim within 3 years from the date you filed your original return, the refund is limited to $200. The estimated tax of $1,000 was paid before the 3 years plus the 6-month extension period.

A notable exception to the 3-year rule is an amended return based on a bad debt or worthless security, which a taxpayer generally must file within seven years after the due date of the return for the tax year in which the debt or security became worthless.

A taxpayer files ***Form 1040X*** with the same IRS Center where he filed his original return in order to claim a credit or refund for an overpayment of tax. Taxpayers use Form 1040X to do the following:

- Correct Forms 1040, 1040A, 1040EZ, 1040EZ-T, 1040NR, or 1040NR-EZ
- Make certain elections after the prescribed deadline
- Change amounts previously adjusted by the IRS
- Make a claim for a carryback due to a loss or unused credit

A taxpayer files Form 1040X only after filing the original return, and before the expiration of the deadline. The taxpayer files a separate form for each year or period involved, and includes an explanation of each item of income, deduction, or credit he uses as a basis for the claim. The taxpayer must attach all appropriate forms and schedules to Form 1040X or it will be returned. A taxpayer who files an erroneous refund claim may be subject to a penalty of 20% of the disallowance.

1.1 Joe files his 2011 income tax return on March 1, 2012. His employer withheld $9,000 from his wages. Joe did not make any other tax payments. What is the last date Joe can file a claim for refund?

Joint and Several Liability

A married taxpayer is ***jointly and severally liable*** for the tax and any additions to tax, interest, or penalties that arise because of a joint return, even after divorce. Joint and several liability means that each taxpayer is legally responsible for the entire liability. One spouse may be held responsible for all the tax due, even if the other spouse earned all the income or claimed improper deductions or credits. Relief from joint liability, such as ***innocent spouse relief***, is different from an ***injured spouse claim***.

Injured Spouse Relief

Sometimes a liability belongs only to one spouse. A taxpayer is an *"injured spouse"* if he files a joint return and all or part of his share of the refund was, or will be, applied against the separate past-due federal tax, state tax, child support, or federal non-tax debt (such as a student loan) of his spouse with whom he filed the joint return. An injured spouse may be entitled to recoup their share of the refund.

The injured spouse files ***Form 8379*** with a jointly filed tax return when the joint overpayment was—or is expected to be—applied to a past-due obligation of the other spouse. By filing Form 8379, the injured spouse may be able to get back his or her share of the joint refund. The taxpayer may file form 8379 with a joint return, with an amended return, or by itself at a later time.

Tom and Lucy expect a refund of $5,000 when they jointly file their tax return. Tom has $60,000 in past-due taxes that he accumulated prior to getting married. To prevent the entire refund from being applied against his past-due obligation, they can file Form 8379, to protect Lucy's share of the refund.

Extensions

A taxpayer may request an ***automatic six-month extension*** by filing Form 4868 (via paper or electronically) by the due date of the return or by paying all or part of the income tax due using a credit or debit card. For most taxpayers, this extends the due date until October 15.

Please note that this is NOT an extension of time to pay taxes. The taxpayer must estimate the taxes due and can submit the payment with the extension request.

- **Serving in a Combat Zone** – When individuals serve in a qualified combat zone, the filing deadline increases by 180 days after the latter of the last day in a qualified combat zone or the last day of a continuous hospitalization related to injury from service. In addition to the 180 days, a service member in a qualified combat zone can receive a deadline extension of up to three and a half months, based on the number of days remaining to file upon entering the combat zone. This period is representative of the time normally allotted for filing taxes (January 1–April 15). If entering the combat zone before the first of the year, the service member may add the entire three and a half months to the 180-day extension.

- **Individuals Outside the United States** – A taxpayer who is a U.S. citizen (or resident) may receive an automatic two-month extension to file a return and pay any federal income tax due if—on the due date of the return—he is in the military or naval service on duty outside the United States and Puerto Rico, or lives and maintains a main place of business outside the United States and Puerto Rico. Interest applies from the due date until paid. The taxpayer must attach a statement to his return explaining which situation applies.

Accounting Periods and Methods

The typical period covered by personal income tax returns is the 12-month period from January 1 through December 31, also known as a ***calendar year***. A ***fiscal year*** is another typical accounting period. A regular fiscal year is a 12-month period that ends on the last day of any month except December. A taxpayer will choose the type of accounting period (tax year) when he files his first income tax return.

Cash Method

Most individual taxpayers use the ***cash method***. A taxpayer using this method reports interest income in the year of ***constructive receipt***. Constructive receipt occurs when the income is available for the taxpayer's unrestricted withdrawal. Physical possession is not a requirement. Examples of constructive receipt include the following:

- Garnished wages (considered income received for the year)
- Debt canceled or paid for a taxpayer but not as a gift or loan (gross income to the recipient)
- Income payments paid directly to a third party from property owned by a taxpayer (treated as received by the taxpayer and paid to the third party)
- Income paid in advance (includable in gross income for the year received)
- Checks received and available to the taxpayer without restriction

Exception: Do not report interest on Series E and EE U.S. savings bonds until the final maturity date.

Jill is a cash basis taxpayer. To earn extra money she works as a photographer in the month of December. Jill shot a family portrait for the Johnson family on December 15, 2011 and receives a check for her work on that date. The Johnsons dated the check January 2, 2012 and asked Jill not to cash it until that time. Jill does not recognize this income in 2011 because of the restriction on withdrawal.

Accrual Method

Another method is the ***accrual method***. When using the accrual method, report interest income when earned, whether the taxpayer has received it or not. Income is earned when all the events have occurred that fix the right to receive it and the amount can be determined with reasonable accuracy.

1.2 Using the same facts as previous example, in what year would Jill recognize income from her photo shoot if she uses the accrual method to account for income and expenses?

Filing Requirements

Individuals

The ***gross income threshold*** determines if a taxpayer must file a return. It is the sum of the standard deduction and personal exemption amounts for each filing status. Generally, if gross income is not greater than the allowable deductions, the taxpayer need not file a return. See Table 1-1.

Table 1-1. 2011 Filing Requirements for Most Taxpayers

IF filing status is...	AND at the end of 2011, the taxpayer was ...	THEN file a return if the gross income was at least ...
Single	younger than 65	$9,500
	65 or older	$10,950
Married Filing Jointly	younger than 65 (both spouses)	$19,000
	65 or older (one spouse)	$20,150
	65 or older (both spouses)	$21,300
Married Filing Separately	any age	$3,700
Head of Household	younger than 65	$12,200
	65 or older	$13,650
Qualifying Widow(er) with Dependent Child	younger than 65	$15,300
	65 or older	$16,450

Dependents

Factors such as marital status, age, income, and blindness affect the need for a dependent to file a return. Dependents must file individual returns under the circumstances described in Table 1-2. ***Earned income*** includes salaries, wages, tips, professional fees, taxable scholarships, and fellowship grants. ***Unearned income*** includes unemployment compensation, taxable Social Security benefits, taxable pensions, annuity income, canceled debt, unearned income from a trust, taxable interest, dividends, and capital gains. ***Gross income*** is the total of *earned* and *unearned income*.

Table 1-2. 2011 Filing Requirements for Single Dependents

Single dependents – Were you either age 65, older, or blind?

□ **No.** You must file a return if any of the following apply.
- Your unearned income was more than $950.
- Your earned income was more than $5,800.
- Your gross income was more than the larger of:
  - $950, or
  - Your earned income (up to $5,500) plus $300.

□ **Yes.** You must file a return if any of the following apply.
- Your unearned income was more than $2,400 ($3,850 if 65 or older and blind).
- Your earned income was more than $7,250 ($8,700 if 65 or older and blind).
- Your gross income was more than the larger of:
  - $2,400 ($3,850 if 65 or older and blind), or
  - Your earned income (up to $5,500) plus $1,750 ($3,200 if 65 or older and blind).

Certain Children Younger than 19 Years of Age or Full-time Students

Parents can elect to include a child's income on the parent's return (Form 8814) when a child's only income is interest, dividends or capital gain distributions. If making this election, the child does not have to file a return. The child must meet the following conditions to qualify:

- At the end of the year, must be younger than age 19 or a full-time student younger than age 24
- Must have gross income of less than $9,500
- Must be required to file a return unless the election is made

- Must not file a joint return for the year
- Must not have made estimated tax payments for the tax year, and no overpayment from the previous year can apply to the tax year under his name and Social Security number
- Must not have any federal income tax taken out of his income under the backup withholding rules

Additional Filing Requirements

A taxpayer is required to file a return if any of the four conditions listed below apply, even if income is less than the amount shown in Table 1-1 or Table 1-2:

- Special taxes are owed, or certain credits must be recaptured
- The taxpayer received earned income credit (EIC) payments from an employer in advance
- Net earnings from self-employment are at least $400
- Wages are $108.28 or more from a church or qualified church-controlled organization that is exempt from employer Social Security and Medicare taxes

Aliens

The IRS considers a ***resident alien*** (not a U.S. citizen) as someone who spends more than 183 days in the United States during the tax year or has a "green card." Resident aliens must file a tax return following the same rules that apply to U.S. citizens. A ***nonresident alien*** must file special forms and adhere to a different set of rules. Most U.S. source income a nonresident alien receives is subject to withholding with a tax rate of 30%. A nonresident who receives U.S. income must file a return (Form 1040NR) if additional taxes are due or if conducting a business in the United States. A nonresident alien who is married to a U.S. citizen or resident at the end of the year can choose tax treatment as a U.S. resident.

Form 1040 and Schedules

A citizen or resident of the United States who is required to file a tax return will use Form 1040 to report information to the IRS. There are three variations: Form 1040EZ, Form 1040A, or Form 1040.

- **Form 1040EZ** – Form 1040EZ is the simplest form to use. The taxpayer must use the tax table to figure tax due, and cannot use Form 1040EZ to report any other tax.
- **Form 1040A** – Those who do not qualify to use Form 1040EZ may be able to use Form 1040A.
- **Form 1040** – All other taxpayers must use Form 1040.

Form 1040EZ

As the name suggests, Form 1040EZ is the easiest to file, but it does not apply to all situations. Only single and joint filers with no dependents are able to use Form 1040EZ. It is a tax return in its most basic form. A taxpayer does not attach any additional schedules to form 1040EZ. In order to file with form 1040EZ the taxpayer must meet all of the following conditions:

- Taxable income must be less than $100,000
- Cannot claim any dependents

- Filing status must be single or married filing jointly. If the taxpayer was a nonresident alien at any time in 2011, their filing status must be married filing jointly
- The taxpayer (and their spouse if married filing a joint return) must be under age 65 and not blind at the end of 2011
- Income is only from wages, salaries, tips, unemployment compensation, Alaska Permanent Fund dividends, taxable scholarship and fellowship grants, and taxable interest of $1,500 or less
- Cannot receive any advance earned income credit (EIC) payments
- The taxpayer cannot claim any adjustments to income, such as a deduction for IRA contributions or student loan interest
- No credits allowed other than the *earned income credit*
- The taxpayer cannot owe household *employment taxes on* wages for a household employee
- Cannot claim the additional standard deduction

TIP

Form 1040-EZ is useful only for taxpayers with simple returns. Of the three choices, Form 1040-EZ is the most limited in scope. A taxpayer who can benefit from the Head of Household filing status or claiming dependents should use Form 1040 or Form 1040A.

Form 1040A

A taxpayer of any age or filing status may use Form 1040A. Even if a taxpayer can use Form 1040EZ, using Form 1040A may be beneficial. A common reason to file Form 1040A is to claim the head of household filing status, which usually results in a lower tax than filing with a status of single. While form 1040A applies to a greater number of taxpayers, it is not available to all taxpayers. A taxpayer using Form 1040A must meet all the following conditions:

- Taxable income must be less than $100,000
- In addition to the income available for a 1040EZ filer, those using form 1040A may also have income from the following sources: IRA distributions, pensions and annuities, interest, ordinary dividends, capital gain distributions (but not unrecaptured section 1250 gain, section 1202 gain, or collectibles gain), taxable social security and railroad retirement benefits
- Adjustments to income cannot be for anything other than the following items:
    1) IRA deduction
    2) Student loan interest deduction
    3) Educator expenses
    4) Tuition and fees deduction
- The taxpayer cannot itemize deductions

- Taxes can only come from the following items:
  1) Tax Table
  2) Alternative minimum tax
  3) Advance earned income credit (EIC) payments
  4) Recapture of an education credit
  5) Form 8615, Tax for Certain Children Who Have Investment Income of More Than $1,900
  6) Qualified Dividends and Capital Gain Tax Worksheet
- The taxpayer can only claim the following tax credits:
  1) The credit for child and dependent care expenses
  2) The credit for the elderly or the disabled
  3) The child tax credit
  4) The additional child tax credit
  5) The education credits
  6) The retirement savings contributions credit
  7) The earned income credit
- The taxpayer cannot have an alternative minimum tax adjustment on stock acquired from the exercise of an incentive stock option

---

TIP Form 1040A is more flexible than 1040EZ with respect to sources of income, deductions, credits, and tax; however, it is not without limits. Substantial limitations of Form 1040A include the lack of ability to itemize deductions or report business income. As a result, taxpayers most often use Form 1040.

Form 1040

A taxpayer who cannot use Form 1040EZ or Form 1040A must use Form 1040 to report <u>all</u> types of income, deductions, and credits. The tax calculation is no different from one form to another; however, it is possible that a taxpayer may pay less tax by filing Form 1040 because of the ability to claim itemized deductions, additional adjustments to income, and credits not available on Form 1040A or Form 1040EZ. A taxpayer <u>must use</u> form 1040 if any of the following apply:

- Taxable income is $100,000 or more
- The taxpayer will itemize deductions
- The taxpayer has income that cannot be reported on Form 1040EZ or Form 1040A, including tax-exempt interest from private activity bonds issued after August 7, 1986.
- The taxpayer claims any credits or adjustments to gross income not allowed on Form 1040A.
- The taxpayer has Form W-2 that shows either of the following:

1) Uncollected employee tax (social security and Medicare tax) on tips or group-term life insurance
2) Income from Nonqualified deferred compensation plans (box 12 with a code Z)

- The taxpayer received $20 or more in unreported tips in any 1 month
- The taxpayer was a bona fide resident of Puerto Rico and excludes income from Puerto Rico sources
- The taxpayer owes excise tax on insider stock compensation from an expatriated corporation
- The taxpayer has a qualified health savings account funding distribution from their IRA
- The taxpayer is an employee and their employer did not withhold social security and Medicare tax
- It is necessary to file other forms with the return to report certain exclusions, taxes, or transactions
- The taxpayer is a debtor in a bankruptcy case filed after October 16, 2005
- The taxpayer has a net disaster loss attributable to a federally declared disaster
- The taxpayer must recapture the first-time homebuyer credit
- The taxpayer received a refund or credit of certain taxes or net disaster loss claimed as part of their standard deduction

---

1.3 Ramona is 70 years old and receives $20,000 in social security benefits. Taxes are not withheld from the payments. She has no other income or deductions. What is the easiest form she is required to file?

Form 1040 Schedules

A taxpayer may file certain schedules along with Form 1040, and in certain cases Form 1040A. Assemble any schedules and forms behind Form 1040 (or 1040A) in order of the "Attachment Sequence No." shown in the upper right corner of the schedule or form. A taxpayer filing with Form 1040 <u>or</u> 1040A can attach the following schedules to their return:

- **Schedule B, Interest and Ordinary Dividends** – A taxpayer completes this schedule if any of the following conditions apply:

  1) The taxpayer has <u>over</u> $1,500 of taxable interest or ordinary dividends
  2) Receipt of interest from a seller-financed mortgage and the buyer used the property as a personal residence
  3) He has accrued interest from a bond
  4) He reports original issue discount (OID) less than the amount shown on Form 1099-OID
  5) He reduces interest income on a bond by the amount of amortizable bond premium
  6) He claims an exclusion of interest from series EE or I U.S. savings bonds issued after 1989
  7) He receives interest or ordinary dividends as a nominee
  8) He has certain interest in a financial account in a foreign country or a foreign trust

- **Schedule EIC, Earned Income Credit** – A taxpayer with one or more qualifying children can file this schedule to claim the earned income credit.
- **Schedule R, Credit for the Elderly or the Disabled** – A U.S. citizen or resident alien with limited income who is age 65 or older at the end of the year can file this schedule to receive a credit.

The following schedules are only available when using Form 1040 to file a tax return:

- **Schedule A, Itemized Deductions** – When itemized deductions exceed the amount of the standard deduction, a taxpayer attaches Schedule A to Form 1040 in order to claim the higher amount.
- **Schedule C, Net Profit or Loss from Business** – A "self-employed" taxpayer files Schedule C with Form 1040 to report income and deductions resulting from their trade or business. To file this schedule the taxpayer must operate a business as one of the following:
    1) Sole proprietor or disregarded entity (single member LLC treated as a sole proprietor)
    2) Qualified joint venture
    3) Statutory employee
- **Schedule C-EZ, Net Profit from Business** – This is really just a simplified version of Schedule C. It is available if a taxpayer has a small business that does not have a loss. Other requirements for a taxpayer using this schedule include:
    1) Business expenses of $5,000 or less
    2) Must use the cash method of accounting
    3) Cannot have an inventory at any time during the year
    4) Must have only one business as a sole proprietor, qualified joint venture, or statutory employee
    5) Cannot have employees
    6) Cannot deduct expenses for business use of home
    7) Cannot have prior year disallowed passive activity losses from the business
    8) Cannot be required to file form 4562, Depreciation and Amortization for the business
- **Schedule D, Capital Gains and Losses** – A taxpayer uses Schedule D to report the sale or exchange of capital assets. Most property held for personal purposes, pleasure, or investment is a capital asset. Many transactions that, in previous years, would have been reported on Schedule D or D-1 must be reported on ***Form 8949*** if they occur in 2011. Schedule D-1 is no longer in use as Form 8949 replaces it. A taxpayer must now use Form 8949 to list all capital gain and loss transactions; the subtotals from this form will then be carried over to Schedule D (Form 1040), where gain or loss will be calculated in aggregate. The transactions reportable on this schedule include the following:
    1) Sales, exchanges, or involuntary conversions of capital assets
    2) Capital gain distributions not reported directly on Form 1040
    3) Nonbusiness bad debts

- **Schedule E, Supplemental Income and Loss** – A taxpayer attaches Schedule E to report income or loss from rental real estate, royalties, partnerships, S corporations, estates, trusts, and residual interests in REMICs.

- **Schedule F, Profit or Loss From Farming** – Farmers use Schedule F to figure net profit or loss from regular farming operations. This includes farm products raised for sale or products bought for resale.

- **Schedule J, Income Averaging for Farmers and Fishermen** – Use Schedule J to elect to figure income tax by averaging, over the previous 3 years (base years), all or part of current year taxable income from farming or fishing. This election does not apply when figuring alternative minimum tax.

- **Schedule SE, Self-Employment Tax** – Withholding tax for social security or Medicare does not apply to net earnings from self-employment. A self-employed taxpayer uses Schedule SE to figure the tax due on net earnings from self-employment. The taxpayer uses ***Schedule SE*** and calculates self-employment tax, which is essentially social security and Medicare tax for the self-employed. A taxpayer must include their share of certain partnership income and guaranteed payments as income from self-employment. In 2011, a tax rate of 13.3% applies to the first $106,800 of income from self-employment. A tax rate of 2.9% applies to the excess. Schedule SE is required under either of the following circumstances:

    1) Net earnings from self-employment of $400 or more

    2) Wages are $108.28 or more from a church or qualified church-controlled organization that is exempt from employer Social Security and Medicare taxes. Income from services performed as a minister or a member of a religious order is not church employee income.

1.4 Jasmine has taxable income of $150,000 in 2011. She is single, has no dependents, and claims the standard deduction. Which tax form(s) can she use to report her income for tax year 2011?

Tax Withholding and Estimated Tax

Federal income tax is a "pay-as-you-go" system. Failure to pay or a significant under-estimation of the amount owed may lead to the assessment of penalties and interest. There are two payment methods, withholding and estimated tax.

Withholding

An employer withholds income tax from an employee's pay and deposits with the IRS in the name of the employee. In order to determine the proper amount of withholding, an employee completes ***Form W-4, Employee's Withholding Allowance Certificate*** indicating the number of personal allowances and provides the form to the employer. A taxpayer may indicate an additional amount of tax to withhold from their pay. An exemption from withholding is possible by writing the word "EXEMPT" on line 7, if the taxpayer can meet both of the following conditions for exemption:

- Last year they had no tax liability, and a right to a refund of all federal income tax withheld, and

- This year they expect a refund of all federal income tax withheld because they expect no tax liability

Individuals may withhold tax on income sources like pensions, bonuses, commissions, and gambling winnings. Recipients of pensions, annuities (including commercial annuities), and certain other deferred compensation will use ***Form W-4P, Withholding Certificate for Pension or Annuity Payments*** to tell payers the correct amount of federal income tax to withhold, to choose not to have any federal income tax withheld, or to have an additional amount of tax withheld. Like Form W-4, a taxpayer indicates the proper number of personal allowances on the form. The taxpayer can check a box and elect not to withhold. The withholding agent does not send these forms to the IRS unless there is a written request.

A taxpayer who receives certain government payments may elect voluntary withholding of federal income tax using ***Form W-4V, Voluntary Withholding Request***. The following payments are eligible:

- Unemployment compensation (including Railroad Unemployment Insurance Act (RUIA) payments)
- Social security benefits
- Social security equivalent Tier 1 railroad retirement benefits
- Commodity Credit Corporation loans
- Certain crop disaster payments under the Agricultural Act of 1949 or the Disaster Assistance Act

For unemployment compensation, the payer is permitted to withhold 10% from each payment. No other percentage or amount is allowed. For any other government payment listed above, the taxpayer may choose to have the payer withhold federal income tax of 7%, 10%, 15%, or 25% from each payment.

Estimated Tax

Income from dividends, interest, capital gains, rent, royalties, and self-employment is not subject to withholding. A taxpayer with income from these sources must make estimated quarterly payments.

An individual with no tax liability in the previous full year is not required to pay estimated tax. Estimated tax liability exists when both the following conditions exist:

- Individuals will owe at least $1,000 in tax, after subtracting withholding and credits
- Withholding and credits will be less than the smaller of one of the following:
    1) 90% of the tax to be shown on this year's tax return
    2) 100% of the tax shown on last year's return (110% if AGI more than $150,000)

Jason earns $130,000, and his tax liability for the current year is $10,000, double what it was the prior year. He can avoid a penalty if his combined payments are at least $5,000 (100% of prior year liability).

The IRS may issue a penalty even if a refund is due when a sufficient amount of tax is unpaid by the due date for each of the periods as indicated in the following table (next business day if on holiday). Non-business taxpayers use Form 1040-ES to make estimated payments to the IRS.

For the period:	Due date:
Jan. 1–Mar. 31 (3 months)	April 15 (fourth month)
Apr. 1–May 31 (2 months)	June 15 (sixth month)
Jun. 1–Aug. 31 (3 months)	September 15 (ninth month)
Sep. 1–Dec. 31 (4 months)	January 15 (first month following tax year)

Margaret sold an investment property in July. She has no other income and did not owe taxes the prior year. She estimates owing $25,000 in taxes because of the transaction. If she is required to pay estimated tax, she must make her fist payment by September 15. However, she had no tax liability in the prior year, and is not required to make estimated payments.

Filing Status

In general, filing status depends on marital status. A person is considered unmarried for the whole year if–on the last day of the tax year–he is unmarried or legally separated from a spouse under a divorce or separate maintenance decree. If a spouse dies during the year, the IRS considers the surviving spouse married for the whole year and allows married filing jointly as the filing status.

Single (S)

An individual is "single" if–on the last day of the year–he is unmarried or legally separated from a spouse under a final court decree and does not qualify for another status.

Head of Household (HH)

Filing as ***head of household*** usually results in lower tax rates than those for single or married filing separately. To qualify, a person must be unmarried or ***considered unmarried*** (file a separate return and spouse did not live in home the last 6 months of the tax year) on the last day of the year and pay more than half the cost of keeping up a home for the year. A ***qualifying person*** must live with the taxpayer more than half of the year, with the exception of a mother or father. A *qualifying person* must be a ***qualifying child*** or ***qualifying relative*** for whom the taxpayer can claim an exemption. A qualifying relative must be a member of the taxpayer's family (not merely a member of the household) in order to be a qualifying person for this status. The taxpayer must pay more than half the cost of maintaining the parent's home (or the cost of a facility), if claiming based on a dependent parent.

Married Filing Jointly (MFJ)

Taxpayers may choose ***married filing jointly*** as the filing status if they are married and agree to file a joint return. Both are responsible, jointly and individually, for the tax and any interest or penalty due. While different accounting methods are allowable, both must use the same accounting period and are generally required to sign the return. All combined income and allowable expenses must be reported. They may file a joint return even if one spouse has no income or deductions. When a court decree of annulment reverses a marriage, they must amend previous joint returns. If one spouse is a nonresident alien, they must have either a SSN or an ITIN to file a joint return.

1.5 Jane and her husband Greg are eligible to file a joint return. Greg died on January 2, 2011, and Jane did not remarry. She has a 10-year old son. Can she file jointly with her deceased husband in 2011?

Married Filing Separately (MFS)

Married couples can choose ***married filing separately*** as a status if they want to be responsible only for their respective taxes. They will *usually* pay more total tax on separate returns than when using another filing status. When choosing this filing status, the following special rules apply:

- Cannot take the credit for child and dependent care expenses in most cases, and the limit on income excluded under an employer's dependent care assistance program is $2,500.
- No earned income credit.
- No exclusion or credit for adoption expenses in most cases.
- Cannot take the education credits (Lifetime Learning or American Opportunities), the deduction for student loan interest, or the tuition and fees deduction.
- No exclusion on interest income from U.S. savings bonds when used for education expenses.
- If the taxpayer lived with a spouse at any time during the tax year, the following conditions apply:
    1) Cannot claim the credit for the elderly or the disabled
    2) Must include in income more (up to 85%) of any Social Security the taxpayer received
- The *child tax credit* and *retirement savings contribution credit* reduce at a level of income equal to one-half of the amount allowable to joint filers.
- The deduction limit for a capital loss is $1,500 (instead of $3,000 for joint returns).
- The first-time homebuyer credit is limited to $4,000 (instead of $8,000 for joint returns).
- The standard deduction is half that allowed to joint filers. If one spouse itemizes deductions, the other cannot claim the standard deduction.
- The exemption amount for the alternative minimum tax is half that allowed to joint filers.

Qualifying Widow(er) with Dependent Child (QW)

If one spouse dies during the tax year, the survivor can file jointly (MFJ) if he otherwise qualifies for that status. The year of death is the last year to file jointly with a deceased spouse. In certain cases, ***qualifying widow(er) with dependent child*** is the filing status for two tax years following the year a spouse dies. This filing status entitles the surviving spouse to use joint return tax rates and the highest standard deduction amount (if not itemizing deductions). To file as a qualifying widow(er) with dependent child, a taxpayer must meet all of the following tests:

- Must be entitled to file a joint return with his spouse for the year the spouse dies
- Must not remarry before the end of the tax year
- Must have a child or stepchild (not a foster child) for whom he can claim an exemption
- A child must live in the person's home all year, except for temporary absences
- The taxpayer and the deceased spouse paid more than half of the cost of maintaining a home

---

Jane files a joint return the year her husband dies (2011). If her son meets the requirements discussed above, she can choose Qualifying Widow with Dependent Child as her status for 2012 and 2013.

Personal Exemptions and Dependents

There are two types of exemptions: ***personal exemptions*** and ***exemptions for dependents***. While each is worth the same amount **($3,700 for 2011)**, different rules apply. In 2011, taxpayers will not lose any part of the deduction for exemptions, regardless of AGI.

Personal Exemptions

Single taxpayers generally receive one *personal exemption*. If another taxpayer can claim an individual as a dependent, that individual is unable to claim a personal exemption. This is true even if the other taxpayer does not actually claim him as a dependent.

- **Joint return (MFJ)** – An additional exemption is available for a spouse.
- **Separate return (MFS)** – On a separate return, claim an additional exemption for a spouse who has no gross income, does not file a return, and is not the dependent of another taxpayer.
- **Death of spouse** – If a spouse dies and the surviving spouse does not remarry that year, the survivor can claim an exemption for the deceased spouse. An individual without gross income who remarries in the year of a spouse's death can be claimed as an exemption on both the final separate return of a deceased spouse and the separate return of a new spouse. If filing a joint return with a new spouse, the exemption is appropriate only for that return.
- **Divorced or separated spouse** – An exemption for a former spouse is not available in the year a decree of divorce or separate maintenance is final. This rule applies even for those who provide all of a former spouse's support.

Exemptions for Dependents

To claim an exemption for a dependent, a taxpayer must meet all three of the following tests:

- **Dependent Taxpayer Test** – The taxpayer cannot qualify as a dependent of another person.
- **Joint Return Test** – A taxpayer cannot claim a married person who files a joint return as a dependent, unless the married person files the return only as a claim for refund.
- **Citizenship or Resident Test** – A dependent must be a U.S. citizen, U.S. resident alien, U.S. national, or a resident of Canada or Mexico, for some part of the year.

In general, a taxpayer cannot claim a person as a dependent unless he provides more than half of the total annual support and that person is a ***qualifying child*** or ***qualifying relative***.

- **Qualifying Child** – There are additional tests for a child to be a qualifying child:
  1) *Relationship Test* – The child must be a son, daughter, stepchild, foster child, brother, sister, half brother, half sister, stepbrother, stepsister, or a descendant of any of them.
  2) *Age Test* – To meet this test, a child must be younger than the taxpayer and meet one of the following conditions:
     A) Younger than age 19 at the end of the year
     B) Younger than age 24 at the end of the year and a full-time student

C) Any age if permanently and totally disabled

3) *Residency Test* – Child must live with taxpayer more than half of year. A child who is born or dies during the year qualifies if the home was the child's home the entire time he was alive. A child is considered to live with a taxpayer when at the hospital following birth, or temporary absences due to special circumstances such as illness, education, business, vacation, or military service. If born alive but living for a moment (not stillborn) official documentation must prove live birth.

4) *Support Test* – The child cannot provide more than half of his own support.

Special rule for qualifying child of more than one person – If a child can be a qualifying child of more than one person, the taxpayer taking the exemption must be the person entitled to claim the child as a qualifying child. In most cases, because of the residency test, a child of divorced or separated parents is the qualifying child of the custodial parent. The custodial parent is generally the parent with whom the child lived for the greater number of nights during the year. A noncustodial parent may claim the exemption only if the custodial parent agrees in writing (Form 8332). The release of claim may be for the current year, and/or future years. The noncustodial parent must attach Form 8332 or similar acceptable statement to their tax return for each year they claim the exemption for the child.

- **Qualifying Relative** – Unlike a qualifying child, a qualifying relative can be any age. There are four tests that must be met:

1) *Not a qualifying child test* – The child cannot be a qualifying child.

2) *Support Test* – A taxpayer generally must provide more than half of a person's total support during the year. Under a written ***multiple support agreement***, if two or more persons together provide more than half of the support, they can agree that one will claim the exemption. The person claiming the dependency exemption must provide at least 10% of the total support for the qualifying individual, and no other person can pay over half of the total support. Each eligible person who pays over 10% of support must provide the taxpayer with a signed statement agreeing not to claim the qualifying individual as a dependent. The taxpayer will file *Form 2120, Multiple Support Declaration* with their tax return attesting to the agreement.

3) *Gross Income Test* – The person's gross income for the year must be less than **$3,700**.

4) *Member of Household or Relationship Test* – To meet this test, a person must meet one of the following conditions:

A) Live with the taxpayer all year as a member of the household, or

B) Must be related in one of the following ways:

(a) A child, stepchild, foster child, or a descendant of any of them (for example, a grandchild). Treat a legally adopted child the same as a child.

(b) A brother, sister, half brother, half sister, stepbrother, or stepsister.

(c) A father, mother, grandparent, or other direct ancestor, but not foster parent.

(d) A stepfather or stepmother.

(e) A son or daughter of the taxpayer's brother or sister.

(f) A brother or sister of the taxpayer's father or mother.

(g) A son or daughter-in-law, father or mother-in-law, brother or sister-in-law.

TIP

A qualifying relative must be related in one of the ways listed above, or live with the taxpayer all year as a member of the household. If the relationship does not violate local law, any person meeting the tests above can be a "qualifying relative," even if not a blood relative. A qualifying relative by virtue of family lineage need not live with the taxpayer.

Tax Return Preparer Competency Exam – Chapter 1 Quiz

Circle the letter next to the best answer. Remember to read the question carefully.

1) Form 4868, Application for Automatic Extension of Time to File U.S. Individual Income Tax Return, will provide the taxpayer with the following:

   a. An automatic extension of two months for taxpayers out of the country on April 15

   b. An automatic extension of four months to pay the taxes due

   c. An automatic extension of six months to file the return

   d. An automatic extension of four months to file the return

2) Which of the following statements is true regarding the filing of a Form 4868, Application for an Automatic Extension of Time to File?

   a. Interest is not assessed on any income tax due if a Form 4868 is filed.

   b. Form 4868 provides the taxpayer with an automatic additional two-month extension to file.

   c. Even though a taxpayer files Form 4868, he will owe interest and may be charged a late payment penalty on the amount owed if he does not pay the tax due by the regular due date.

   d. A U.S. citizen, who is out of the country on April 15, will be allowed an additional 12 months to file as long as "Out of the Country" is written across the top of Form 4868.

3) Lisa was married with two dependent children in 2011. Her husband died in April 2011, and she did not remarry before the end of 2011. Which filing status should Lisa use for her tax return in 2011?

   a. Single

   b. Married Filing Jointly

   c. Head of Household

   d. Qualifying Widow(er) With Dependent Child

4) Who would not be a qualifying person for purposes of filing as Head of Household in 2011?

   a. Your mother whom you can claim as a dependent.

   b. Your adopted child who lives with you, is married, and can be claimed as your dependent.

   c. Your foster child who lived with you all year and is your dependent.

   d. Your aunt, related to you by blood. She does not live with you but is your dependent.

5) You do not have to pay estimated taxes if:

a. Your tax liability for the previous year was less than $1,000.

b. Your withholding covers 90% of the tax liability for the previous year.

c. Your earned income credit will exceed your tax liability for the current year.

d. All of the above.

6) Thomas and Rebecca are the parents of four children, ages 10, 12, 15, and 22. Their 22-year-old child is a full-time student with an income of $5,600. Thomas and Rebecca provided more than 50% of the support for all their children. If they file a joint return, how many exemptions can they claim for the above family members?

a. Five

b. Four

c. Six

d. Three

7) Milton is 39 years old. He is divorced from his wife since March 1 of the tax year. They have two minor children. One child lives with Milton and the other child lives with the mother. The children have been with their respective parents from March through December of the tax year. Milton provides all of the support for the minor child living with him. The filing status with the lowest rate that Milton qualifies for is:

a. Married filing separately

b. Single

c. Head of household

d. Married filing jointly

8) John is the sole support of his mother. To claim her as a dependent on his Form 1040A for 2011, she must be a resident of which of the following countries for some part of calendar year 2011?

a. United States

b. Mexico

c. Canada

d. Any of the above

Tax Return Preparer Competency Exam – Chapter 1 Quiz Rationale

For more practice questions, visit fastforwardacademy.com and access our **FREE** online question bank.

1) **c** A request for an automatic six-month extension may be filed (via Form 4868, paper or electronically) by the due date of the return. For most taxpayers, this allows until October 15 to submit a return. The IRS will automatically allow a taxpayer who is out of the country on April 15 an extra two months to file his return and pay any tax due. Form 4868 also provides those out of the country with an additional automatic four-month extension. This is an actual question from the exam. While D is also right, the IRS considers C as the correct answer.

2) **c** Form 4868 is NOT an extension of time to pay taxes. Taxpayers must estimate the taxes due and submit the payment with the request. A taxpayer who is a U.S. citizen (or resident) may receive an automatic two-month extension to file a return and pay any federal income tax due if, on the due date of the return, he is in the military on duty or lives (and maintains a primary place of business) outside the United States and Puerto Rico. Interest is charged from the due date until date paid.

3) **b** If one spouse dies, the survivor can file jointly if he would otherwise qualify to use that status. The year of death is the last year to file jointly with a deceased spouse. In certain cases, *qualifying widow(er) with dependent child* is the filing status for two tax years following the year of death.

4) **d** To qualify for *head of household*, a person must be unmarried or *considered unmarried* (file a separate return and spouse did not live in home the last six months of the tax year) on the last day of the year and pay more than half the cost of keeping up a home for the year. A *qualifying person* must live with the taxpayer more than half of the year, with the exception of a mother or father. A *qualifying person* is a *qualifying child* or *qualifying relative* for whom they can claim an exemption. The aunt did not meet the residency test, even though she is a qualifying relative for purposes of the dependency exemption.

5) **c** U.S. citizens with no tax liability in the previous full year are not required to pay estimated tax. Estimated tax liability exists if a taxpayer will owe at least $1,000 in tax, after subtracting withholding and credits, and withholding and credits will be less than the smaller of 90% of the tax liability, or 100% of the tax liability on prior year's return (110% if AGI is more than $150,000).

6) **c** The children are dependents as they meet the definition of a qualifying child. **Relationship Test** – The child must be a son, daughter, stepchild, foster child, brother, sister, half brother, half sister, stepbrother, stepsister, or a descendant of any of them. **Age Test** – To meet this test, a child must be younger than age 19 at the end of the year, or younger than age 24 at the end of the year and a full-time student, or any age if permanently and totally disabled. **Residency Test** – The child must live with the taxpayer for more than half of the year. A child who is born or dies during the year passes this test if the home was the child's home the entire time he or she was alive during the year. **Support Test** – The child cannot provide more than half of their own support.

7) **c** Since Milton is not married at the end of the year, he cannot file either MFS or MFJ. HOH is better than Single as a filing status in terms of tax rates, and all tests for HOH are met.

8) **d** A dependent must be a U.S. citizen, U.S. resident alien, U.S. national, or a resident of Canada or Mexico, for some part of the year.

FASTFORWARD ACADEMY

It is unlikely that answering eight questions per chapter will prepare you for this exam. Fortunately, there are hundreds of questions available in our online test bank that you can access for FREE. The online test bank is an important part of our proven ***Best Strategy to Pass***.

Register for the FREE Online Question Bank

Register online at **fastforwardacademy.com** and gain access to a number of free resources that will help you prepare for your exam. In addition to our free online question bank, we have a variety of tools to help you measure your performance and overall readiness to sit for the exam:

- The ***momentum indicator*** displays your overall performance trend.
- Discover how you measure up against other users with our ***Community vs. You*** feature.
- Track your ***study time***, including time per question.
- Our ***section analysis*** report and ***opportunities filter*** help you understand your weak areas.
- The ***answers report*** tracks each question, answer, and rationale that you see.

2 Gross Income

Wage, Salaries, and Other Earnings · Tip Income · Interest Income · Dividends and Other Corporate Distributions · Rental Income and Expenses · Retirement Plans, Pensions and Annuities · Social Security · Other Income

This chapter summarizes the various forms of gross income that a taxpayer must report on a tax return. This information is based on IRS Publications 17, 527, 925, and 4681.

Wages, Salaries, and Other Earnings

Wages

Gross income includes wages, salaries, and other forms of employee compensation. Generally, the employer reports annual employee compensation to employees on Form W-2, which the employer must provide to the employee by the end of January each year.

Self-employment Income

A self-employed taxpayer reports business income and expenses on Schedule C. The net income or loss is part of gross income on his personal tax return. The IRS defines net earnings from self-employment as the gross income from a trade or business, less business deductions. A partner's distributive share of ordinary income or loss is also self-employment income. A self-employed taxpayer must withhold and pay self-employment tax on net earnings from self-employment. A self-employed taxpayer may take a deduction on his personal return for one-half of the employment tax paid. For 2011, the self-employment tax rate is reduced from 15.3% to 13.3%, accordingly, in determining net earnings from self-employment, take account of the deduction for the "employer-equivalent" part of self-employment tax (rather than "one-half"). The Internal Revenue Code lists income from the following sources as specifically <u>not</u> income from self-employment:

- Income earned as an employee
- Income from rental real estate (unless a real estate dealer)
- Dividends from stocks or bonds (unless a securities dealer)
- Payments to a retired partner that continue until death
- Income received for services as an employee of a state (one example is a notary)

Partnership and S Corporation Income

Generally, certain flow-through entities such as partnerships or S corporations do not pay tax on income. Instead, the entity files an informational return with the IRS and distributes a Schedule K-1 to each partner or shareholder. The income, gains, losses, deductions, and credits pass through to the owners based on their respective shares.

Childcare Providers

When taxpayers provide childcare, regardless of location, the pay received must be included in gross income. Taxpayers who are not employees must include payments for services on Schedule C (Form 1040). The same rules apply for persons babysitting, even if only periodically and/or just for relatives.

Foreign Income

U.S. citizens and resident aliens must report income from sources outside the United States (foreign income) on their tax return unless it is exempt by U.S. law. This applies to earned income (such as wages and tips) as well as unearned income (such as interest, dividends, capital gains, pensions, rents, and royalties). U.S. citizens and resident aliens residing outside the United States may be able to exclude all or part of their foreign source earned income.

Advance Commissions

Under the cash method, a taxpayer receiving advance commissions or other amounts for future services must include these amounts as income in the year received.

Cost-of-living Allowances and Reimbursements

Cost-of-living allowances are generally included in income. However, allowances for a federal civilian or federal court employee stationed in Alaska, Hawaii, or outside the United States are exempt from the rule and are <u>not</u> included as income. Allowances that increase an employee's basic pay as an incentive for taking a less desirable assignment are part of compensation and must be included in income.

Back Pay

Amounts awarded in a settlement or judgment for back pay should be included in income. These include payments made to a person for damages, unpaid life insurance premiums, and unpaid health insurance premiums. Employers should report on Form W-2.

Bonuses and Awards

Bonuses or awards received from an employer are included in income and should appear on Form W-2. If the award is goods or services, include the fair market value in income.

Severance Pay

Severance pay and any payment received due to the cancellation of an employment contract must be included in income. This includes any payment received for accrued leave and monies withheld from severance for outplacement services.

Sick Pay

Pay received from an employer while sick or injured is part of salary or wages. In addition, employees must include in income sick pay benefits received from any of the following payors:

- A welfare fund
- A state sickness or disability fund
- An association of employers or employees
- An insurance company, if the employer paid for the plan

However, if the employee paid the premiums on an accident or health insurance policy, the benefits received under the policy are not taxable.

Disability Income

Generally, employees must report as income any amount received for personal injury or sickness through an accident or health plan when the employer pays plan premiums. If both the employee and employer pay for the plan, the employee must report only the amount received that is due to the employer's payments. However, certain payments may not be taxable to the employee. For example, a taxpayer need not report as income any reimbursement for medical expenses incurred after the plan was established. A taxpayer may need to include reimbursements for medical expenses deducted on a prior return as income in the current year.

Accident or Health Plan

Generally, the value of accident or health plan coverage provided by taxpayers or their employers are not included in income. Benefits received from the plan may be taxable.

Fringe Benefits

An employee must include fringe benefits received in connection with the performance of services in income as compensation unless the employee paid fair market value for the benefits or law specifically excludes the payment. The IRS treats abstaining from the performance of services (for example, under a covenant not to compete) as the performance of services for purposes of these rules.

Group Term Life Insurance

Generally, the cost of up to $50,000 of group term life insurance coverage provided by an employer (or former employer) is not included in income. However, the cost of employer-provided insurance that exceeds the cost of $50,000 of coverage reduced by any amount paid toward the purchase of the insurance must be included in income. If an employer provides more than $50,000 of coverage, the employer must report the amount included in income as part of wages in box 1 of Form W-2. Employer-paid premiums for whole life or permanent insurance are included in the employee's income.

Transportation

For 2011, if an employer provides a qualified transportation fringe benefit, the taxpayer may exclude it from income, up to certain limits. A qualified transportation fringe benefit includes the following:

- Transportation in a commuter highway vehicle between the employee's home and workplace, as well as the following items:

    1) A transit pass – Include the excess more than $230 per month in gross income.

    2) Qualified parking – Include the excess more than $230 a month in gross income.

    3) Qualified bicycle commuting – Up to $20 reimbursement for each month the taxpayer uses a bicycle regularly for a substantial portion of travel between home and place of employment. Can cover expenses incurred during the year for the purchase of a bicycle and bicycle improvements, repair, and storage.

Restricted Property

Generally, the fair market value of property received for services is income in the year the taxpayer receives the property. A taxpayer does not include the value of stock or other property in income if there are certain restrictions that affect its value, e.g., a substantial risk of forfeiture. The taxpayer must report the property as income once it substantially vests (is no longer restricted). A taxpayer can choose to include the value of the property in income in the year the transfer occurs if making a proper ***83(b) election*** within 30 days of the grant date. The IRS treats restricted stock dividends as compensation and not as dividend income unless the taxpayer has recognized the stock as income. The holding period begins when the taxpayer includes the amount in income. The benefit of the 83(b) election is that future income or gains may receive more preferential dividend and capital gain tax treatment.

Employee Stock Options

Stock options grant the holder–typically an employee–the right to purchase shares of stock for a set period of time. The period is usually ten years, during which the employee can purchase the stock for a specified price determined at the date of grant. Generally, an employer grants ***statutory stock options*** under an employee stock purchase plan or an incentive stock option (ISO) plan. ***Non-statutory stock options*** (NSO) are not granted under an employee stock purchase plan or an ISO plan.

- If an employee receives a non-statutory stock option that has a readily determinable fair market value at the time it is granted, the option is treated similarly to other property received as compensation. Otherwise, the amount of income to include (and the time to include it) depends on the fair market value of the option when the employee does one of the following:

    1) Exercises the option (uses it to buy or sell the stock or other property)

    2) Sells or otherwise disposes of the option

- However, if the option is a statutory stock option, the employee will <u>not</u> have any income until he sells or exchanges the stock. The tax treatment for ISOs is more favorable than that of NSOs. Capital gain tax rates apply to a gain from ISOs if an employee holds the stock more than one year from the date of exercise and more than two years from the option grant date prior to disposing of the stock; otherwise ordinary income rates apply to the gain at the time of sale.

In 2005, Doug was granted non-statutory options giving him the right to purchase 1,000 shares of MicroMedia stock for a price of $25 per share. On the grant date, MicroMedia shares traded at $5. Douglas does not recognize income when he receives the options because his exercise price is above the current share price; therefore, there is no readily determinable market value. In 2011, Douglas exercises his options when the price of the stock is $95. He receives $70,000 in compensation, which is the difference between what he pays ($25,000) and the value of the stock at exercise ($95,000). MicroMedia should include the compensation on Doug's W-2, and withhold any applicable social security and Medicare tax.

Tip Income

All tips received are income and are subject to federal income tax. Include in gross income all tips received directly, charged tips paid by an employer, and any tips received under a tip splitting or tip pooling arrangement. The IRS also considers non-cash tips such as tickets, passes, or other items of value as taxable income, based on their value. To report tip income correctly, employees must:

- Keep a daily tip record
- Report tips to employer by the 10th of the following month if more than $20
- Report <u>all</u> tips on the income tax return

Tip income is subject to social security and Medicare tax. The taxpayer must give his employer a written report of cash and charge tips if he receives $20 or more in tips during a month. A taxpayer uses ***Form 4137*** to figure the social security and Medicare tax owed on tips he did not report to his employer, including any allocated tips shown on Form(s) W-2 that he must report as income.

Special Rules for Certain Employees

Clergy

Members of the clergy must include in income any salary and fees received for masses, marriages, baptisms, funerals, etc. Payments to the religious institution are not taxable. Members of religious organizations who give outside earnings to the organization must include the earnings as income and may take a charitable deduction for the amount paid to the organization.

- **Pension** – Pension or retirement pay for a clergy member usually receives normal treatment.
- **Housing** – The rental value of a home (including utilities) or any designated ***housing allowance*** is excludable from income. The exclusion cannot be more than the reasonable pay for services rendered. Any allowance designated for the cost of utilities is excludable, up to the actual utility cost. The home or allowance must represent compensation for services rendered as an ordained, licensed, or commissioned minister. However, the rental value of the home or the housing allowance must be included as earnings from self-employment (on Schedule SE) if self-employment tax is applicable.

2.1 Randy Lee is an ordained minister of a tax-exempt church. Randy receives a salary plus a housing allowance for rent and utilities. What does Randy report as income?

Members of Religious Orders

The treatment of renounced earnings turned over to a religious order by a member under a vow of poverty depends on whether or not the member performed the services specifically for the order.

- **Services performed for the order** – If the member performed services as an agent of the order in the exercise of duties required by the order, the amounts turned over to the order should not be included as income. If the member performed services for another agency of the supervising church or an associated institution, and the order mandated said service, the IRS considers the member to have performed the services as an agent of the order. Any wages a member earns as an agent of an order and turns over to the order are not included as income.
- **Services performed outside the order** – If a member of an order is directed to work outside the order, the services rendered are not an exercise of duties required by the order unless they meet both of the following requirements:
    1) The services are the kind of services that are ordinarily the duties of members of the order.
    2) They are part of the duties that the member must exercise for the religious order as its agent.

Foreign Employer

Special rules apply if the employer is a foreign employer. A U.S. citizen who works in the United States for a foreign government, an international organization, a foreign embassy, or any foreign employer must include salary in income. Employees of an international organization or a foreign government in the United States are exempt from Social Security and Medicare employee taxes. However, such an employee must pay self-employment taxes on earnings from services performed in the United States, even though the employee is not self-employed.

Military Pay

A member of a military service must generally report payments received as a service member as wages for tax purposes, except for retirement pay, which is taxable as a pension.

Interest Income

Taxable Interest

A taxpayer must generally report taxable interest from Form 1099-INT or Schedule K-1 for partnerships and S corporations. Taxable interest includes income from various sources such as the following:

- Bank, savings and loan, or credit union accounts
- Money market funds
- Certificates of deposit
- U.S. treasury bills, notes, and bonds (exempt from all state and local income taxes)
- Loans made to others
- Gifts more than $10 for opening financial accounts. ($20 if the account is more than $5,000)
- Interest received on tax refunds
- U.S. Savings Bond Interest
    1) Series H and HH – Report semi-annual interest payments in the year received.
    2) Series I, E, and EE – Interest is credited at maturity. Taxpayers who use the cash method of accounting may elect to defer reporting interest until maturity; those using the accrual method must report interest on U.S. savings bonds each year as it accrues.

TIP: Interest from Series I or EE bonds may be tax free if used to pay for qualified education expenses the same year. This exclusion is known as the Education Savings Bond Program, and is not available when married filing separately. A taxpayer uses Form 8815 to figure the exclusion and attaches the form to Form 1040 or Form 1040A.

Nominees

Generally, if someone receives interest as a nominee for you, that person will give you a Form 1099-INT showing the interest received on your behalf. If you receive a Form 1099-INT that includes amounts belonging to another person, report the full amount shown as interest on Schedule B. Then, below a subtotal of all interest income listed, enter "Nominee Distribution" and the amount that actually belongs to someone else. Subtract that amount from the interest income subtotal. An example of when this occurs is with a joint account with one owner indicated as the tax-reporting holder.

A taxpayer who receives interest as a nominee in 2011 must file a Form 1099-INT for that interest with the IRS with a Form 1096, Annual Summary and Transmittal of U.S. Information Returns, by March 1,

2012 (March 31, 2012, if filing Form 1099-INT electronically). In addition, the actual owner of the interest must receive Copy B of the Form 1099-INT by February 1, 2012.

In certain circumstances, a shareholder may receive dividends as a nominee on form 1099-DIV. When this occurs, the same rules apply except the taxpayer must submit form 1099-DIV to the actual owner.

Original Issue Discount (OID)

Original issue discount (OID) is a form of interest. Taxpayers include a portion of the discount as income as it accrues over the term of the debt instrument, even if they do not receive any payments from the issuer. A debt instrument generally has OID when the debtor issues the instrument for a price that is less than its stated redemption price at maturity. OID is the difference between the stated redemption price at maturity and the issue price. The IRS presumes that all debt instruments that do not pay interest before maturity are issued at a discount. Zero coupon bonds are one example of these instruments.

The OID accrual rules generally do not apply to short-term obligations (those with a fixed maturity date of one year or less from date of issue). The taxpayer may treat the discount as zero if it is less than one-fourth of 1% (.0025) of the stated redemption price at maturity multiplied by the number of full years from the date of original issue to maturity. This small discount is known as "*de minimis*" OID.

2.2 Guadalupe purchases a zero coupon bond on the advice of her broker on July 1. She pays $850 for the bond, which has a face value of $1,000 and has 5 years left to maturity. What amount of OID does she include as interest in the initial year of purchase?

Exceptions to Reporting OID

The OID rules discussed in this chapter do not apply to the following debt instruments:

- Tax-exempt obligations
- U.S. savings bonds
- Short-term debt instruments (with a fixed maturity date one year or less from the date of issue)
- Obligations issued by an individual before March 2, 1984
- Loans between individuals, if all the following are true:
    1) The lender is not in the business of lending money.
    2) All outstanding loans between the same individuals total $10,000 or less.
    3) Avoiding any federal tax is not one of the principal purposes of the loan.

Dividends and Other Corporate Distributions

Ordinary Dividends

Ordinary (taxable) dividends are the most common type of distribution from a corporation. The corporation pays ordinary dividends out of its earnings and profits, and the shareholders must report such payments as ordinary income.

Qualified Dividends

Qualified dividends are subject to the same 0% or 15% maximum tax rate that applies to net capital gain. Qualified dividends are subject to the 15% rate if the regular tax rate that would apply is 25% or higher. If the regular tax rate that would apply is less than 25%, qualified dividends are subject to the 0% rate. To qualify for the 0% or 15% maximum rate, the following must be true:

- The dividends must be paid by a U.S. corporation or a qualified foreign corporation.
- The taxpayer must hold the stock for more than 60 days during the 121-day period that begins 60 days before the ex-dividend date. (Include the day the stock was disposed, but not the day acquired. The ex-dividend date is the first date following the declaration of a dividend on which the buyer of a stock will not receive the next dividend payment. Instead, the seller will get the dividend.)

2.3 Darlene is single and has wages of $25,000 and $5,000 in qualified dividends. How much of the dividends must she include in gross income, and what is the applicable tax rate on the dividends?

Dividends Used to Buy More Stock

Some corporations have a dividend reinvestment plans that allow for the purchase of more stock in the corporation instead of receiving the dividends in cash. Taxpayers who are members of this type of plan must still report the dividends as income. If the plan allows the purchase of more stock at a price less than its fair market value, the taxpayer must report the fair market value of the additional stock as dividend income on the dividend payment date.

Money Market Funds

A taxpayer reports amounts received from money market funds as dividend income. Money market funds are a type of mutual fund, not to be confused with bank money market accounts that pay interest.

Capital Gain Distributions

Capital gain distributions reflect income paid or credited to the taxpayer's account by mutual funds (or other regulated investment companies) and real estate investment trusts (REITs). A taxpayer must report capital gain distributions as long-term capital gains regardless of how long the taxpayer has owned the shares of the mutual fund or REIT. Some mutual funds and REITs keep their long-term capital gains and pay tax on them.

Shareholders receive **Form 2439** reflecting their share of undistributed long-term capital gains. Each must treat his share of gain as a distribution, even if not actually received. Report undistributed capital gains as long-term capital gains on Schedule D. A taxpayer can apply for a refund or credit of any payments made by including the amount in the "Payments" section of their tax return, and checking the appropriate box next to "2439."

Non-dividend Distributions

A ***non-dividend distribution*** (return of capital) is a distribution that is not a payment from the earnings and profits of a corporation. It is a return of an investment in the stock of the company and reduces the basis of the stock. It is <u>not taxable until</u> the taxpayer fully recovers his basis. When stock basis reaches zero, report any additional non-dividend distribution as a capital gain. Whether the taxpayer should report it as a long-term or short-term capital gain depends on his holding period.

Distributions of Stock and Stock Rights

Distributions by a corporation of its own stock or stock rights (also known as "stock options") are generally not taxable, and a holder of such options need not report them on a return. Distributions of stock dividends and stock rights are taxable if any of the following apply:

- Shareholders have the choice to receive cash or other property instead of stock or stock rights.
- The distribution gives cash or other property to some shareholders and an increase in the percentage interest in the corporation's assets or earnings and profits to other shareholders.
- The distribution is in convertible preferred stock, resulting in a change of ownership.
- The distribution is preferred stock for some common shareholders and common stock to others.
- The distribution is on preferred stock.

Rental Income and Expenses

Several factors determine the amount of rental income to include on a taxpayer's return. The IRS allows certain expenses as a deduction against gross rental income, resulting in either a gain or loss from rental activities. Report gross rental income and expenses on Schedule E, and transfer the resulting net gain or allowable loss amount to Form 1040.

Personal Use Property

The IRS treats rental real estate property as a home, if used for personal purposes more than the greater of **14 days or 10% of the total days rented to others.**

- If the taxpayer does not use the property as a home, report all the rental income and deduct all the rental expenses. Deductible rental expenses can be more than gross rental income.
- If the taxpayer uses the property as a home, the rental income and deductions depend on how many days the taxpayer rented the unit at a fair rental price.

    1) If rented **fewer than 15 days** during the year, do not treat that period as rental activity. Do not include any of the rent as income and do not deduct any of the rental expenses.
    2) If rented 15 days or more, include all rental income and allocate expenses between rental and personal use. If resulting in a loss, not all expenses may be deductible.

        A) Personal use is use by owners, family members, or anyone for less than fair value.

        B) Any day that the taxpayer rents the unit at a fair rental price is a day of rental use even if used for personal purposes that day.

        C) Any day that the unit is available but not actually rented is not a day of rental use.

2.4 Delores rents out her summer home for 80 days and uses it personally for 20 days. She pays $600 for repairs and $2,400 for utilities. Rental income is $10,000. What was her net rental income?

Rental Income

Generally, a taxpayer must include all amounts received as rent in gross income. Rental income is any payment received for the use or occupation of property. In addition to amounts received as normal rent payments, other amounts may be rental income.

- **Advance rent** – Advance rent is any amount received before the period that it covers. Include advance rent as rental income during the year the taxpayer received the income, regardless of the period covered or the method of accounting used.
- **Security deposits** – Do not include a security deposit as income when the taxpayer receives the deposit if the taxpayer is to return the deposit to the tenant at the end of the lease. If the taxpayer keeps part or all of the security deposit during any year because the tenant does not live up to the terms of the lease, include the amount kept as income in that year. If the taxpayer designates an amount called a security deposit as a final payment of rent, treat it as advance rent. Include it as income when received.
- **Expenses paid by tenant** – If a taxpayer's tenant pays any of the taxpayer's expenses, the taxpayer must report the payments as rental income. These payments should be included as income. The taxpayer may deduct certain deductible ***rental expenses***.
- **Property or services** – If a taxpayer receives rent in the form of property or services, instead of money, include the fair market value of the property or services as rental income. If the tenant provides the services at an agreed upon or specified price, that price is generally considered the fair market value.
- **Rents from personal property** – If renting out personal property, such as equipment or vehicles, the method for reporting income and expenses depends upon whether or not the rental activity is a business conducted for profit. In general, if the primary purpose is income or profit and the taxpayer is regularly involved in the rental activity, it is a business. Report income and expenses on Schedule C. If a rental activity is not a business, report rental income as other income on Form 1040 and include any expenses as an adjustment to gross income.

Rental Expenses

- **Related expenses** – Deductions from rental income include advertising, cleaning and maintenance, utilities, taxes, interest, commissions for the collection of rent, travel, and transportation.
- **Fire and liability insurance** – If the taxpayer pays insurance premiums for more than one year in advance, the part of the premium payment that will apply to a future year is not a deduction until that year. The taxpayer may not deduct the total premium in the year it was paid.
- **Depreciation** – Depreciate rental property when it is ready and available for rent. Depreciation is a method to recover the cost of income producing property through yearly tax deductions. The property type will dictate the period used. The recovery period for residential real property is 27.5 years. The recovery period for non-residential real property is 39 years. Taxpayers may not depreciate the cost of land.
- **Repairs** – A repair keeps property in good operating condition. It does not materially add to the value of the property or substantially prolong its life. Repainting the property inside or out, fixing gutters or floors, fixing leaks, plastering, and replacing broken windows are examples of repairs. If the taxpayer makes repairs as part of an extensive remodeling or restoration of the property, the whole job is considered an improvement. The taxpayer may deduct the cost of repairs to the rental property. The

taxpayer may not deduct the cost of improvements. Instead, the taxpayer may recover the cost of improvements by taking depreciation.

- **Improvements** – An improvement adds to the value of property, prolongs its useful life, or adapts it to new uses. If the taxpayer makes improvements to the property, the taxpayer must capitalize the cost of the improvement. Examples of improvements include putting a recreation room in an unfinished basement; adding a bathroom or bedroom; building a fence; installing new plumbing, wiring, or cabinets; putting on a new roof; and paving a driveway.

Additional Considerations

- **Local benefit taxes** – Generally, a taxpayer may not deduct charges for local benefits that increase the value of the property. Examples of these charges include charges for putting in streets, sidewalks, or water and sewer systems. These charges are non-depreciable capital expenditures, and the taxpayer must add them to the basis of the property.

- **Vacant rental property** – If holding property for rental purposes, ordinary and necessary expenses may be deducted (including depreciation) for managing, conserving, or maintaining the property while the property is vacant. Income loss due to a vacancy is not deductible.

- **Uncollected rent** – Cash basis taxpayers do not deduct uncollected rent because it was never considered as income. Under the accrual method, taxpayers report income when earned. If the taxpayer is unable to collect the rent, he may be able to deduct it as a bad business debt.

- **Not rented for profit** – If the taxpayer rents a property but does not rent the property to make a profit, the taxpayer may deduct rental expenses, but only up to the amount of the rental income. The taxpayer cannot deduct losses nor carry them forward to the next year if rental expenses are more than the rental income for the year.

- **Property changed to rental use** – If a property converts to rental use at any time after the beginning of the tax year, taxpayers divide yearly expenses such as taxes and insurance between rental and personal use. Only the portion of expenses relative to the rental use is deductible. The IRS does not permit deductions for depreciation or insurance during periods of personal use.

- **Renting part of property** – If the taxpayer rents part of the property, the taxpayer must divide certain expenses between the part of the property used for rental purposes and the part of the property used for personal purposes; it would be as though two separate pieces of property existed. The taxpayer need not divide expenses that belong only to the rental part of the property. The taxpayer may deduct depreciation on the part of the house used for rental purposes as well as on the furniture and equipment used for rental purposes.

Limits on Rental Losses

The following rules may limit the loss deduction allowed on a rental real estate activity. One must consider these rules in the order shown below:

- **At-risk rules** – Apply these rules first if there is investment in the taxpayer's rental real estate activity for which the taxpayer is not at risk. This applies only if the real property was placed in service after 1986. Generally, the IRS allows any loss from an activity subject to the at-risk rules only to the extent of the total amount that is at risk in the activity at the end of the tax year. A taxpayer is at risk in an activity to the extent of cash and the adjusted basis of other property contributions and certain amounts borrowed for use in the activity. Losses disallowed because of the at-risk limits are deductions from the same activity in the next tax year.

- **Passive activity limits** – Generally, the IRS considers rental real estate activities as passive activities, and a loss is not deductible unless income from another passive activity exists to offset it. The taxpayer may carry any excess ***passive activity loss (PAL)*** or credit forward to the next tax year. However, a loss may offset ordinary income if under the following two exceptions:
    1) A ***real estate professional*** may deduct losses against ordinary income, when both of the following conditions exist:
        A) More than half of work is involved in real property trades or businesses in which the taxpayer ***materially participates***
        B) More than **750 hours** of material participation in real property trades or businesses.
    2) If rental losses are ***less than $25,000***, and the taxpayer or spouse ***actively participates*** in the rental activity, the passive activity limits may not apply. Active participation is a less stringent standard than material participation. Active participation includes management decisions such as approving tenants, deciding rental terms, approving expenditures, etc.
    3) If a taxpayer (S or MFJ) has modified adjusted gross income (MAGI) more than $100,000, the $25,000 special allowance is limited to 50% of the difference between $150,000 and MAGI. There is no allowance when MAGI is more than $150,000.

Modified adjusted gross income (MAGI) – Adjusted gross income figured without considering:

- The taxable amount of Social Security or equivalent tier 1 railroad retirement benefits
- The deduction allowed for contributions to IRAs or certain other qualified retirement plans
- The exclusion from income of interest from Series EE and I U.S. savings bonds
- The exclusion of amounts received under an employer's adoption assistance program
- Any passive activity income or loss included on Form 8582
- Any rental real estate loss allowed to real estate professionals
- Any overall loss from a publicly traded partnership
- The deduction allowed for one-half of self-employment tax
- The deduction allowed for interest paid on student loans
- The deduction for qualified tuition and related fees
- The domestic production activities deduction

Pedro and his wife manage the daily activities of his 10-unit apartment building. He collects rent and orders repairs. The loss in 2011 from this rental activity is $40,000. They also own an oil partnership generating $5,000 in passive income. MAGI is $125,000. They actively participate in the rental activity and can deduct $12,500 (50% of difference between MAGI and $150,000) against ordinary income on a jointly filed return. The remaining $27,500 is passive loss. They can apply $5,000 of that loss in the current year against other passive income, and may carry forward the remaining $22,500 into the following year.

Social Security Benefits

Only a portion of Social Security benefits <u>may</u> be included in gross income.

- **Step 1:** Determine provisional income:

    1) **One-half** of Social Security benefits, *plus*

    2) All other income, including tax-exempt interest, *reduced by* all deductions for AGI, except those for tuition and fees, student loan interest or domestic production activities

Compare provisional income to the base amounts for filing status:

Bracket Location	S, HH, QW	MFJ	Taxable SS
Above Upper Base Amount	$34,000 +	$44,000+	85% MAX
Between Base Amounts	$25,000 to $34,000	$32,000 to $44,000	50% MAX
Below Lower Base Amount	0 to $25,000	0 to $32,000	NONE

- **Step 2:** Identify the <u>lowest</u> result from the steps below, and include that in gross income.

    1) Determine the maximum amount of benefits subject to tax as indicated below:

        A) If provisional income is **less than the lower** base amount, **NO** benefits are subject to tax.

        B) If **between** the brackets, a **MAXIMUM of 50%** of benefits is subject to tax.

        C) If it is **more than the upper** base amount, a **MAXIMUM of 85%** of benefits is subject to tax.

    2) Multiply the amount of provisional income between the brackets by 50% and the amount above the upper base amount by 85%, and then add together.

TIP For exam purposes, the chances are slim that you encounter questions with provisional income falling between the upper and lower base amounts. However, you should understand the level where a taxpayer will not pay any tax on benefits, and the level subjecting 85% of benefits to tax.

2.5 ? Gertrude is single. Her income consists of $50,000 in public purpose municipal bond interest, and $10,000 in social security benefits. What is her AGI?

Retirement Plans, Pensions, and Annuities

The taxpayer must include distributions other than the taxpayer's cost (basis) from certain retirement plans or annuities in gross income. The IRS treats distributions of basis as a tax-free return of principal. A loss may arise if the entire account is withdrawn and a taxpayer receives less than his cost basis.

Qualified Retirement Plans and IRAs

For ***qualified retirement plans (QP)*** (401k, 403b, and certain pension plans) and ***individual retirement arrangements (IRA)***, basis equals the amount of after-tax contributions remaining within the plan. Contributions that the taxpayer excludes from income do not constitute basis. Distributions from a qualified plan are usually taxable because most recipients have no cost basis. If the taxpayer has a basis, the pro rata portion of each withdrawal that represents basis is not taxed. Withdrawals, other than required distributions, can maintain tax-deferred treatment if transferred into another qualified plan or

IRA within 60 days. This is commonly referred to as a ***rollover***. Any amount withdrawn and not rolled over within this period is subject to tax. A ***conversion*** is a distribution from a qualified retirement plan or IRA into a Roth IRA. Conversions are taxed as ordinary distributions.

Annuities

An annuity in a qualified plan or IRA will receive the same tax treatment afforded to those plans. If the annuity is a ***non-qualified annuity*** (funded with after-tax dollars), individuals do not receive a tax deduction for the investment; therefore, the initial basis is the total of all contributions to the policy. Factors in addition to cost basis may also determine the tax treatment of withdrawals:

- ***Annuitization*** – The process of converting an annuity into a series of periodic payments.
    1) **Accumulation phase** – Prior to annuitizing, withdrawals are removed earnings first. The IRS treats any amount in excess of basis as ordinary income.
    2) **Distribution phase** – After annuitizing, allocate the periodic payments to income and basis according to an exclusion ratio. The exclusion ratio refers to the basis portion of each payment that is exempt from tax.
        A) Under the Simplified Method, figure the tax-free part of each annuity payment by dividing the cost by the total number of anticipated monthly payments. For an annuity that is payable for the lives of the annuitants, this number is based on the annuitants' ages on the annuity starting date and is determined from a table. For any other annuity, this number is the number of monthly annuity payments under the contract.
- **Exchanges** – During the accumulation phase, a policyholder may exchange an annuity under Sec. 1031 for a policy with another provider without recognition of taxes.

George spends $100,000 for an immediate annuity. The insurance company will pay George $500 each month for the next 20 years. The tax-free portion of each payment is $416.67 ($100,000 / 240).

Qualified Distributions

Withdrawals other than ***qualified distributions*** may be subject to a 10% additional tax on the distribution. This tax applies to the amount received that the person must include in income. The payment or distribution is a qualified distribution if it meets one of the following criteria:

- Made on or after the date the person reaches age 59.5, (55 and separated from service for QP)
- Made because the taxpayer is disabled
- Made as part of a series of substantially equal periodic payments (rule 72t)
- Made to a beneficiary or to the taxpayer's estate after death
- Used to purchase the taxpayer's first home, up to a $10,000 lifetime limit

Mandatory Distributions

An owner of a tax-deferred retirement plan must begin mandatory ***Required Minimum Distributions*** from his account for each year starting with the year he reaches age 70.5 ***(required beginning date)***. The first distribution is due April 1 following the year he reaches 70.5. All other future required distributions must occur by December 31 of each year. Figure the required minimum distribution for each year by dividing the IRA account balance (as of the close of business on December 31) of the preceding year by the applicable distribution period or life expectancy.

TIP Once a taxpayer reaches age 70.5 he can no longer contribute to an IRA, and must begin taking annual withdrawals. The RMD rules prevent people from leaving money in retirement accounts indefinitely. Failure to take RMD can result in a penalty equal to 50% of the required distribution amount. A non-qualified annuity is not subject to the age 70.5 restrictions.

Distributions Due to Death

When inheriting a qualified retirement plan or IRA, surviving spouses can elect to treat it as their own by rolling the account into their names. All other beneficiaries must withdraw the entire balance of the retirement account over a specified period, depending on several factors, including age of decedent, age of beneficiary, and the type of beneficiary (i.e., individual, trust, or estate). A portion of funds within retirement plans or annuities has never been taxed or has accumulated free of tax. This amount, if withdrawn by the original account owner, would be subject to income tax. If the account owner dies, this amount becomes ***income in respect of a decedent*** (IRD) and is taxable to the beneficiary of the account upon withdrawal.

Roth IRAs

- No tax deduction on contributions
- Mandatory distributions are not required when attaining age 70.5
- Earnings inside of the Roth IRA are tax deferred, and qualified distributions are tax free when removed. Distributions from a Roth IRA are qualified only if made after the five-year anniversary of establishing and funding the account.

Other Income

A taxpayer must include certain other sources on income on his tax return. If applicable, the taxpayer should list the type and amount of each source on Form 1040, line 21.

Alimony

Payments to a former spouse that meet the criteria of ***alimony*** are included in the gross income of the recipient. ***Property settlements*** or payments of court ordered ***child support*** are not alimony and do not qualify as income or deduction items. For a more detailed discussion of alimony, see *Adjustments to Gross Income.*

Bartering Income

Bartering is an exchange of property or services. The taxpayer must report the fair market value of property or services received in bartering as income. The fair market value should be determined at the time of the exchange.

Canceled Debt

Generally, if a creditor cancels or forgives a debt, the debtor must report the canceled or forgiven amount as income. If the creditor intends the canceled debt as a gift or bequest, the debtor does not have to report it as income. A debt includes any indebtedness for which the taxpayer is liable or which attaches to property held by the taxpayer. Do not consider canceled debt as income in these cases:

- **Bankruptcy** – Debt canceled in a title 11 bankruptcy case is not included in income.
- **Insolvency** – Immediately before the cancellation, liabilities exceed assets.
- **Certain student loans** – If the creditor canceled the debt due to performance of services.
- **Qualified real property business indebtedness** – Debt used to acquire new business real property or to refinance business real property acquired before 1993.
- **Qualified principal residence indebtedness** – Debt incurred in acquiring, constructing, or substantially improving a principal residence and secured by the principal residence. Also includes any debt resulting from the refinancing of such debt but only to the extent of the prior debt. Cash taken during refinancing is not qualified principal residence indebtedness.
- **Qualified farm indebtedness** – Debt directly related to bus ness of farming, and more than 50% of gross receipts for past three years are from farming.

Unemployment Benefits

The IRS considers the amount of unemployment compensation received to be income. Unemployment compensation generally includes any amount received under an unemployment compensation law of the United States or of a state. The taxpayer should receive a Form 1099-G, Certain Government Payments, showing the amount of unemployment compensation paid.

Gambling Winnings

A taxpayer must report gambling winnings as income. Winnings from lotteries and raffles are gambling winnings. In addition to cash winnings, the fair market value of bonds, cars, houses, and other non-cash prizes should be included as income. A taxpayer may take gambling losses as an itemized deduction on Schedule A but only to the extent of gambling winnings. The taxpayer may not report a net loss from gambling.

Jury Duty Pay

Compensation for jury duty is included in income on Form 1040. If the taxpayer must give the pay to an employer because the employer continues to pay a salary while serving on the jury, he may deduct the amount turned over to the employer as an adjustment to income.

Court Awards and Damages

To determine if settlement amounts received are income, the taxpayer must consider the item that the settlement replaces. Include the following as ordinary income:

- Interest on any award.
- Compensation for lost wages or lost profits in most cases.
- ***Punitive damages*** (punishment). It does not matter if related to a physical injury or sickness.
- Amounts received in settlement of pension rights (if the taxpayer did not contribute to plan).
- Damages for one of the following:

1) Patent or copyright infringement
2) Breach of contract
3) Interference with business operations

- Back pay and damages for emotional distress received to satisfy a claim under Title VII of the Civil Rights Act of 1964.
- Attorney fees and costs where the underlying recovery is included in gross income.

Do <u>not</u> include in income ***compensatory damages*** (compensation) for personal physical injury, physical sickness, or emotional distress.

Tax Return Preparer Competency Exam – Chapter 2 Quiz

Circle the letter next to the best answer. Remember to read the question carefully.

1) Sandy received the following income this year: Wages (Box 1 of W-2) of $50,000, money won at weekly poker games of $1,000, Christmas ham (fair market value) of $22, dependent care benefits (Box 10 of W-2) of $2,000 (spent $3,000 for childcare), and group term life insurance ($40,000 death benefit) of $50. How much gross income must Sandy report?

   a. $50,022

   b. $53,000

   c. $51,000

   d. $53,072

2) John, who is 63 years of age and single, has 2011 wages of $10,000, interest income of $3,000, dividends of $2,000, municipal bond interest of $3,000, state unemployment compensation of $4,000, and Social Security benefits of $4,000. What is John's adjusted gross income?

   a. $26,000

   b. $22,400

   c. $23,000

   d. $19,000

3) Mr. and Mrs. Spice report the following items on their joint return: Net profit on Mrs. Spice's Schedule C of $40,000, Mr. Spice paid court-ordered alimony of $5,000, and Self-Employment Tax of $6,120 on Mrs. Spice's Schedule C profit. Compute their adjusted gross income.

   a. $31,940

   b. $35,000

   c. $28,880

   d. $40,000

4) Which of the following is not rental income in the year received?

   a. Security deposit, equal to one month of rent, to be refunded at the end of the lease if the building passes inspection

   b. Payment to cancel the remaining lease

   c. Repairs paid by the tenant in lieu of rent

   d. January 2012 rent received December 2011

5) The following statements about dividends received from a dividend reinvestment plan are correct except:

a. Reinvested dividends are not taxable if not removed from the plan.

b. Reinvested dividends are taxable in the year paid.

c. Reinvested dividends are taxable and are added to the basis of the stock or mutual fund.

d. Reinvested dividends are treated as ordinary or qualified dividends.

6) At their annual budget meeting, the Downtown Church voted to set the salary package for their pastor as follows: Basic salary of $30,000, housing allowance (at fair rental value) of $10,000, and maximum reimbursement for travel (reports must be filed with receipts attached) of $5,000. How much of the salary package is includible in the pastor's taxable income?

a. $30,000

b. $35,000

c. $40,000

d. $45,000

7) Debby broke her leg this past year and was unable to work for three months. During this time, she received $2,500 in sick pay from her employer. She also received $1,000 from her personally purchased accident policy. How much of these benefits is taxable income to Debby?

a. $-0 –

b. $2,500

c. $1,000

d. $3,500

8) Which of the following items may be considered alimony?

a. Non-cash property settlement

b. Payments you made under a written separation agreement for the mortgage and real estate taxes on a home you owned by yourself and in which your former spouse lived rent-free

c. Payments made to a third party on behalf of the former spouse for the former spouse's medical expense

d. Payments made for the three-month period after the death of the recipient spouse

Tax Return Preparer Competency Exam – Chapter 2 Quiz Rationale

For more practice questions, visit fastforwardacademy.com and access our **FREE** online question bank.

1) **c** Only Sandy's wages and poker game winnings are reportable income. The rest are excluded. If an employer gives employees turkeys, hams, or other items of nominal value at Christmas or other holidays, the value of the gift should not be included in income. Generally, up to $5,000 received from an employer's dependent care assistance program may be excluded from income, provided it is used to pay for eligible dependent care expenses. If the face value of a life insurance policy is $50,000 or less, none of the premiums paid by the employer are taxable income to the employee.

2) **d** Wages, dividends, interest (except municipal bond interest), and taxable unemployment compensation are all part of John's AGI; and they add up to a total of $19,000. Social Security income is not taxable unless the taxpayer's provisional income exceeds minimum base amount. Provisional income is one-half of Social Security received plus all other income (including tax-exempt interest). For single taxpayers, the base amount is $25,000. John's provisional income is $24,000, so none of his Social Security is included in AGI.

3) **a** Self-employed taxpayers (Schedule C) include the Profit or Loss From Business in gross income. A deduction is allowed for one-half of self-employment tax paid. Alimony is a payment to or for a spouse or former spouse under a divorce or separation instrument. It does not include voluntary payments that are not made under a divorce or separation instrument. Alimony is deductible by the payer and must be included in the spouse's or former spouse's income.

4) **a** Do not include a security deposit as income when it is received if it is to be returned to the tenant at the end of the lease. If part or all of the security deposit is kept during any year because the tenant does not live up to the terms of the lease, include the amount kept as income in that year. If an amount called a security deposit is to be used as a final payment of rent, it is to be considered as advance rent. Include it as income when it is received.

5) **a** Dividends are taxable as income when received. The fact that they are re-invested does not matter.

6) **a** Only the base salary is taxable income to the pastor. The housing allowance is specifically excludable from his income (as it is less than his salary and is a reasonable amount), The travel expenses are also non-taxable as they are reimbursed under an accountable plan (reimbursement is based on filed reports with proof of expenditures).

7) **b** Pay received from an employer while sick or injured is part of salary or wages. In addition, employees must include in income sick pay benefits received from a welfare fund, state sickness or disability fund, an association of employers or employees, and an insurance company, if the employer paid for the plan. However, if the employee paid the premiums on an accident or health insurance policy, the benefits received under the policy are not taxable.

8) **c** Property settlements, payments to maintain the payer's property, and payments made after the recipient's death are not alimony.

3 Gains and Losses

Basis of Property · Disposition or Sale of Property · Reporting Gains and Losses

This chapter summarizes data from IRS Publications 17, 523, 527, 537, 550, 551, and 946.

Basis of Property

Cost Basis

Basis is the amount of a taxpayer's investment in a property for tax purposes. A gain or loss is determined by subtracting the adjusted basis from the proceeds of the sale, exchange, or other disposition of property. Basis is used to figure deductions for depreciation, amortization, depletion, and casualty losses. If a taxpayer uses property for business (or investment) purposes and for personal purposes, the taxpayer must properly allocate basis based on the property use. Only the basis allocated to business or investment use of the property is depreciable. The basis of property is usually its cost. The cost is the amount paid in cash, debt obligations, other property, or services. A taxpayer's cost basis also includes (but is not limited to) amounts paid for:

- Commissions
- Sales tax, freight, installation, and testing
- Legal and accounting fees (when they must be capitalized)
- Excise taxes, revenue stamps, recording fees, and real estate taxes (if assuming sellers liability)

The original basis in property is adjusted (increased or decreased) by certain events:

- Improvements to a property will increase basis.
- Deductions for depreciation or casualty losses or claiming certain credits will reduce basis.

3.1 Tito bought a new truck and plow to earn extra money during the winter. The rest of the year, he uses the truck exclusively in his carpentry business. He paid $30,000 for the truck, $10,000 for the plow, and paid $2,400 sales tax. He claims $4,160 in depreciation on the vehicle and plow in 2011. What is his total basis in the property?

Real Property

Real property, also called real estate, is land and generally anything built on, growing on, or attached to the land. Certain fees and other expenses are part of the cost basis in the property. If a taxpayer buys buildings and the land on which the buildings stand for a lump sum, the taxpayer should allocate cost basis among the land and the buildings. The taxpayer should allocate cost basis according to the respective fair market value (FMV) of the land and buildings at the time of purchase. The basis of each asset is calculated by multiplying the lump sum by a fraction. The numerator is the FMV of that asset, and the denominator is the FMV of the whole property at the time of purchase.

TIP Since land is not depreciable, a taxpayer must allocate a portion of the purchase price to land prior to calculating the depreciation deduction. Improvements that increase the value of a structure apply only to the structure and do not increase the basis of the land.

If a taxpayer buys property and assumes an existing mortgage on the property, the basis includes the amount paid for the property plus the amount to be paid on the mortgage. The basis is adjusted by certain settlement cost as described below:

- A taxpayer's basis includes the ***settlement fees*** and ***closing costs*** paid for buying the property. A fee for buying property is a cost that the taxpayer must pay even if he buys the property with cash. Do not include fees and costs for getting a loan on the property in the basis.

  1) Taxpayers may add the following settlement fees or closing costs to the basis:

     A) Abstract fees (abstract of title fees)

     B) Charges for installing utility services

     C) Legal fees (fees for the title search and preparation of the sales contract and deed)

     D) Recording fees

     E) Survey fees

     F) Transfer taxes

     G) Owner's title insurance

     H) Any amounts the buyer agrees to pay for the seller, such as back taxes or interest, recording or mortgage fees, cost of improvements or repairs, and sales commissions

  2) Taxpayers may not add the following settlement fees and closing costs to basis:

     A) Casualty insurance premiums.

     B) Rent for occupancy of the property before closing.

     C) Charges for utilities or other services related the property before closing.

     D) Charges connected with getting a loan, such as points (discount points, loan origination fees), mortgage insurance premiums, loan assumption fees, cost of a credit report, and fees for an appraisal required by a lender.

     E) Fees for refinancing a mortgage. If a taxpayer pays points to get a loan (including a mortgage, second mortgage, line of credit, or a home equity loan), the points may not be added to the basis of the related property. Generally, the taxpayer will deduct points over the term of the loan.

     F) Amounts placed in escrow for the future payment of taxes and insurance.

The term "points" is used to describe certain charges paid to obtain a home mortgage. Points are prepaid interest, and may be deductible as home mortgage interest. Special rules apply to points paid on a mortgage to buy a main home. If certain requirements are met, a taxpayer may deduct the points in full for the year in which they are paid. Points paid for refinancing generally can only be deducted over the life of the new mortgage. Points do not increase basis.

Points charged for specific services, such as preparation costs for a mortgage note, appraisal fees or notary fees are not interest and cannot be deducted. Points paid by the seller of a home cannot be deducted as interest on the seller's return, but they are a selling expense which will reduce the amount of gain realized. Points paid by the seller may be deducted by the buyer provided the buyer subtracts the amount from the basis, or cost, of the residence. Points you pay on loans secured by your second home can be deducted only over the life of the loan.

Adjusted Basis

Before figuring gain or loss on a sale, exchange, or other disposition of property or figuring allowable depreciation, depletion, or amortization, a taxpayer must usually make certain adjustments (increases and decreases) to the cost of the property. The result is the adjusted basis.

- **Increase** the basis of any property by all items properly added to a capital account. These include (but are not limited to) the following items:

  1) **Capital improvements** – The costs of improvements having a useful life of more than one year, which increase the value of the property, lengthen its life, or adapt it to a different use. Improvements include the following:

     A) Putting a recreation room in an unfinished basement

     B) Adding another bathroom or bedroom

     C) Building a fence

     D) Installing new plumbing or wiring

     E) Installing a new roof

     F) Paving the driveway

  2) **Assessments for local improvements** – Add property assessments for improvements that increase the value of the property assessed to the basis. Do not deduct these assessments as taxes. Examples of assessments are as follows:

     A) Roads

     B) Sidewalks

     C) Water connections

     D) Extending utility service lines to the property

- **Decrease** the basis of any property by all items that represent a return of capital for the period during which the taxpayer held the property. Examples of items that decrease basis include (but are not limited to) the items discussed below:

1) **Non-taxable corporate distributions** – Also known as non-dividend distributions. This amount reflects a return of capital and reduces basis.

2) **Casualty and theft losses** – Decrease the basis of property by any insurance proceeds or other reimbursement and by any deductible loss not covered by insurance. Increase the basis in the property by the amount spent on repairs that restore the property to its pre-casualty condition.

3) **Depreciation and Section 179 deduction** – The basis of a taxpayer's qualifying business property will be decreased by any Section 179 deductions taken and the depreciation deducted, or could have deducted (including any special depreciation allowance), on the taxpayer's returns under the method of depreciation selected.

4) **Easements** – Generally, the IRS considers compensation for granting an easement proceeds from the sale of an interest in real property. Reduce basis of the property by the amount received.

5) **Certain Credits** – Basis may be reduced by the amount of credits received for one of the following:

    A) Alternative motor vehicle credit

    B) Alternative fuel vehicle refueling property credit

    C) Residential energy efficient property credit

3.2 The city of Auburndale assessed $3,500 to each resident on Park Street for new sidewalks and a community boat ramp. Ariel pays her bill in 2011. What is the amount of her tax deduction?

Property Received for Services

If a taxpayer receives property for services rendered, its FMV must be included in income. The amount included in income becomes the basis. If the taxpayer performed the services for a price agreed on beforehand, the IRS will accept that price as the FMV of the property if there is no evidence to the contrary. If the property is subject to certain restrictions, the basis in the property is its FMV when it vests substantially. However, this rule does not apply if the taxpayer makes an election to include in income the FMV of the property at the time the transfer of property occurs, less any amount the taxpayer paid for it. Property is substantially vested when it is transferable or when it is not subject to a substantial risk of forfeiture (the taxpayer does not have a good chance of losing it).

Bargain Purchases

A bargain purchase is a purchase of an item for less than its FMV. If, as compensation for services, a taxpayer buys goods or other property at less than FMV, the difference between the purchase price and the property's FMV must be included in income. The basis in the property is its FMV (the purchase price plus the amount included in income).

Involuntary Conversions

If a taxpayer receives replacement property because of an ***involuntary conversion***, such as a casualty, theft, or condemnation, the basis of the replacement property is calculated by using the basis of the converted property.

- **Similar or related property** – If a taxpayer receives replacement property similar or related in service or use to the converted property, the replacement property's basis is the same as the converted property's basis on the date of the conversion, with the following adjustments:
  1) The basis is decreased by the following:
     A) Any loss recognized on the involuntary conversion
     B) Any money received that the taxpayer does not spend on similar property
  2) The basis is increased by the following:
     A) Any gain recognized on the involuntary conversion
     B) Any cost of acquiring the replacement property
- **Money or property not similar or related** – If a taxpayer receives money or property not similar or related in service or use to the converted property, and he buys replacement property similar or related in service or use to the converted property, the basis of the replacement property will be its cost decreased by the gain not recognized on the conversion.

Bill's dog knocks over a glass of milk destroying his work laptop. His basis in the laptop is $2,000. He receives a $2,500 insurance reimbursement and purchases another laptop for $2,200. Bill recognizes a gain of $500, increasing his basis. He does not spend $300 of the proceeds on the replacement property, reducing his basis. His adjusted basis in the new laptop is $2,200 ($2,000 + $500 - $300).

Property Received as a Gift

To establish the basis of property received as a gift, a taxpayer must know the adjusted basis to the ***donor*** (source of gift), its fair market value (FMV) at the time the donor gifted the property, and any gift tax paid on it. The annual exclusion is $13,000 in 2011. The relationship between the FMV and the donor's basis determines the applicable rule. If a taxpayer receives a gift of property and the donor's adjusted basis determines the basis, the IRS considers the taxpayer's holding period to have started on the same day the donor's holding period started. If the fair market value of the property determines the basis, the holding period starts on the day after the date of the gift.

- **FMV <u>less</u> than donor's adjusted basis** – Basis depends on whether a gain or a loss occurs when the property is disposed of. The following ***dual basis rules*** prevent taxpayers from shifting unrealized losses to other taxpayers:
  1) The basis for figuring gain is the same as the donor's adjusted basis.
  2) The basis for figuring loss is its FMV when the taxpayer received the gift.
- **FMV <u>equal to or greater</u> than donor's adjusted basis** – Basis is the donor's adjusted basis at the time the taxpayer received the gift.
  1) If the donor paid gift tax on the transfer, basis increases by the part of the gift tax that is due to the net increase in value of the gift. The net increase in value of the gift is the FMV of the gift minus the donor's adjusted basis. Figure the increase by multiplying the gift tax paid by a fraction.

$$Gift\ Tax\ Paid\ x\ \frac{FMV\ at\ time\ of\ gift - Donor's\ basis}{Amount\ of\ gift\ (after\ annual\ exclusion)}$$

3.3 Jennifer's mother gave her a painting recently appraised at $12,000. Her mother originally paid $25,000 for the painting at auction. Several years later, Jennifer sells the painting to a local art dealer for $20,000. What is the amount of gain or loss that Jennifer must recognize on the painting?

Property Transferred From a Spouse

The basis and holding period of property transferred to a taxpayer or transferred in trust for the taxpayer's benefit by the taxpayer's spouse is the same as the spouse's adjusted basis. The same rule applies to a transfer by a taxpayer's former spouse that is incident to divorce. The taxpayer does not recognize any gain or loss on property transferred to a spouse or former spouse incident to divorce. This is true even if receiving cash or other consideration.

Inherited Property

With the exception of 2010 transfers electing modified carryover basis, a gain on inherited property is always long-term. Basis of an inherited capital asset is generally the FMV of the property on the date of death or an alternate valuation date, if elected by the personal representative. A ***step-up*** in basis occurs when the FMV is greater than the ***decedent's*** (person who died) basis.

The form of ownership can affect the amount of the step-up:

- ***Qualified Joint Interest*** – A qualified joint interest is any interest in property held by a husband and wife as ***tenants by the entirety*** or ***tenants with rights of survivorship***. One-half of the value of the property receives a step up in basis to FMV.
- ***Joint tenancy with rights of survivorship (JTWROS)*** – Joint tenants with rights of survivorship share an equal interest in property. As such, they participate equally in income and deductions. If one owner dies, only the portion included in the decedent's estate receives a step-up in basis. The amount is dependent upon the percentage of total consideration for the property the decedent provided and whether or not a decedent made a gift. Where the capital contribution was 75%, and the decedent did not gift any portion of the property, 75% of the property receives a step-up in basis.
- ***Community Property*** – In community property states (Arizona, California, Idaho, Louisiana, Nevada, New Mexico, Texas, Washington, and Wisconsin), the husband and wife each usually own half of the community property. When either spouse dies, the total value of all community property, even the part belonging to the surviving spouse, can receive a step-up in basis, provided the decedent's share is part of their gross estate.

3.4 Louie inherited a house from his father in 2008. His father paid $15,000 for the house in 1962. When his father died the house appraised at $625,000. Louie rented the house for three years and sold it in 2011 for $375,000. Without considering depreciation, what is the amount and character of Louie's gain or loss on the sale?

Property Changed From Personal to Business or Rental Use

If a taxpayer holds property for personal use and then changes it to business use or uses it to produce rent, the taxpayer may begin to depreciate the property at the time of the change. To do so, calculate the property's basis for depreciation. An example of changing property held for personal use to business or rental use would be renting a former personal residence. The basis for depreciation is the lesser of the following amounts:

- The FMV of the property on the date of the change
- The adjusted basis on the date of the change

If the taxpayer sells the property at a loss, the FMV on date of conversion (with adjustments) is the cost for purposes of determining basis. If the taxpayer sells the property at a profit, the original basis (with adjustments) is used. This rule prevents a taxpayer from shifting nondeductible losses on personal property to deductible losses on business property.

Securities

The rules explained below apply to most investors. Dealers in securities and day-traders may utilize different methods to account for their transactions.

- **Stocks or bonds** – The basis of purchased stocks or bonds is generally the purchase price and any costs of purchase, such as commissions and recording or transfer fees.

    1) **Nontaxable stock dividends or stock splits** – In this situation, a shareholder's percentage of ownership does not change. Allocate the total adjusted basis of all shares *pro rata* to each share. Reduce the basis of existing shares by the amount of basis allocated to the new shares. This rule applies only when the additional stock received is identical to the stock held.

    2) **Return of capital** – Also known as non-dividend distributions. This amount reflects a return of capital and reduces basis.

    3) **Subsequent Transactions** – If a person buys and sells securities at various times in varying quantities and cannot adequately identify the shares sold, the basis used is the basis of the securities acquired first. This is the ***first in, first out (FIFO)*** method. If adequate identification is possible, the taxpayer may elect to report the specific shares sold, regardless of their order of purchase.

- **Mutual Funds** – The rules for other securities also apply to mutual funds with one addition.

    1) **Subsequent Transactions** – In addition to FIFO or specific identification, a mutual fund may use the ***average cost method*** to calculate basis. Average cost reflects the average basis of all shares. Accounting for re-invested dividends or capital gains is easier with this method.

- **Options** – Gain or loss from the expiration, ***closing transaction*** (sale or trade to close position) of an option to buy or sell property, is reported as a capital gain or loss in the year these events occur. Upon expiration, if the option to buy or sell is unexercised, the IRS considers the taxpayer to have sold or traded the option on the date that it expired. The tax treatment of transactions is <u>different</u> if the taxpayer ***exercises*** the options. The option is <u>not</u> reported separately; instead, the option's cost (or proceeds) modifies the basis (or amount realized) on the underlying stock. A ***put option*** is the right to sell to the ***writer** (seller)*, at any time before a specified future date, a stated number of shares at a specified price. Conversely, a ***call option*** is the right to buy from the writer of the option, at any time before a specified future date, a stated number of shares of stock at a specified price. This adjustment depends on several factors:

    1) **Put buyer** – Reduces the amount realized on the sale of stock by the cost of the put

    2) **Call buyer** – Adds the cost of call to the basis of stock purchased

3) **Put writer** – Reduces the basis of the stock purchased by the amount received for the put

4) **Call writer** – Increases the amount realized on sale of stock by the amount received for call

Wash Sales

A taxpayer may not deduct losses from sales of stock or securities in a ***wash sale***. A wash sale occurs when the taxpayer sells securities at a loss and, within 30 days before or after the sale, the taxpayer obtains the same securities or rights (options) to acquire identical securities. Do not include the date of sale in the calculation of the 30 days. Add the basis of any disallowed loss to the cost of the new securities. This adjustment postpones the loss deduction until the disposition of the new stock or securities.

Moe buys 1,500 shares of Acme stock on December 7, 2011. He sells the shares on December 31, 2011 at a loss of $3,000. Regretting his decision, he buys 1,000 shares of Acme stock on January 29, 2012. This partial wash sale prevents him from claiming the entire loss. He can deduct only $1,000 of the loss due to the 500 shares he did not replace. The remaining loss of $2,000 increases the basis of the replacement stock. On Form 8949, he should report the entire loss with the appropriate box checked; enter "W" in column (b); enter as a positive number in column (g) the amount of the loss not allowed.

Disposition or Sale of Property

Worthless Securities

Stocks, stock rights, and bonds (other than those held for sale by a securities dealer) that became completely worthless during the tax year are treated as though they were sold on the last day of the tax year. Worthless securities also include securities abandoned after March 12, 2008. To abandon a security, the taxpayer must permanently surrender and relinquish all rights in the security and receive no consideration in exchange for it. Consider all the facts and circumstances to determine whether the taxpayer should characterize the transaction as abandonment or another type of transaction, such as an actual sale or exchange, contribution to capital, dividend, or gift.

Non-business Bad Debt

A taxpayer who is owed money that he cannot collect is said to have a bad debt. The bad debt may be deductible during the year it becomes worthless. There are two kinds of bad debts—business and non-business. A business bad debt, generally, is one that comes from operating a trade or business and is deductible as a business loss. All other bad debts are non-business bad debts and are deductible as short-term capital losses, if the debt meets the following conditions:

- A debt must be totally worthless.
- The debt must be genuine. A debt is genuine if it arises from a debtor-creditor relationship based on a valid and enforceable obligation to repay a fixed or determinable sum of money.
- There must be an intention at the time of the transaction to make a loan and not a gift. If a taxpayer lends money to an individual with the understanding that individual does not have to pay it back, it is a gift and not a loan. A taxpayer may not take a bad debt deduction for a gift. There cannot be a bad debt unless there is a true creditor-debtor relationship between the taxpayer and the individual or organization that owes the money.

- There is no genuine debt when minor children borrow from their parents to pay for their basic needs. A taxpayer may not take a bad debt deduction for such a loan.
- To deduct a bad debt, the taxpayer must have a basis in it. The amount must have already been included in income or loaned out in cash. For example, a taxpayer cannot claim a bad debt deduction for unpaid court-ordered child support. A cash method taxpayer (most individuals) generally may not deduct unpaid salaries, wages, rents, fees, interest, dividends, and similar items.
- A taxpayer can only take a bad debt deduction in the year the debt becomes worthless. A taxpayer does not have to wait until a debt is due to determine whether it is worthless. A debt becomes worthless when there is no longer any chance that the debtor will pay the amount owed.
- It is not necessary to go to court if the taxpayer can show that a judgment from the court would be uncollectible. A taxpayer need only show that he has taken reasonable steps to collect the debt. Bankruptcy of the debtor is generally good evidence of the worthlessness of a debt.
- If a taxpayer guarantees a debt that becomes worthless, he may not take a bad debt deduction for payments on the debt unless it can be shown that either the reason for making the guarantee was to protect the investment or that the taxpayer entered the guarantee transaction with a profit motive. If the taxpayer made the guarantee as a favor to friends without any consideration in return, the IRS will treat the payments as a gift and the taxpayer may not take a bad debt deduction.

Sale of Property

Calculate the gain or loss on the sale property by subtracting the adjusted basis from the amount ***realized*** to get the gain or loss. The amount realized is the selling price minus selling expenses. Selling expenses include commissions, advertising fees, legal fees, and loan charges paid by the seller, such as loan placement fees or "points." A taxpayer may exclude from income a gain up to certain levels on the sale of his ***main home*** (*see Exclusions*). A taxpayer may not deduct a loss on the sale of his main home; however, the taxpayer must report the loss on Schedule D even though it is not deductible.

Involuntary Conversion

A taxpayer has had a disposition when property is destroyed or ***condemned*** and the taxpayer receives another property or money in payment, such as insurance or a condemnation award. The IRS treats this as a sale, and the taxpayer may be able to exclude all or part of any gain from the destruction or condemnation of the main home, as explained above.

Reporting Gains and Losses

Holding Period

In general, the holding period for investment property begins the day after the day the property is acquired (trade date) or receipt of title and includes the date of disposition, transfer, or sale. Gain or loss is ***short-term*** on property held less than one year; otherwise, the holding period is ***long-term***.

Gain Recognition

TIP: Pay careful attention to the language of each exam question. Multiple questions will test your understanding of the difference between realized and recognized gains.

- **Amount realized** – The amount ***realized*** from a sale or trade of property is everything received for the property. This includes the money, the fair market value of any property or services, and debt or other liabilities assumed by the buyer.

- **Realized gains** – The difference between the ***adjusted basis*** (discussed later) and the amount realized in a sale is the realized gain (or loss) on the transaction.

- **Amount recognized** – The amount of income or loss ***recognized*** is the amount a taxpayer includes in taxable income for the tax year. Certain transactions such as ***like-kind exchanges*** and ***installment sales*** (discussed later) may defer recognition of gain.

Capital Assets

Generally, a sale or trade of a ***capital asset*** results in a ***capital gain*** or loss. A sale or trade of a non-capital asset results in ***ordinary gain*** or loss. In some situations, part of the gain or loss may be a capital gain or loss and part may be an ordinary gain or loss. For the most part, everything owned and used for personal purposes, pleasure, or investment is a capital asset.

Examples of capital assets include stocks or bonds held in a personal account, a house owned and used by the taxpayer and the taxpayer's family, household furnishings, a car used for pleasure or commuting, coin or stamp collections, gems and jewelry, gold, silver, or any other metal.

Investment Property

Investment property is a capital asset. Any gain or loss from its sale or trade is generally a capital gain or loss, unless a dealer holds them for sale. Examples include gold, silver, stamps, coins, gems, stocks, bonds, etc. The taxpayer recaptures depreciation on investment property when he sells the property.

Personal Use Property

Property held for personal use only is a capital asset. If a taxpayer sells personal use property, he must report the difference between the sale price and the basis in the asset, if positive, as a capital gain. The IRS does not permit a deduction for capital loss on the sale of personal use property.

Capital Gains Rates

If a taxpayer has a taxable gain or a deductible loss from a transaction, it may be either a capital gain or loss or an ordinary gain or loss, depending on the circumstances. Capital gains receive more favorable tax treatment than ordinary gains, to which ordinary income tax rates apply. The tax rates that apply to a ***net capital gain*** are generally lower than the tax rates that apply to other income. These lower rates are the ***maximum capital gain rates***.

Table 3-1. What Is the Maximum Capital Gain Rate?

IF the net capital gain is from ...	THEN the maximum capital gain rate is ...
Gain on collectibles or qualified small business stock	28%
Un-recaptured Section 1250 gain	25%
Other gain and the regular tax rate that would apply is 25% or higher	15%
Other gain and the regular tax rate that would apply is lower than 25%	0%

Long-term capital gains (other than gains on collectibles, small business stock, or un-recaptured §1250 gains) receive special tax treatment and a maximum rate of 15%. Ordinary income tax rates apply to short-term capital gains. Report overall capital gains and losses on Schedule D, unless reporting only capital gain distributions, which are reportable directly on Form 1040 without the use of Schedule D.

Form 8949 —*New*

Many transactions that, in previous years, would have been reported on Schedule D or D-1 must be reported on ***Form 8949*** if they occur in 2011. Schedule D-1 is no longer in use as Form 8949 replaces it. A taxpayer must now use Form 8949 to list all capital gain and loss transactions; the subtotals from this form will then be carried over to Schedule D (Form 1040), where gain or loss will be calculated in aggregate. Short-term gains are listed together in part I, while long-term gains are listed in part II. There are three categories for each part of the new form:

(A) Transactions reported on Form 1099-B with basis reported to the IRS
(B) Transactions reported on Form 1099-B but basis not reported to the IRS
(C) Transactions for which you cannot check box A or B

A taxpayer with transactions in multiple categories must complete a separate part of Form 8949, for each of the three categories above.

A taxpayer uses Form 8949 to report:

- The sale or exchange of a capital asset not reported on another form or schedule,
- Gains from involuntary conversions (other than from casualty or theft) of capital assets not held for business or profit, and
- Nonbusiness bad debts.

Calculating Net Gains and Losses

Tax rates differ, depending upon the nature of the gain and the type of property involved. Combine gains and losses in each category to arrive at a net gain or loss.

- **Short-term gains and losses** – Sale or trade of investment property held one year or less. Combine the taxpayer's share of short-term capital gain or loss from partnerships, S corporations, fiduciaries, and any short-term capital loss carryover with other short-term capital gains and losses to figure the ***net short-term capital gain*** (NSTCG) or loss (NSTCL).
- **Long-term gains and losses** – Sale or trade of investment property held more than one year is a long-term capital gain or loss. Combine the taxpayer's share of long-term capital gain or loss from partnerships, S corporations, and fiduciaries, as well as any long-term capital loss carryover with other long-term capital gains and losses, to figure ***net long-term capital gain*** (NLTCG) or loss (NLTCL).
- **Total net gain or loss** – A taxpayer may calculate total net gain or loss by comparing the net short-term capital gain or loss to the net long-term capital gain or loss. If a taxpayer has a:
  1) **Net gain and a net loss** (NLTCG and NSTCL or NLTCL and NSTCG) – The resulting gain or loss maintains the character of the larger item. Example: If net short-term losses exceed net long-term gains, the character of the resulting net loss is short-term

2) **Both short and long-term losses** (NLTCL and NSTCL) – Each loss maintains its character, either long or short-term

3) **Both short and long-term gains** (NLTCG and NSTCG) – Each gain is taxed at the tax rates described in table 3-1

3.5 Sheila has the following gains and losses for the year: $500 short-term gain, $1,200 long-term gain, $600 short-term loss, $1,000 long-term loss. What is the amount and character of her net gain or loss?

Capital Loss Carryover

If capital losses are more than capital gains, a taxpayer may claim a capital loss deduction. The allowable capital loss deduction, figured on Schedule D, is the lesser of the following:

- $3,000 ($1,500 if taxpayer is married and files a separate return)
- The taxpayer's total net loss, as shown on Schedule D

A taxpayer may use his total net loss to reduce income dollar for dollar, up to the $3,000 limit. If the total net loss exceeds the yearly limit on capital loss deductions, carry the unused part over to the next year and treat it as though it had incurred in that next year. If part of the loss is still unused, the taxpayer may carry the unused part over to later years until none of the loss remains. When calculating the amount of any capital loss carryover to the next year, consider the current year's allowable deduction, whether or not the taxpayer has claimed the allowable deduction. When a taxpayer carries over a loss, it remains long term or short term. Any long-term capital losses carried over to the next tax year will reduce that year's long-term capital gains before it reduces that year's short-term capital gains. In calculating the capital loss carryover, a taxpayer should use the short-term capital losses first, even if the taxpayer incurred those losses after a long-term capital loss. If a taxpayer has not reached the limit on the capital loss deduction after using the short-term capital losses, use the long-term capital losses until the taxpayer has reached the limit.

Sheila has both long and short- term capital losses in 2011. Her net STCL is $5,000 and a net LTCL is $10,000. She can only deduct $3,000 in the current year and must use her short-term loss first. She carries $2,000 STCL and $10,000 LTCL forward to 2012.

Passive Activity Losses

Taxpayers report capital gains or losses from a passive activity on Form 8582. Passive activities occur when there is income from certain businesses where no material participation occurs. Passive losses are not deductible unless the taxpayer has offsetting income from other passive activities.

Section 1244 Small Business Stock

Certain eligible C corporations with gross assets under $50 million may qualify for special treatment under ***Section 1244*** as ***qualified small business stock (QSB)***. If so, any gain on the sale of stock is a capital gain if the stock is a capital asset. A taxpayer may deduct the loss on the sale, trade, or worthlessness of Section 1244 stock as an ordinary loss, rather than as a capital loss.

- **Ordinary loss limit** – The amount a taxpayer may deduct as an ordinary loss is limited to $50,000 each year. On a joint return, the limit is $100,000, even if only one spouse has this type of loss.

- Certain corporations do not qualify, such as a REIT, REMIC, RIC, DISC, FASIT, cooperative, or corporation electing treatment as a possessions corporation.
- The C corporation must be an active business using at least 80% of assets in the active conduct of a qualified trade or business. The following trades or businesses do not qualify:
    1) Services performed in the fields of health, law, engineering, architecture, accounting, actuarial science, performing arts, consulting, athletics, financial services, or brokerage services
    2) One whose principal asset is the reputation or skill of one or more employees
    3) Any banking, insurance, financing, leasing, investing, or similar business
    4) Any farming business (including the business of raising or harvesting trees)
    5) Oil or gas operations if percentage depletion can be claimed
    6) Any business of operating a hotel, motel, restaurant, or similar business

Section 1202 Exclusion

A taxpayer selling QSB stock held for more than five years can exclude up to 50% of the gain from income. Prior to 2009, QSB stock did not have a big advantage from a tax perspective because taxpayers would report gains on Schedule D (Form 1040) subject to the 28% rate. The result was an effective tax rate of 14%, not far from the maximum 15% tax rate on capital gains.

TIP For stock acquired after September 27, 2010, and before January 1, 2011, the *2010 Small Business Jobs Act* provides an exclusion of 100%. The *2010 Tax Relief Act* extends this through January 1, 2012, allowing QSB shareholders to exclude 100% of gains. Since the rule depends on date of aquisitions, you should pay extra attention to the date the shareholder aquires his shares.

Tax Return Preparer Competency Exam – Chapter 3 Quiz

Circle the letter next to the best answer. Remember to read the question carefully.

1) After a year of ownership, George and Marie sold a personal pleasure boat for $50,000. They bought the boat from a dealer for $100,000. What is the amount of loss they recognize on the sale?

   a. None

   b. $50,000

   c. $40,000

   d. $30,000

2) Connor purchased Flora stock in 2004 and sold it in 2011. In 2011, he also traded in a copy machine that he had been using in his business since 2004 for a new model. On December 15, 2011, he inherited 35 shares of Fauna Laboratories stock. What is the holding period for these properties?

   a. All short term.

   b. Flora stock long term, copy machine and Fauna stock short term.

   c. Flora and Fauna stock long term; copy machine short term.

   d. All long term.

3) If you purchase stock of a small corporation meeting the requirements of Section 1244 (small business) stock, and you sell that stock at a loss, the loss from that stock will be reported as:

   a. Long-term loss.

   b. Ordinary loss.

   c. Short-term loss.

   d. Ordinary loss subject to limitations.

4) If 100 shares of stock are purchased February 14, 2010, what is the earliest date on which the stock can be sold and the gain or losses qualify for the long-term holding period?

   a. August 14, 2011

   b. February 15, 2011

   c. February 14, 2011

   d. August 15, 2011

5) Rose has the following transactions during the year:

- Sale of ACB stock (basis $400) $800, commission pa d on sale of ACB stock. $50
- Received 200 extra shares of DEF in stock split (fair market value). $800
- Decrease in value of GHI mutual Fund. $600
- JKL stock declared worthless (basis $700). (no stock value) $0

What is the net gain or loss Rose will claim on her Schedule D?

a. $350 loss

b. $1,000 gain

c. $300 gain

d. $650 loss

6) For 2011, a taxpayer in the 15% tax bracket who has net long term capital gains on the sale of publicly traded stocks will pay a maximum rate of:

a. 15%

b. 20%

c. 28%

d. 0%

7) The state condemned Joe's property. Joe did not hold the property for use in a trade or business or for investment. The adjusted basis of the property was $26,000. The state paid Joe $36,000 in 2011. Joe realized a gain of $10,000. Joe bought like-kind property for $35,000 in 2011 for the purpose of replacing the condemned property. Joe also made a proper Internal Revenue Code Section 1033 election to defer gain from the condemnation on his 2010 tax return. In 2011, what is the net taxable gain and where must Joe report it?

a. $36,000 on Form 8949

b. $10,000 on line 21 of the Form 1040

c. $1,000 Form 8949

d. $26,000 on Form 4797 – Sale of Business Property

8) To determine net capital gains/losses for the year:

a. Net all capital gains, both long-term and short-term, together

b. Net short-term gains/losses and long-term gains/losses separately, then combine

c. Net short-term gains/losses and long-term gains/losses and report only any net gains

d. Net all gain transactions together and all loss transactions together, then combine

Tax Return Preparer Competency Exam – Chapter 3 Quiz Rationale

For more practice questions, visit fastforwardacademy.com and access our FREE online question bank.

1) **a** Property held for personal use only is a capital asset. If a taxpayer sells personal use property, he must report the difference between the sale price and the basis in the asset, if positive, as a capital gain. The IRS does not permit a deduction for capital loss on the sale of personal use property.

2) **d** The gain on inherited property is always a long-term gain or loss when sold, no matter how long you actually hold it. The stock bought in 2004 and sold in 2011 was held long-term. The copier was also held long-term.

3) **d** Certain C corporations with gross assets under $50 million may qualify under *Section 1244* as *qualified small business stock*. If so, any gain on the sale of stock is a capital gain if the stock is a capital asset. A taxpayer may deduct as an ordinary loss, rather than as a capital loss, the loss on the sale, trade, or worthlessness of Section 1244 stock. Limited to $50,000/yr ($100,000/yr MFJ).

4) **b** If you hold investment property more than 1 year, any capital gain or loss is a long-term capital gain or loss. If you hold the property 1 year or less, any capital gain or loss is a short-term capital gain or loss. To determine how long you held the investment property, begin counting on the date after the day you acquired the property. The day you disposed of the property is part of your holding period.

5) **a** No gain or loss is realized when a stock splits or investments decrease in value. The net gain on the ABC transaction is $350. The JKL transaction is a $700 loss. The NET of these is a $350 loss.

6) **d** For 2011, the maximum capital gain rate is 0% for a taxpayer in the 15% bracket.

28% Gain on collectibles or qualified small business stock
25% Un-recaptured section 1250 gain
15% Other gain and the regular tax rate that would apply is 25% or higher
0% Other gain and the regular tax rate that would apply is lower than 25%

7) **c** Joe has a taxable gain of $1,000 (received $36,000 from the state and bought like-kind property for $35,000). Long or short-term gains are reported on Form 8949, and carried to Schedule D.

8) **b** A taxpayer may calculate total net gain or loss by comparing the net short-term capital gain or loss to the net long-term capital gain or loss. The resulting gain or loss maintains the character of the larger item. If both are gains, each is taxed at the applicable rates. If both are losses, each maintains its character, either long or short-term.

4 Items Excluded from Gross Income

Items Excluded from Gross Income · Municipal Bond Interest · Gain on Sale of Main Home · Discharge of Qualified Principal Residence Indebtedness · Employee Achievement Awards · Fringe Benefits · Housing Allowance for Members of Clergy · Military and Government Disability Pensions · Education Related Benefits · Workers' Compensation · Compensation for Sickness and Injury · Life Insurance · Foreign Earned Income Exclusion

This chapter summarizes the items specifically excluded from gross income as outlined in Publications 15B, 17, 54, 547, and 970.

Items Excluded from Gross Income

Certain forms of income are not subject to federal income tax. An ***exclusion*** item is any income that is specifically not taxed. A few of the major exclusions from income are as follows:

- **Municipal bond interest** – Interest from state and local government bonds is generally excluded.
- **Gain on sale of main home** – Up to $500,000 for qualifying married filers.
- **Discharge of debt due to bankruptcy or insolvency**
- **Discharge of qualified principal residence indebtedness** – Up to $2 million.
- **Social Security benefits** – Up to 85% of benefits may be included in gross income; therefore, exclude a minimum of 15% from gross income.
- **Employee achievement awards** – Up to $1,600 for length of service or safety achievement.
- **Fringe benefits** – Certain employer-provided fringe benefits are specifically excluded.
- **Housing allowance for member of clergy** – A reasonable housing allowance may be excluded.
- **Military and government disability pensions** – Must not be based on years of service.
- **Veterans (VA) benefits** – Does not include <u>any</u> veterans' benefits paid under any law, regulation, or administrative practice administered by the Department of Veterans Affairs (VA) in income.
- **Gifts and inheritances** – Generally, property received as a gift, bequest, or inheritance.
- **Scholarships and fellowships** – Exempt if used for qualified educational expenses.
- **Distributions from Coverdell ESA or 529 Plan** – When taxpayer uses distributions to pay for qualified educational expenses of the designated beneficiary.
- **Interest on Series EE and I savings bonds** – When used for qualified higher education expenses.
- **Workers' compensation** – Payments for occupational sickness or injury under the workers' compensation act.

- **Compensation for sickness or injury** – Compensatory damages from a lawsuit, benefits under a health insurance plan where taxpayer paid the premiums or reimbursements for medical care.
- **Welfare or public assistance** – Exclude unless payment for services or obtained fraudulently.
- **Life insurance proceeds** – Death payouts are generally tax free to beneficiary.
- **Accelerated death benefits** – Exclude payments to the terminally or chronically ill.
- **Casualty insurance** – Exclude insurance settlements received to compensate for damaged or stolen property from income. However, include in income any payments for living expenses that are more than the temporary increase in actual living expenses.
- **Qualified disaster relief payments** – Due to terrorist or military action, federally declared disaster area, or an accident involving a common carrier determined to be catastrophic.
- **Property settlements** – A taxpayer does not recognize any gain on a transfer of property to a spouse due to divorce. However, any gain on later distribution or sale of the property may be taxable.
- **Child support** – Child support payments are excluded.
- **Foster care** – In general, exclude payments received as a provider of foster care.
- **Reimbursements for certain employment-related expenses** – Exclude from the employee's income any ordinary and necessary business expenses related to travel, meals, and entertainment paid by the employee and later reimbursed under an employer's ***accountable plan***.
- **Foreign earned income exclusion** – Up to $92,900 ($185,800 MFJ) of foreign earnings in 2011.

Municipal Bond Interest

Generally, interest on a bond used to finance government operations is not taxable if a state, the District of Columbia, a U.S. possession, or any of their political subdivisions issues the bond for a public purpose. Even if interest is not subject tax, capital gain or loss may apply when sold. Political subdivisions include:

- Port authorities
- Toll road commissions
- Utility services authorities
- Community redevelopment agencies
- Qualified volunteer fire departments (for certain obligations issued after 1980)

Interest on bonds used for most private activities is not exempt from income tax. A bond is generally considered a ***private activity bond*** if the amount of the proceeds to finance loans to persons other than government units is more than 5% of the proceeds or $5 million (whichever is less). Private activity bonds are often used to build a sports facility or industrial park, airport, for profit hospital, etc.

Interest on a bond to finance a bridge is exempt from federal income tax. Interest on a bond to build a new sports arena is taxable. Report both on Form 1040, but exclude exempt interest from income.

Gain on Sale of Main Home

A taxpayer who meets certain qualifications may exclude gains on the sale of a principal residence. This is a ***Section 121 exclusion***. Usually, the home in which the taxpayer lives most of the time is the main home. In addition to a house, a main home may also be a condominium, cooperative apartment, houseboat, or mobile home. If a taxpayer uses only part of the property as a main home, these rules apply only to the gain or loss on the sale of that part.

The taxpayer must own and live in the property as his ***main home*** for at least two years during the five-year period ending on the date of sale.

Ownership and Use Tests

During the five-year period ending on the date of the sale, the taxpayer must meet the following ownership and use tests in order to claim the exclusion:

- **Ownership test** – Owned the home for at least two years.
- **Use test** – Lived in the home as a main home for at least two years. Occupancy does not have to be consecutive so long as periods of residence total 24 months (730 days). Occupancy does not have to begin on, or end on, the dates of purchase or sale of the property.
    1) Taxpayers with occupancy of less than two years may claim a reduced exclusion if the move is due to unexpected changes in employment, health, or other unforeseen circumstances.
    2) Certain members of the military, intelligence community, or Peace Corps volunteers may suspend the five-year test by up to 10 additional years if on qualified official extended duty.

Maximum Exclusion

- Taxpayers may exclude up to $250,000 of the gain if all of the following are true:
    1) The taxpayer meets the ownership test.
    2) The taxpayer meets the use test.
    3) The taxpayer did not exclude the gain from the sale of another home during the two-year period ending on the date of the sale.
- Taxpayers may exclude up to $500,000 of the gain if all of the following are true:
    1) The taxpayer is married and files a joint return for the year.
    2) Either the taxpayer or spouse meets the ownership test.
    3) Both the taxpayer and spouse meet the use test.
    4) During the two-year period ending on the date of the sale, neither taxpayer nor spouse excluded gain from the sale of another home.

4.1 Lucas and Lila sell their summer home (they spent 4 months there every summer for the past 10 years) for $750,000. Their original cost was $175,000. How much gain do they recognize in the year of sale?

Periods of Nonqualified Use

Generally, the gain from the sale or exchange of a main home will not qualify for the exclusion to the extent that the taxpayer allocates gains to periods of nonqualified use. Nonqualified use is any period after December 31, 2008, during which the taxpayer does not use the property as his main home. Allocate the gain resulting from the sale of the property between qualified and nonqualified use periods based on the amount of time the taxpayer held property for qualified and nonqualified use. Gain from the sale or exchange of a main home allocable to periods of qualified use will continue to qualify for the exclusion for the sale of a main home. Gain from the sale or exchange of property allocable to nonqualified use will not qualify for the exclusion.

- A period of nonqualified use does not include:
    1) Any portion of the five-year period ending on the date of the sale or exchange that is after the last date the taxpayer (or spouse) used the property as a main home
    2) Any period (not to exceed an aggregate period of 10 years) during which taxpayer or spouse is serving on qualified official extended duty:
        A) As a member of the uniformed services,
        B) As a member of the Foreign Service of the United States, or
        C) As an employee of the intelligence community; and
        D) Any other period of temporary absence (not to exceed an aggregate period of two years) due to change of employment, health conditions, or such other unforeseen circumstances as may be specified by the IRS.
- To figure the portion of the gain that is allocated to the period of nonqualified use, multiply the gain by the following fraction:

$$\frac{total\ nonqualified\ use\ during\ period\ of\ ownership\ after\ 2008}{total\ period\ of\ ownership}$$

Business Use or Rental of Home

A taxpayer may be able to exclude gain from the sale of a home that he has used for business or to produce rental income. However, a taxpayer must meet the ownership and use tests. If a taxpayer is entitled to take depreciation deductions because his main home was used for business purposes or as rental property (even if he did not actually claim them), he may not exclude the part of the gain equal to any depreciation allowed or allowable as a deduction for periods after May 6, 1997. If the taxpayer can show, by adequate records or other evidence, that the depreciation allowed was less than the amount allowable, the amount a taxpayer may not exclude is the amount allowed.

4.2 Sarah who is single, paid $250,000 for her residence in March 2007 and lived in it until July 2010. She then moved away and rented her home from August 2010 until she sold it August of 2011 for $340,000. While it was rental property, she deducted $20,000 of depreciation. What amount of gain on the sale of her residence is excludable from income?

Discharge of Qualified Principal Residence Indebtedness

A taxpayer may be able to exclude from gross income a ***discharge of qualified principal residence indebtedness***. This exclusion applies to discharges made after 2006 and before 2013. If a taxpayer chooses to exclude this income, reduce the basis of the principal residence by the amount excluded from the gross income (not less than zero).

- **Principal residence** – The principal residence is the home where the taxpayer ordinarily lives most of the time. There can only be one principal residence at any one time.
- **Qualified principal residence indebtedness** – Debt that the taxpayer incurs while acquiring, constructing, or substantially improving a principal residence, for which the principal residence serves as security. Also includes any debt resulting from the refinancing of such debt but only to the extent of prior debt. Cash taken during refinancing is not qualified principal residence indebtedness.
- **Amount eligible for the exclusion** – The exclusion applies only to debt discharged after 2006 and before 2013. The maximum amount that the taxpayer may treat as qualified principal residence indebtedness is $2 million ($1 million if married filing separately). The taxpayer may not exclude discharge of qualified principal residence indebtedness from gross income if the discharge was for services performed for the lender or because of any other factor not directly related to a decline in the value of the residence or to the taxpayer's financial condition.

Employee Achievement Awards

Generally, if tangible personal property is received (other than cash, a gift certificate, or an equivalent item) as an award for length of service or safety achievement, its value may be excluded from the taxpayer's income. However, the amount the taxpayer may exclude is limited to an employer's cost and cannot be more than $1,600 ($400 for awards that are not qualified plan awards) for all such awards received during the year. The award must be part of a meaningful presentation, under conditions and circumstances that do not create a significant likelihood of it being disguised pay. This exclusion does <u>not</u> apply to the following awards:

- A length-of-service award for less than five years of service or if already received another length-of-service award during the previous 4 years,
- A safety achievement award for managers, administrators, clerical employees, or other professional employees or if more than 10% of eligible employees previously received safety achievement awards during the year.

Fringe Benefits

Fringe benefits received in connection with the performance of services are included in income as compensation unless the employee pays fair market value for the benefits or the law specifically excludes them. The IRS treats abstaining from the performance of services (for example, under a covenant not to compete) as the performance of services for purposes of these rules.

- **Accident or health plan** – Generally, the values of an accident or health plan coverage that an employer provided to a taxpayer are not to be included as income. Benefits received from the plan may be taxable, as explained later under *Sickness and Injury Benefits*.
- **Long-term care coverage** – Contributions by employers to provide coverage for long-term care services generally are not included as income. However, contributions made through a flexible

spending or similar arrangement (such as a cafeteria plan) must be included in income. This amount appears as wages in box 1 of Form W-2.

- **Archer MSA contributions** – Employer contributions to an Archer MSA generally are not included as income. The total of these contributions appears in box 12 of Form W-2 with code R. The taxpayer must report this amount on Form 8853, Archer MSAs and Long-Term Care Insurance Contracts. A taxpayer should file Form 8853 with his returns. If a taxpayer does not enjoy employer contributions to his MSA, the taxpayer may make his own contributions

- **Meals and lodging** – An employee can exclude the value of employer provided meals or lodging from gross income if provided on the employer's premises for the employer's convenience.

- **Health flexible spending arrangement (health FSA)** – If an employer provides a health FSA that qualifies as an accident or health plan, the amount of salary reduction and reimbursements of medical care expenses for the employee and those of the employee's spouse and dependents are not included in income.

- **Health reimbursement arrangement (HRA)** – If the employer provides an HRA that qualifies as an accident or health plan, coverage and reimbursements of medical care expenses and those of a spouse and dependents generally are not included in income.

- **Health savings accounts (HSA)** – Employer contributions are not included in income. Distributions from the HSA that the taxpayer uses to pay qualified medical expenses are not included in income. Distributions not used for qualified medical expenses are included in income and may be subject to early withdrawal penalties.

- **De Minimis (Minimal) benefits** – If an employer provides employees with products or services where the cost of it is so small that it would be unreasonable for the employer to account for it, the value is not included in income. Examples of this would include coffee, doughnuts, etc.

- **Holiday gifts** – If an employer gives employees turkeys, hams, or other items of nominal value at Christmas or other holidays, the value of the gift should not be included in income. However, if the employer gives an employee cash, gift certificates, or similar items that may easily be exchanged for cash, the employee should include the value of that gift as extra salary or wages regardless of the amount involved.

- **Dependent care assistance** – Generally, employees may exclude from income up to $5,000 received from an employer's dependent care assistance program.

- **Adoption assistance** – Employees may exclude from income any amounts paid or expenses incurred by an employer for qualified adoption expenses in connection with the adoption of an eligible child.

- **Educational assistance** – For tax year 2011, employees may exclude from income up to $5,250 of qualified employer-provided educational assistance (payments of tuition, fees, books, supplies, and equipment for either undergraduate or graduate education). Employees may not exclude expenses for meals, lodging, supplies, tools, or transportation. Exclusion is generally not available for education related to sports, games or hobbies unless it has a relationship to the business of the employer or is otherwise required to obtain a degree.

- **Group-term life Insurance** – Generally, the cost of up to $50,000 of group-term life insurance coverage provided by an employer (or former employer) is not included in income. However, the cost of employer-provided insurance that is more than the cost of $50,000 of coverage reduced by any amount the employee pays toward the purchase of the insurance should be included as income. If a group-term life insurance policy includes permanent benefits, such as a paid-up or cash surrender value, an employee should include the cost of the permanent benefits minus the amount paid for them as income in the form of wages. The exclusion is for term life insurance protection (insurance for a fixed period of time), meeting all of the following conditions:

1) The insurance must provide a general death benefit
2) The insurance must be provided to a group of employees
3) Is insurance must be under a policy carried by the employer
4) The insurance must provide an amount of insurance to each employee based on a formula that prevents individual selection

- **Retirement planning services** – Qualified retirement planning services that an employer provides to employees are not included in income. Qualified services include retirement planning advice, information about the employer's retirement plan, and information about how the plan may fit into the overall individual retirement income plan. Employees may not exclude the value of any tax preparation, accounting, legal, or brokerage services provided by the employer.
- **Transportation** – Employees may exclude employer-provided qualified transportation fringe benefits from income, up to certain limits. Qualified transportation fringe benefits include the following:
    1) A ***transit pass*** or transportation in a commuter highway vehicle (such as a van) between the home and workplace (up to $230/m).
    2) Qualified parking (up to $230/m).
    3) Qualified bicycle commuting – Up to $20 reimbursement for each month the taxpayer uses a bicycle regularly for a substantial portion of travel between home and place of employment. This can include expenses for bicycle purchase, improvements, repair, and storage.
- **No additional cost services** – Employees may exclude the value of certain employer-provided services from income when the services do not cause the employer any substantial additional costs. The employee must offer the services to customers in the ordinary course of the line of business in which the employee performs substantial services. Generally, no-additional-cost services are excess capacity services, such as airline, bus, or train tickets; hotel rooms; or telephone services provided free or at a reduced price to employees working in those lines of business.
- **Athletic facilities** – Employees may exclude the value of using employer-owned athletic facilities if substantially all use is by employees, spouses, and dependent children.
- **Employee discounts** – Employees may exclude discounts on either of the following:
    1) Merchandise up to the employer's gross profit percentage
    2) Services up to 20% of the price charged to non-employees
- **Qualified retirement plan contributions** – Employer contributions to a qualified retirement plan for employee accounts are not included in income at the time contributed. Although not immediately taxed, these contributions are not excluded from income when withdrawals occur from the plan.
    1) **Elective deferrals** – An employee contribution is treated the same as an employer contribution to a qualified plan. An elective deferral, other than a designated Roth contribution, is not included in wages subject to income tax at the time contributed. However, it is included in wages subject to Social Security and Medicare taxes.

Housing Allowance for Members of Clergy

A member of the clergy should not include the rental value of a home (including utilities) or a designated housing allowance provided to the member as part of income. However, the exclusion may not be more than the reasonable pay for services. If the member pays for the utilities, he may exclude any allowance designated for utility cost, up to the actual cost. The home or allowance must represent compensation for services rendered as an ordained, licensed, or commissioned minister. If the taxpayer is subject to the self-employment tax, he must include the rental value of the home or the housing allowance as earnings from self-employment on Schedule SE (Form 1040).

Military and Government Disability Pensions

Service-connected Disability

Taxpayers may exclude from income amounts received as a pension, annuity, or similar allowance for personal injury or sickness resulting from active service in one of the following government services:

- The armed forces of any country
- The National Oceanic and Atmospheric Administration
- The public health service
- The foreign service

Conditions for Exclusion

Disability payments should not be included in income if ***any*** of the following conditions apply:

- The taxpayer is entitled to receive a disability payment before September 25, 1975.
- The taxpayer was a member of a listed government service or its reserve component, or was under a binding written commitment to become a member, on September 24, 1975.
- The taxpayer receives the disability payments for a combat-related injury or sickness that meets one of the following criteria:
    1) Results directly from armed conflict
    2) Takes place while engaged in extra-hazardous service
    3) Occurs under conditions simulating war, including training exercises such as maneuvers
    4) Is caused by an instrumentality of war
- The taxpayer would be entitled to receive disability compensation from the Department of Veterans Affairs (VA) upon the filing of an application. Exclusion under this condition is equal to the amount the taxpayer would be entitled to receive from the VA.

Pension Based on Years of Service

Generally, if a taxpayer receives a disability pension based on years of service, the pension must be included in income. However, if the pension qualifies for exclusion for a service-connected disability as listed above, the part of the pension based on a percentage of disability should not be included as income. The rest of the pension should be included in income.

Education-related Benefits

Scholarships and Fellowships

A candidate for a degree may exclude amounts received as a qualified scholarship or fellowship. A qualified scholarship or fellowship is any amount received that is for one of the following:

- Tuition and fees to enroll at or attend an educational institution
- Any fees, books, supplies, and equipment required for courses at the educational institution.

Amounts used for room and board do not qualify for the exclusion. A taxpayer must include in income the part of any scholarship or fellowship that represents payment for past, present, or future teaching, research, or other services. This applies even if all candidates for a degree must perform the services to receive the degree. Scholarship prizes won in a contest are not scholarships or fellowships if a taxpayer does not have to use the prizes for educational purposes. Include these amounts as income on Form 1040, whether or not the taxpayer used them for educational purposes.

Education Savings Bond Program

Under the Education Savings Bond Program, a taxpayer may exclude all or part of the interest received on the redemption of qualified U.S. savings bonds during the year if the taxpayer uses that interest to pay for qualified higher educational expenses during the same year. Taxpayers will not qualify for this exclusion if their filing status is married filing separately.

- **Qualified U.S. savings bonds** – A qualified U.S. savings bond is a series EE bond issued after 1989 or a series I bond. The bond must be in the taxpayer's name (sole owner) or jointly held with a spouse. The taxpayer must be at least 24 years old before the bond's issue date. The issue date of a bond may be earlier than the date the taxpayer purchased the bond because the issue date assigned to a bond is the first day of the month in which it is purchased.
- **Qualified expenses** – Qualified higher educational expenses are tuition and fees required for a taxpayer and dependents (for whom an exemption is claimed) to attend an eligible educational institution. Qualified expenses include any contribution made to a qualified tuition program or to a Coverdell education savings account.
    1) Qualified expenses do not include expenses for room and board or for courses involving sports, games, or hobbies that are not part of a degree or certificate-granting program.
- **Eligible educational institutions** – These institutions include most public, private, and nonprofit universities, colleges, and vocational schools that are accredited and are eligible to participate in student aid programs run by the Department of Education.
- **Reduction for certain benefits** – A taxpayer must reduce his qualified higher-educational expenses by all of the following tax-free benefits:
    1) Tax-free part of scholarships and fellowships
    2) Expenses used to figure the tax-free portion of distributions from a Coverdell ESA
    3) Expenses used to figure the tax-free part of distributions from a qualified tuition program
    4) Any tax-free payments (other than gifts or inheritances) received for educational expenses:
        A) Veterans' educational assistance benefits

B) Qualified tuition reductions

C) Employer-provided educational assistance

5) Any expense used for the American Opportunity and Lifetime Learning credits

- **Amount excludable** – If the total proceeds (interest and principal) from the qualified U.S. savings bonds redeemed during the year are not more than the adjusted qualified higher educational expenses for the year, it is possible for the taxpayer to exclude all of the interest. If the proceeds are more than the expenses, the taxpayer may exclude only part of the interest. To determine the amount to exclude from income, divide the qualified expenses by the total bond proceeds. Multiply this percentage by the amount of bond interest to arrive at the amount excluded from income. The remainder of the interest is included in income.

- **Modified adjusted gross income limit** – The interest exclusion is limited if 2011 modified adjusted gross income (MAGI) is as follows:

  1) $71,100 to $86,100 for taxpayers filing single or head of household

  2) $106,650 to $136,650 for married taxpayers filing jointly or for a qualifying widow(er) with dependent child

---

4.3 ? LaQuanta has expenses of $20,000 in tuition and $10,000 for her dorm room for her current semester in college. She cashes in $30,000 of her Series EE bonds to pay these expenses. The accumulated interest for the bond was $6,000. How much of the interest can she exclude from her income?

Qualified Education Expenses

For purposes of the ***Coverdell ESA*** and ***qualified tuition programs (QTP)***, qualified education expenses are the amounts paid for tuition, fees, books, supplies, and equipment required for enrollment or attendance at an eligible educational institution. They also include the reasonable costs of room and board for a designated beneficiary who is at least a half-time student. The cost of room and board qualifies only to the extent that it is not more than the greater of the following two amounts:

- The allowance for room and board, as determined by the eligible educational institution, that was included in the cost of attendance (for federal financial aid purposes) for a particular academic period and living arrangement of the student

- The actual amount charged if the student is residing in housing owned or operated by the eligible educational institution

Adjust qualified education expenses to take into account certain credits, such as the ***American Opportunity credit*** or ***Lifetime Learning credit***, and any other tax-free benefits received to pay for expenses. If a designated beneficiary receives distributions from both a QTP and a Coverdell ESA in the same year, and the total of these distributions is more than the beneficiary's adjusted qualified higher education expenses, allocate the expenses between the distributions. For purposes of this allocation, disregard any qualified elementary and secondary education expenses.

TIP Qualified education expenses include the cost of room and board for ESAs and QTPs, but not for other purposes such as the education credits, education savings bond program, scholarships and fellowships.

Coverdell Educational Savings Account (ESA)

A Coverdell ESA is a trust or custodial account created or organized in the United States only for paying the qualified education expenses of the designated beneficiary of the account. While there is no tax deduction for contributions, earnings are tax deferred. Exclude distributions from a Coverdell ESA from income up to the amount of qualified education expenses for the year, adjusted for other benefits received. The expenses may be qualified higher education expenses or qualified elementary and secondary education expenses.

- The account must be a designated Coverdell ESA when the taxpayer created the account.
- Account documents must be in writing and must satisfy the following requirements:
    1) The trustee or custodian must be a bank or an entity approved by the IRS.
    2) The trustee or custodian may only accept contributions that meet the following conditions:
        A) The contribution is in cash.
        B) The contribution is made before the beneficiary (other than a special needs beneficiary) reaches age 18.
        C) Contributions for the year (not including rollovers) may not be more than $2,000.
    3) The taxpayer cannot invest the money in the account in life insurance contracts.
    4) The taxpayer cannot combine the money in the account with other property except in a common trust fund or common investment fund.
        A) The account balance must be distributed within 30 days after the earlier of the following:
            (a) The beneficiary reaches age 30, unless a special needs beneficiary
            (b) The beneficiary's death
- If modified adjusted gross income (MAGI) is between $95,000 and $110,000 (between $190,000 and $220,000 if filing a joint return), then the $2,000 contribution limit for each designated beneficiary is gradually reduced. If MAGI is $110,000 or more ($220,000 or more if filing a joint return), the taxpayer cannot contribute to anyone's Coverdell ESA.
- Calculate the reduced contribution amount by multiplying $2,000 by a fraction. The numerator (top number) is the MAGI minus $95,000 ($190,000 if filing a joint return). The denominator (bottom number) is $15,000 ($30,000 if filing a joint return). Subtract the result from $2,000. The taxpayer may contribute this amount for each beneficiary.

Qualified Tuition Programs (QTPs)

A qualified tuition program (also known as a ***529 program***) is a program set up to allow the taxpayer to either prepay or contribute to an account established for paying a student's qualified higher education expenses at an eligible educational institution. A state, a state agency, an instrumentality of a state, or an eligible educational institution can establish and maintain a QTP.

- The part of a distribution representing the amount paid or contributed to a QTP is not included in income. This is a return of the investment in the program.

- The beneficiary generally does not include earnings distributed from a QTP in income if the total distribution is less than or equal to adjusted qualified higher education expenses. Income is reported to the recipient on Form 1099Q. The beneficiary is the recipient when distributions are made either directly to the beneficiary or to an eligible educational institution for his benefit. Consequently, taxable distributions constitute income to the beneficiary when paid either directly to the beneficiary or to an eligible educational institution for his benefit. Otherwise, the account owner is the recipient.
- The designated beneficiary is generally the student (or future student) for whom the QTP is intended to provide benefits. The taxpayer <u>can change</u> the designated beneficiary.
- Contributions to a QTP on behalf of any beneficiary cannot be more than the amount necessary to provide for the qualified education expenses of the beneficiary.
- There are <u>no income restrictions</u> on the individual contributors.

TIP An ESA and a QTP are similar in that neither offers a tax deduction for contributions to the plan, earnings accumulate free of tax until withdrawn, and withdrawals are excluded from income if used for qualified education expenses. A QTP is different from an ESA in the following ways: the beneficiary of a QTP can be any age and can even change, QTP does not have age-based distribution requirements, contributions can be far more than allowed in an ESA, and there are no income restricitions.

Workers' Compensation

An amount received as workers' compensation for an occupational sickness or injury is fully exempt from tax if paid under a workers' compensation act or similar statute. The exemption also applies to the victim's survivors. The exemption does not apply to retirement plan benefits received based on age, length of service, or prior contributions to the plan, even if an occupational sickness or injury caused retirement. If a taxpayer returns to work after qualifying for workers' compensation, salary payments received for performing light duties are taxable as wages.

Compensation for Sickness or Injury

Many other amounts taxpayers receive as compensation for sickness or injury are not taxable. These include the following amounts:

- Compensatory (not punitive) damages received from a lawsuit for physical injury or physical sickness, whether paid in a lump sum or in periodic payments.
- Benefits under an accident or health insurance policy on which either a taxpayer paid the premiums or the taxpayer's employer paid the premiums and those premiums were included in income.
- Disability benefits received for loss of income or earning capacity because of injuries under a no-fault car insurance policy.
- Compensation for permanent loss (or loss of use) of a part or function of the body, or for permanent disfigurement. This compensation must be based only on the injury and not on the period of absence from work. These benefits are not taxable, even if an employer pays for the accident and health plan that provides these benefits.
- A reimbursement for medical care is generally not taxable. However, it may reduce the medical expense deduction.

Life Insurance Proceeds

Life insurance proceeds paid because of the death of the insured person are <u>not taxable</u> unless the taxpayer sold the policy to another for a price (*see Viatical Settlements*). This is true even if the taxpayer received proceeds under an accident or health insurance policy or an endowment contract.

- If the taxpayer receives death benefits paid in a ***lump sum*** or other than at regular intervals, include in income only the benefits that are more than the amount payable at the time of the death.

- If the taxpayer receives payment of life insurance proceeds in installments, exclude part of each installment from income. To determine the excluded part, divide the amount held by the insurance company (generally the total lump sum payable at the death of the insured person) by the number of installments to be paid. Include anything more than this excluded part in income as interest.

    1) If the spouse of the taxpayer died before October 23, 1986, and the taxpayer receives payment in installments of insurance proceeds because of the death, the taxpayer may exclude up to $1,000 a year of the interest included in the installments, even if the taxpayer remarries.

- ***Endowment contract proceeds*** – An endowment contract is a policy under which the taxpayer receives a specified amount of money on a certain date. If the taxpayer dies before that date, the money goes to the designated beneficiary. Endowment proceeds paid in a lump sum at maturity are taxable only if the proceeds are more than the cost of the policy. To determine the cost, take any amount previously received under the contract (and excluded from income) and subtract that from the total premiums (or other consideration) paid for the contract. Include the part of the lump sum payment that is more than the cost in income.

- ***Accelerated death benefits*** – Exclude certain amounts paid as accelerated death benefits under a life insurance contract or viatical settlement before the insured's death if the insured is terminally or chronically ill.

    1) **Exclusion for terminal illness** – Accelerated death benefits are fully excludable if the insured is a terminally ill individual, certified by a physician as having an illness or condition reasonably expected to result in death within 24 months from the date of the certification.

    2) **Exclusion for chronic illness** – If the insured is a chronically ill individual, who is not terminally ill, accelerated death benefits paid based on costs incurred for qualified long-term care services are fully excludable. Accelerated death benefits paid on a *per diem* or other periodic basis are excludable up to a limit.

    3) **Viatical settlement** – This is the sale or assignment of any part of the death benefit under a life insurance contract to a ***viatical settlement provider*** in the business of buying insurance contracts on the lives of insured individuals who are terminally or chronically ill.

4.4 Mark has a whole life insurance policy with a face value of $50,000. He paid a lump sum of $5,000 for the policy 20 years ago. He dies in 2011, and his wife Marlene, as the named beneficiary of the policy, elects to receive a $50,000 lump sum payment. How much must Marlene include in her income?

Foreign Earned Income Exclusion and Foreign Housing Exclusion

A U.S. citizen or resident alien of the United States who lives abroad pays taxes on his worldwide income. However, he may qualify to exclude some or all of his foreign earnings from income. For tax year 2011, the exclusion cannot be more than the smaller of the following:

- $92,900 ($185,800 MFJ and both meet the requirements)
- Foreign earned income for the tax year minus the amount of foreign housing exclusion

The taxpayer may exclude or deduct certain foreign housing amounts, limited to the lesser of the foreign housing costs paid for with employer-provided amounts or the amount of foreign earned income. A calendar year taxpayer with $92,900 or less of foreign earned income covering a 12-month period can use ***Form 2555-EZ*** to claim the exclusion. A taxpayer with self-employment income, business or moving expenses, or those claiming the foreign housing exclusion or deduction must use ***Form 2555***.

To claim the ***foreign earned income exclusion***, the ***foreign housing exclusion***, or the ***foreign housing deduction*** (deduction only available if the taxpayer is self-employed), a taxpayer must meet all three of the following requirements:

- The ***tax home*** must be in a foreign country. A tax home is the place where a taxpayer permanently or indefinitely engages to work as an employee or self-employed individual. The tax home is not in a foreign country for any period in which the taxpayer's abode is in the United States. An abode is one's home, habitation, residence, domicile, or place of dwelling.
- The taxpayer must have foreign earned income.
- The taxpayer must meet one of the following tests:

    1) **Bona Fide Residence Test** – A taxpayer does not automatically acquire bona fide resident status merely by living in a foreign country for one year. The length of stay and the nature of the job are additional factors that determine whether a taxpayer meets the test. A taxpayer who travels to a foreign country to work on a particular construction job for a specified period-of-time ordinarily is not a bona fide resident of that country even if working there for more than one tax year. To be a bona fide resident a taxpayer must be:

        A) A U.S. citizen who is a bona fide resident of a foreign country or countries for an uninterrupted period that includes an entire tax year, or

        B) A U.S. resident alien who is a citizen or national of a country with which the United States has an income tax treaty in effect and who is a bona fide resident of a foreign country or countries for an uninterrupted period that includes an entire tax year

    2) **Physical Presence Test** – A U.S. citizen or a U.S. resident alien physically present in a foreign country or countries for at least 330 full days during any period of 12 consecutive months. The physical presence test is based only on how long the taxpayer is in a foreign country. This test does not depend on the kind of residence established, intentions about returning, or the nature and purpose of the stay abroad.

TIP: There is a differece between the *Physical Presence Test* and the *Substantial Presence Test* used to determine U.S. residency status. Aside from the number of days required, the former measures time in a foreign country while the latter measures time in the United States.

4.5 ? Noah is a U.S. Citizen. He moved to Brazil in 2010 to work on several construction projects as the country prepares for the world cup in 2014. He sold his house and rented an apartment in Brazil, where he remained through the first six months of 2011 when he left prematurely. Noah earns $80,000 in 2011 while working in Brazil. How much can he exclude from his income on his Form 1040?

Tax Return Preparer Competency Exam – Chapter 4 Quiz

Circle the letter next to the best answer. Remember to read the question carefully.

1) Derek Dunn received three employee achievement awards during the year: a nonqualified plan award of a watch, which cost $250, and two qualified plan awards of a computer, which cost $1500 and a radio, which cost $400. The requirements for qualified plan awards are satisfied. What amount, if any, must Derek include in income?

   a. $0

   b. $1,150

   c. $550

   d. $1,500

2) Mr. Red is a college student working on a degree in accounting. He received the following in 2011:

   - A $4,000 scholarship used for tuition at State University
   - A $1,000 scholarship used for fees and books
   - An $8,000 fellowship used for his room and board

   Compute the amount Mr. Red must include in income for 2011.

   a. $8,000

   b. $5,000

   c. $13,000

   d. $9,000

3) The following items of income are specifically excluded from gross income, EXCEPT:

   a. $600 interest from municipal bond used to build a sports arena

   b. $350 employee achievement award

   c. $2,000 in veterans benefits

   d. $250 of workers' compensation

4) All the following statements are true of the foreign earned income exclusion except:

   a. Tax home must be in a foreign country.

   b. Must have foreign earned income.

   c. If residing outside the country, must return to the United States before the end of the tax year.

   d. Must be a US citizen or US resident alien.

5) Which of the following does not qualify for exclusion from income of all or part of the gain from the sale of their main home in 2011?

a. You sold a personal residence January 1, 2010 and excluded all the gain. You sold another personal residence December 30, 2011. You did not sell because of health problems or a change in employment.

b. You owned and lived in your house from January 1, 2007 until February 15, 2008 when you moved out and lived with your friend. You moved back into your house July 12, 2009 and then sold it October 20, 2011. The sale was not due to health problems or a change of employment.

c. Betty sells her house (that she had owned and lived in since 1999) in February 2011 and gets married one month later. Her husband had excluded the gain on the sale of his residence on his 2010 return.

d. A taxpayer and his wife are divorced in 2005 and his spouse is allowed to live in the house until sold. The house sells on July 15, 2011.

6) Joe and Jean purchased their primary residence in 1982 for $100,000. While they lived there, they made renovations at a cost of $125,000. They lived there until July 1, 2008. On June 15, 2011, the residence was sold for $800,000. From July 1, 2008, until June 15, 2011, the home was unoccupied. Joe and Jean file a joint return, and they have never excluded a gain from the sale of another home. What is their maximum taxable gain?

a. $575,000

b. $0

c. $75,000

d. $200,000

7) The following fringe benefits are non-taxable except:

a. Employer paid premiums on $100,000 face value life insurance policy.

b. The value of accident or health plan coverage provided to you by your employer

c. Long-term care coverage contributions made by your employer to provide coverage for long-term care services.

d. Contributions by your employer to your medical savings account.

8) In 2001, Joe and Peg refinanced the $275,000 remaining balance on a loan used to build their principal residence and took cash out amounting to $50,000 to pay off their credit cards. The bank forgave the entire loan in 2011 when they became insolvent. Which statement is correct?

a. The entire amount of the discharged debt is included in income for 2011.

b. The entire amount is qualified principal residence indebtedness and is excluded from income.

c. They may recognize the amount included in income over a 5-year period.

d. Cash taken during refinancing is not qualified principal residence indebtedness.

For more practice questions, visit fastforwardacademy.com and access our FREE online question bank.

1) **c** Each award by itself would qualify for an exclusion from gross income. However, total awards of $2,150 ($250 in non-qualified plan awards and $1,900 in awards under a qualified plan) are more than the $1,600 annual limit of all combined awards. He must report $550 in income.

2) **a** The two scholarship items are not taxable income as the full amount of the proceeds were used for qualified educational expenses. The fellowship income is fully taxable because it was not used for a qualified educational expense (room and board is not a qualified expense).

3) **a** Interest on bonds used for private activities is <u>not</u> exempt from income tax. A bond is generally considered a *private activity bond* if the amount of the proceeds to be used to make or finance loans to persons other than government units is more than 5% of the proceeds or $5 million (whichever is less).

4) **c** The earned income exclusion is for U.S. citizens or resident aliens of the United States who live abroad and are taxed on their worldwide income. There is no time-period requirement for them to return to the US.

5) **a** Choice A does not indicate meeting the 2-year use and ownership tests or any allowed exceptions, and more importantly, the taxpayer excluded gain on another home in the previous 2 years. Items B, C and D all meet the 2-year use and ownership rule.

You are considered to have used property as your main home during any period when:

- You owned it, and
- Your spouse or former spouse is allowed to live in it under a divorce or separation instrument and uses it as his or her main home.

6) **c** The couple meets the tests (owned over 2 years and lived in at least 24 of prior 60 months) to exclude up to $500,000 of gain. The total gain on the sale was $575,000 ($800,000 proceeds minus $225,000 basis), less the $500,000 exclusion, leaves a taxable gain of $75,000. The period of nonqualified use does not apply within 5 years of the date of sale. Report the gain on Form 8949.

7) **a** Exclude life insurance fringe benefits up to $50,000 in face value.

8) **d** Cash taken during refinancing is not qualified principal residence indebtedness.

5 Adjustments to Gross Income

Individual Retirement Arrangements (IRAs) · Health Account Deductions · Moving Expenses · Self-employed Health Insurance · Self-employed SEP, SIMPLE, and Qualified Plans · Alimony · Education-related Adjustments · Miscellaneous Adjustments

This chapter summarizes adjustments to gross income referenced in Publications 17, 521, 590, and 969.

Individual Retirement Arrangements (IRAs)

An ***individual retirement account*** is a trust or custodial account set up in the United States for the exclusive benefit of a taxpayer or his beneficiaries. A taxpayer creates this account with a written document. The document must show that the account meets all of the following requirements:

- The trustee or custodian must be a bank, a federally insured credit union, a savings and loan association, or an entity approved by the IRS to act as trustee or custodian.
- The trustee or custodian generally cannot accept contributions of more than the deductible amount for the year. However, rollover contributions and employer contributions to a simplified employee pension (SEP) can be more than this amount.
- Contributions, except for rollover contributions, must be in cash.
- The taxpayer must have a non-forfeitable right to the amount at all times.
- The account holder cannot use money in the account to buy a life insurance policy.
- The account holder cannot combine assets with other property, except in a common trust or investment fund.
- Distributions must begin by April 1 of the year after the taxpayer reaches age 70.5.

Traditional IRAs

A traditional IRA (sometimes called an ordinary or regular IRA) is any IRA that is not a Roth IRA or a SIMPLE IRA. A traditional IRA can be an individual retirement account or annuity. It can be part of either a simplified employee pension (SEP) or an employer or employee association trust account. Two advantages of a traditional IRA are as follows:

- Contributions may be tax deductible, depending on the circumstances
- Amounts in the IRA, including earnings and gains, are not taxed until distributed

Taxpayers can set up and contribute to a traditional IRA only if the following conditions exist:

- Taxpayer or spouse received ***taxable compensation*** during the year
- Taxpayer is <u>younger than age 70.5</u> at the end of the year

Individuals can have a traditional IRA even if covered by another retirement plan. Contributions may not be deductible if the taxpayer (or spouse) is covered by an employer retirement plan. If both a taxpayer and a spouse have compensation and are younger than age 70.5, each can set up an IRA; however, they cannot participate in the same IRA. If filing a joint return, only one spouse needs to have compensation.

- **Compensation** – Generally, compensation is the amount earned from working. Compensation includes wages, salaries, tips, professional fees, bonuses, and other amounts individuals receive for providing personal services. For IRA purposes, compensation includes amounts considered taxable alimony and nontaxable combat pay. For the ***self-employed*** (a sole proprietor or a partner), compensation is the ***net earnings*** (do not consider a net loss) from a trade or business (provided the personal services are a material income-producing factor) reduced by the total of the following:
    1) The deduction for contributions made on the taxpayer's behalf to retirement plans
    2) The deduction allowed for one-half of self-employment taxes
- Compensation does NOT include any of the following:
    1) Earnings and profits from property, such as rental, interest, and dividend income
    2) Pension or annuity income
    3) Deferred compensation received (compensation payments postponed from a past year)
    4) Income from a partnership if taxpayer does not provide services that are a material income-producing factor
    5) Amounts excluded from income (other than combat pay), such as foreign earned income

Contribution Deadlines

A taxpayer can make contributions to a traditional IRA at any time during the year or by the due date for filing the return for that year, not including extensions. For most taxpayers, this is April 15.

Jim makes a contribution to his IRA on February 3, 2011. Jim can apply his contribution to 2010 or 2011. He can apply the contribution to the 2010 tax year since it is made before the due date of his 2010 tax return. He can apply the contribution to 2011, the actual year of deposit.

General Limit on IRA Contributions

For 2011, an individual taxpayer's maximum contribution to a traditional IRA is the smaller of the following:

- $5,000 ($6,000 if 50 or older, due to a $1,000 catch-up contribution)
- 100% of taxable compensation for the year

5.1 Benjamin impresses his father during take your child to work day and is offered a job doing office tasks in the family business during his summer break. He earns $800 during his vacation, and receives a W-2 reflecting this income. Benjamin also has a weekly allowance of $20 for taking out the trash, and dividend income of $3,000 for the year. Benjamin is 10 years old. What is the maximum amount Benjamin can contribute to an IRA?

Spousal IRA Limit

If filing a joint return with a spouse, the IRA contribution for the person with the lowest compensation cannot exceed:

- $5,000 ($6,000 if 50 or older)
- The total compensation includible in the gross income of both spouses for the year, reduced by the following two amounts:
    1) The other spouse's IRA contribution for the year to a traditional IRA
    2) Any contribution for the year to a Roth IRA on behalf of the other spouse

The total combined contributions that a taxpayer can make for the year to both IRAs can be as much as $10,000 ($11,000 if one is 50 or older, or $12,000 if both are 50 or older).

5.2 Mary is 52 and her husband Gary is 48. Mary earns $65,000 at her job. Gary is unemployed. What is the maximum that Mary and Gary can contribute to IRAs if they file a joint return?

Tax on Excess Contributions

Contributions above the allowed limits are ***excess contributions***. If the taxpayer does not withdraw excess contributions by the date of the return (including extensions), a taxpayer is subject to a 6% tax and must pay the 6% tax each year on excess amounts that remain in the traditional IRA.

Deduction Limits

Generally, the deduction is the lesser of the following:

- The actual contributions to a traditional IRA for the year
- The general limit (or the spousal IRA limit, if it applies)

The deduction may be limited if an employer retirement plan covers either spouse at any time during the year for which contributions are made. The deduction limitation does not affect the amount that the taxpayer can contribute. The deduction amount is decreased (phased out) when income rises above a certain amount, and it is eliminated altogether when it reaches a higher amount. These amounts vary depending on filing status. To determine if the deduction is subject to phase-out, compare modified adjusted gross income (MAGI) to the base amounts.

- When MAGI is less than the lower base amount, taxpayers receive a full deduction.
- If MAGI is more than the upper base amount, the IRS does not allow any deduction.
- If MAGI is between the base amounts, a partial deduction amount is determined by subtracting MAGI from the upper base amount and multiplying it by a percentage, according to filing status:
    1) **Married Filing Jointly** – The total IRA deduction is 25% (30% if 50 or older) of the difference between MAGI and the upper base amount.
- **All others** – The total IRA deduction is 50% (60% if 50 or older) of the difference between MAGI and the upper base amount.

Table 5-1. Effect of MAGI on Deduction if Taxpayer Is Covered by a Retirement Plan at Work – 2011

IF your filing status is	**AND** your modified AGI is	**THEN** you can take
single or **head of household**	$56,000 or less	a full deduction
	between $56,000 – $66,000	a partial deduction
	$66,000 or more	no deduction
married filing jointly or **qualifying widow(er)**	$90,000 or less	a full deduction
	between $90,000 – $110,000	a partial deduction
	$110,000 or more	no deduction
married filing separately	less than $10,000	a partial deduction
	$10,000 or more	no deduction

Table 5-2. Effect of MAGI on Deduction if Taxpayer Is **NOT** Covered by a Retirement Plan at Work – 2011

IF your filing status is	**AND** your modified AGI is	**THEN** you can take
single, head of household, or **qualifying widow(er)**	any amount	a full deduction
married filing jointly or **separately** and spouse is not covered by a plan at work	any amount	a full deduction
married filing jointly and spouse is covered by a plan at work	$169,000 or less	a full deduction
	between $169,000 – $179,000	a partial deduction
	$179,000 or more	no deduction
married filing separately with a spouse who is covered by a plan at work	less than $10,000	a partial deduction
	$10,000 or more	no deduction

Nondeductible Contributions

Although the deduction for IRA contributions may be reduced or eliminated, contributions can be made up to the general limit or, if it applies, the spousal IRA limit. The difference between the total permitted contributions and the IRA deduction is a ***nondeductible contribution***. A nondeductible contribution increases the basis of the IRA and is not taxable when withdrawn.

TIP

To designate contributions as nondeductible, individuals must file ***Form 8606***, even if they are not required to file a tax return for the year. If a taxpayer does not report nondeductible contributions, the IRS treats all contributions to a traditional IRA as deductible contributions–meaning they are taxed!

A traditional IRA consisting only of deductible contributions and earnings does not have a basis. If the IRA has a basis resulting from nondeductible contributions, distributions consist partly of nondeductible contributions (basis) and partly of deductible contributions, earnings, and gains (if any). Until the entire basis has been distributed, each distribution is partly nontaxable and partly taxable. To determine the nontaxable percentage of the distribution, divide the basis at the beginning of year (*plus* contributions for the tax year) by the total value of all IRAs at the end of the year (*plus* distributions in the tax year).

Jim makes a $6,000 nondeductible contribution in 2011 to his IRA and properly files Form 8606. His prior year deductible contributions to the account total $15,000. The balance in his IRA at the end of 2011 is $50,000. Jim withdraws $10,000 during 2011. The nontaxable portion is $1,000, reflecting 10% of the distribution amount. $6,000 /($50,000+$10,000) = 10%

Age 59.5 Rule

Generally, if a taxpayer is younger than age 59.5, he must pay a 10% additional tax on the distribution of any assets (money or other property) from a traditional IRA. Distributions before age 59.5 are called early distributions. The 10% additional tax applies to the part of the distribution the taxpayer must include in gross income. It is in addition to any regular income tax on that amount. A number of exceptions to this rule include the following:

- The taxpayer has unreimbursed medical expenses that are more than 7.5% of AGI.
- The distributions are not more than the cost of medical insurance.
- The taxpayer is disabled.
- The taxpayer is the beneficiary of a deceased IRA owner.
- The taxpayer receives distributions as an annuity, or series of substantially equal periodic payments.
- The distributions are not more than the taxpayer's qualified higher education expenses
- The distribution is to buy, build, or rebuild a first home:
    1) Up to $10,000 for qualified acquisition costs if used within 120 days of distribution.
    2) $10,000 for each spouse if both are *first-time homebuyers.* A first-time homebuyer cannot own a main home during the two-year period ending on the date of acquisition of the home.
    3) Must be used on qualified acquisition costs for the main home of a taxpayer, spouse, child, grandchild, parent, or other ancestor.
- The distribution is due to an IRS levy of the qualified plan.
- The distribution is a qualified reservist distribution.
- The amount is rolled into another retirement plan within 60 days.

5.3 Oscar is 31 years old. He does not have family dental insurance, so in June of 2011 he withdraws $5,000 to pay for his daughter's braces. He deposits $5,000 back into his IRA on December 21, 2011. His AGI for 2011 is $30,000. What amount, if any, is his penalty for early distribution?

Age 70.5 Rule

Money cannot remain in a traditional IRA indefinitely. Distributions must begin by April 1 of the year after the taxpayer reaches age 70.5. The amount of the distribution is referred to as the ***required minimum distribution (RMD).*** The taxpayer must make the RMD for any year after the year attaining age 70.5 by December 31 of that later year. If distributions are less than the RMD for the year, taxpayers may have to pay a 50% excise tax on the amount not distributed as required. Figure the RMD for each year by dividing the IRA account balance as of the close of business on December 31 of the preceding year by the applicable distribution period or life expectancy. To calculate the divisor, compare the taxpayer's age at the end of the year to the corresponding number in the ***Uniform Lifetime Table***, or the ***Joint Lifetime Table*** if a spouse is more than 10 years younger.

TIP The penalty may be waived if the account owner establishes that the shortfall in distributions was due to reasonable error and that reasonable steps are being taken to remedy the shortfall. In order to qualify for this relief, the taxpayer must file ***Form 5329*** and attach a letter of explanation.

Qualified Charitable Distribution

A qualified charitable distribution (QCD) is a nontaxable distribution made directly by the trustee of an IRA (other than a SEP or SIMPLE IRA) to an organization eligible to receive tax-deductible contributions. The taxpayer must have been at least age 70.5 when making the distribution. The taxpayer must keep the same type of acknowledgement of the contribution that he would need to claim a deduction for a charitable contribution. Total QCDs for the year cannot be more than $100,000 ($200,000 if MFJ). The amount of the QCD is limited to the amount of the distribution that would otherwise be included in income. If the IRA includes nondeductible contributions, the distribution is first considered to be paid out of otherwise taxable income. This treatment expires after 2011.

Inherited IRAs

Beneficiaries must begin withdrawals from a traditional IRA by December 31 of the year following the IRA owner's death. For non-spouse ***designated beneficiaries*** (not a trust or estate), these required distributions must occur under one of the following methods:

- **Lump sum** – Distribute entire account immediately.
- **Life expectancy** – Use the divisor from the ***Single Life Table***, minus one each year.
- **Five-year deferral** – If the IRA owner is older than 70.5 at time of death, this method is not allowed.

A taxpayer who inherits an IRA from a deceased spouse can elect to treat the IRA as his own and move the account into his own name, or begin withdrawals as described previously.

Prohibited Transactions

Generally, a prohibited transaction is any improper use of a traditional IRA account or annuity by a taxpayer, a beneficiary, or any disqualified person. Disqualified persons include the fiduciary and members of a taxpayer's family (spouse, ancestor, lineal descendant, and any spouse of a lineal descendant). The following are examples of prohibited transactions with a traditional IRA:

- Borrowing money from it
- Selling property to it
- Receiving unreasonable compensation for managing it
- Using it as security for a loan
- Buying property for personal use (present or future) with IRA funds

Generally, if there is a prohibited transaction in connection with a traditional IRA account at any time during the year, the account stops being an IRA as of the first day of that year. At that time, the entire account balance is considered a distribution, and the taxpayer may need to pay a 10% penalty if under age 59.5. If someone other than the owner or beneficiary of a traditional IRA engages in a prohibited transaction, that person may be liable for certain taxes. There is a 15% tax on the amount of the prohibited transaction and a 100% additional tax if not corrected.

Roth IRAs

The deductions mentioned in this chapter are adjustments to gross income, otherwise known as "above the line" deductions. A taxpayer subtracts above the line deductions from total income to arrive at AGI. Roth IRAs contributions or distributions usually do not impact the return of a taxpayer. A Roth IRA contribution is never deductible and is not an adjustment to gross income. The Roth IRA rules appearing below are there to help you absorb its differences and similarities to a traditional IRA.

Regardless of age, individuals may be able to establish and make nondeductible contributions to a Roth IRA retirement plan. The taxpayer must designate the account as a Roth IRA when establishing the IRA. A Roth IRA is an individual retirement plan that is subject to the rules that apply to a traditional IRA, with the following exceptions:

- Contributions to a Roth IRA are not tax deductible. Do not report them on the tax return.
- Can contribute after age 70.5, and amounts can remain in the account until taxpayer dies (no RMD).
- Certain ***qualified distributions*** may be tax free. A qualified distribution meets the following requirements:
    1) Made after the five-year period beginning with the first year a contribution was made
    2) Meets one of the following criteria:
        A) Made on or after the date the taxpayer reaches age 59.5
        B) Made because the taxpayer is disabled
        C) Made to a beneficiary or to estate after death
        D) Meets the requirements listed for a first-time homebuyer ($10,000 lifetime)

Table 5-3. Effect of MAGI on Roth IRA Contributions – 2011

IF your filing status is	**AND** your modified AGI is	**THEN** you can make
married filing jointly or **qualifying widow(er)**	$169,000 or less	a full contribution
	between $169,000 – $179,000	a partial contribution
	$179,000 or more	no contribution
married filing separately and live with spouse	0	a full contribution
	between $0 – $10,000	a partial contribution
	$10,000 or more	no contribution
All others	$107,000 or less	a full contribution
	between $107,000 – $122,000	a partial contribution
	$122,000 or more	no contribution

Sam is 40 years old files jointly with his spouse. He contributes $5,000 to his Roth IRA on July 1, 2011, which grows to $6,000 and his MAGI for the 2011 year is $176,000. He does not contribute to any other retirement plans. He has excess income of $9,000 ($176,000 - $167,000) and must reduce his contribution and any earnings by 90% ($9,000 / $10,000). He must remove $5,400 from the account by the due date for his return or he is liable for the 6% excise tax.

If a taxpayer contributes to both Roth IRAs and traditional IRAs, the limit for Roth IRAs generally is the same as the limit would be if contributions were made only to Roth IRAs. However, it is reduced by all contributions for the year to all IRAs other than Roth IRAs. Employer contributions under a SEP or SIMPLE IRA plan do not affect this limit. The contribution limit is the lesser of the following:

- $5,000 ($6,000 if age 50 or older) minus all contributions (other than employer contributions under a SEP or SIMPLE IRA plan) for the year to all IRAs other than Roth IRAs
- Taxable compensation minus all contributions (other than employer contributions under a SEP or SIMPLE IRA plan) for the year to all IRAs other than Roth IRAs. If modified AGI is above a certain amount, the contribution limit is reduced as indicated below:
    1) Modified AGI minus the following:
        A) $169,000 if filing a joint return (MFJ)or qualifying widow(er)(QW)
        B) $-0- if married filing a separate return (MFS) and the taxpayer lived with his spouse at any time during the year
        C) $107,000 for all other individuals
    2) Divide the result by $15,000 ($10,000 if filing status is MFJ, MFS, or QW)
    3) Multiply the resulting percentage by the maximum contribution limit (before reductions)
    4) Subtract the result and all contributions (other than employer contributions to a SEP or SIMPLE IRA plan) for the year to all IRAs other than Roth IRAs from the maximum contribution limit. The result is the reduced Roth IRA contribution limit.

A <u>6% excise tax</u> applies to any excess contribution to a Roth IRA. For purposes of determining excess contributions, any contribution that is withdrawn on or before the due date (including extensions) for filing the tax return for the year is treated as an amount not contributed. This treatment only applies if any earnings on the contributions are also withdrawn. The earnings are considered earned and received in the year the excess contribution was made.

Roth Conversions

A taxpayer can withdraw all or part of the assets from a traditional IRA and reinvest them (within 60 days) in a Roth IRA. The amount that the taxpayer withdraws and timely contributes (converts) to the Roth IRA is called a conversion contribution. If properly (and timely) rolled over, the 10% additional tax on early distributions will not apply. The taxpayer must roll over into the Roth IRA the same property received from the traditional IRA. The taxpayer can roll over part of the withdrawal into a Roth IRA and keep the rest of it. The amount kept will generally be taxable (except for the part that is a return of nondeductible contributions) and may be subject to the 10% additional tax on early distributions.

The IRS treats the converted amount as a taxable distribution in the year of the conversion. A taxpayer recognizes the entire amount of a 2011 conversion (other than basis) in income. The IRS removed the income limitation for Roth IRA conversions, where previously only those with modified AGI less than $100,000 could convert to a Roth IRA. For conversions done in tax year 2011, taxpayers with any filing status may convert a traditional IRA or Simple IRA into a Roth IRA.

Half of any income that results from a rollover or conversion to a Roth IRA from another retirement plan in 2010 is included in income in 2011, and the other half in 2012, unless the taxpayer elects to include all of it in 2010. A taxpayer may choose to include the entire amount in income in 2010 simply by reporting it on his 2010 tax return. If a taxpayer converts a traditional IRA to a Roth IRA in 2010 and did not elect to include the taxable amount in income for 2010, the taxpayer must include the taxable amount in income for 2011 and 2012, generally half in 2011 and half in 2012.

Distributions from a Roth IRA

If a taxpayer receives a distribution that is not a qualified distribution, he may have to pay the 10% additional tax on early distributions. The 5-year period used for determining whether the 10% early distribution tax applies to a distribution from a conversion or rollover contribution is separately determined for each conversion and rollover, and is not necessarily the same as the 5-year period used for determining whether a distribution is a qualified distribution. For example, if a calendar-year taxpayer makes a conversion contribution on February 25, 2011, and makes a regular contribution for 2010 on the same date, the 5-year period for the conversion begins January 1, 2011, while the 5-year period for the regular contribution begins on January 1, 2010.

- **Ordering Rules** – If a distribution from the Roth IRA is not a qualified distribution, part of it may be taxable. There is a set order in which contributions (including conversion contributions and rollover contributions from qualified retirement plans) and earnings are considered to be distributed from the Roth IRA. For these purposes, disregard the withdrawal of excess contributions and the earnings on them. Order the distributions as follows:

    1) Regular contributions

    2) Conversion and rollover contributions, on a first-in, first-out basis (generally, total conversions and rollovers from the earliest year first). Take these conversion and rollover contributions into account as follows:

        A) Taxable portion (the amount required to be included in gross income because of the conversion or rollover) first, and then the

        B) Nontaxable portion

    3) Earnings on contributions

Designated Roth Accounts

Designated Roth accounts are separate accounts under 401(k), 403(b), or 457(b) plans that accept elective deferrals that are referred to as Roth contributions. A taxpayer includes these elective deferrals in income, but qualified distributions from these accounts are not included in income. Designated Roth accounts are not IRAs and should not be confused with Roth IRAs. Contributions, up to their respective limits, can be made to Roth IRAs and designated Roth accounts according to a taxpayer's eligibility to participate. A contribution to one does not impact eligibility to contribute to the other.

Health Savings Accounts (HSAs)

A health savings account (HSA) is a tax-exempt trust or custodial account established with a qualified HSA trustee to pay or reimburse certain medical expenses. The maximum contribution to an HSA depends on the type of ***high deductible health plan (HDHP)*** coverage, age, the date the taxpayer became an eligible individual, and the date a taxpayer ceases to be an ***eligible individual***. For 2011, taxpayers who have self-only HDHP coverage can contribute up to $3,050. For family HDHP coverage, the maximum contribution is up to $6,150. The benefits of an HSA are as follows:

- The taxpayer receives a tax deduction for contributions that he or someone other than an employer made to the HSA even if not itemizing deductions on Form 1040.
- A taxpayer may exclude employer contributions to an HSA from gross income.
- The contributions remain in the HSA account from year to year until used.
- The interest or other earnings on the assets in the account accumulate tax-free.
- Distributions may be tax-free if used to pay for ***qualified medical expenses*** (costs that would generally qualify for the medical and dental expenses deduction). However, the additional tax on distributions not used for qualified medical expenses is **20%**
- An HSA is "portable" so it stays with the taxpayer if he changes employers or leaves the work force.

To qualify for an HSA, an individual must meet all the following requirements:

- Must be covered under a high deductible health plan (HDHP) on the first day of the month:
    1) Under the last-month rule, individuals are eligible for the entire year if covered on the first day of the last month of the tax year (December 1 for most taxpayers).
- Must not have other health coverage
- Must not be enrolled in Medicare
- Must not be claimed as a dependent on someone else's tax return

If a taxpayer meets these requirements, he is an eligible individual even if his spouse has non-HDHP family coverage, provided the spouse's coverage does not cover the taxpayer.

An HDHP has the following features:

- A higher annual deductible than typical health plans.
- A maximum limit on the sum of the annual deductible and out-of-pocket medical expenses that the taxpayer must pay for covered expenses. Out-of-pocket expenses include copayments and other amounts, but do not include premiums.

Table 5-4. HDHP Requirements

Type of Coverage	Minimum Annual Deductible		Maximum Annual Deductible and Other Out-of-pocket Expenses	
	2010	**2011**	**2010**	**2011**
Self-only	$1,200	$1,200	$5,950	$5,950
Family	$2,400	$2,400	$11,900	$11,900

Self-employed Health Insurance

A self-employed taxpayer may make an adjustment on his personal income tax return for the amount of medical, dental, and qualified long-term care insurance premiums (limited) that he pays on behalf of himself, his spouse, his dependents, and his child who was under age 27 at the end of 2011, even if the child was not a dependent. For this purpose, a taxpayer is considered self-employed if he is a general partner (or a limited partner receiving guaranteed payments) or if he receives wages from an S corporation in which he is more than a 2% shareholder. The deduction cannot be more than the earned income from the business. The taxpayer must establish the plan under the business. A taxpayer establishes a plan under a business if the policy is in the name of the following:

- A self-employed individual who files Schedule C, or his trade or business
- A partnership or S corporation
- Partners, if the partnership reimburses the partner for premiums paid, and the amount of the reimbursement is included in the partner's income on the K-1 as a guaranteed payment
- More than 2% shareholders, if S corporation reimburses them for the premiums paid, and the amount of the reimbursement is included in the shareholders' wages on Form W-2

A taxpayer cannot deduct payments for medical insurance for any month in which he was eligible to participate in a health plan subsidized by his employer, his spouse's employer, or an employer of his dependent or child under age 27 at the end of the year.

Moving Expenses

To qualify as an adjustment to gross income, moving expenses must closely relate–both in time and in place– to the start of work at a new job location.

The taxpayer must meet the specific requirements of the ***Distance Test*** and the ***Time Test***:

- **Closely related in time** – Expenses incurred within one year from the date first reporting to work at a new location relate closely in time to the start of work. It is not necessary for a person to arrange to work before moving, as long as he actually goes to work in that location.
- **Closely related in place** – The distance from the new home to the new job location is not more than the distance from the former home to the new job location. If the move does not meet this requirement, an individual may still deduct moving expenses if he meets one of the following:
    1) Is required to live in the new home as a condition of employment
    2) Spends less time or money commuting from the new home to the new job location
- **Distance test** – The new main job location must be at least 50 miles farther from the taxpayer's former home than the old main job location. For example, if the old job was 3 miles away from the former home, the new job location must be at least 53 miles away.
- **Time test** – The requirements for the time test will vary depending on employment. If married filing jointly, only one spouse must satisfy this test.
    1) **For employees** – Work full time in the same general area for at least 39 weeks during the first 12 months after arriving in the area of the new job location.
        A) Taxpayer does not need to work for the same employer for all 39 weeks.
        B) Do not have to work 39 weeks in a row.

2) **For self-employed person** – Work full time for at least 39 weeks during the first 12 months and for a total of at least 78 weeks during the first 24 months

A taxpayer who <u>expects</u> to meet the requirements may deduct moving expenses even if the taxpayer does not satisfy the time test by the due date of the return. If a taxpayer fails to meet the time test requirements, he must report the moving expense deduction as other income on Form 1040 for the year he cannot meet the test, or amend the prior return, figuring tax without the moving expense deduction.

5.4 John's employer of 15 years has a job opening with a substantial pay raise available in Tampa. The new job location is 40 miles away from his house, so he decides to relocate his family. He spends $5,000 to move his household furniture and $50 in gas driving his family car to Tampa. Previously his daily commute to work was 10 miles. His new home is only 3 miles away from his office. What amount of moving expenses can John claim on his tax return as an adjustment to income?

Deductible Moving Expenses

Taxpayers may deduct the reasonable expenses of the following:

- Moving household goods and personal effects, including the following:
  1) The cost of packing, crating, and transporting household goods and personal effects
  2) Storing and insuring household goods and personal effects within any period of 30 consecutive days after moving the items from the former home (includes in-transit or foreign-move storage)
- Traveling to a new home, consisting of:
  1) Transportation and lodging for the taxpayer and household members. This includes expenses for the day of arrival. There is no deduction for meals.
  2) If traveling by car, a taxpayer may deduct actual expenses such as gasoline or oil if he keeps an accurate record of each expense. There is no deduction for certain automobile expenses such as general repairs, general maintenance, insurance, or depreciation. An alternative is to use the 2011 standard mileage rate of <u>19 cents per mile</u> (23 1/2 cents after June 30, 2011). Taxpayers can deduct parking fees and tolls regardless of the method used.

Nondeductible Expenses

A taxpayer cannot deduct the following items as moving expenses:

- Meals while traveling
- Any part of the purchase price of a new home
- Car tags
- Driver's license
- Expenses of buying or selling a home (including closing costs, mortgage fees, and points)
- Expenses of entering into or breaking a lease
- Home improvements to help sell a home
- Loss on the sale of a home

- Losses from disposing of memberships in clubs
- Mortgage penalties
- Pre-move house hunting expenses
- Real estate taxes
- Refitting of carpet and draperies
- Return trips to a former residence
- Security deposits (including any given up due to the move)
- Storage charges except those incurred in transit and for foreign moves

Alimony

Alimony is a payment to (or for) a spouse or former spouse under a divorce or separation instrument. It does not include voluntary payments made by the taxpayer that are not under a divorce or separation instrument. Alimony is deductible by the taxpayer and must be included in the spouse's or former spouse's income. Not all payments under a divorce or separation instrument are alimony. Alimony does not include the following items:

- Child support
- Noncash property settlements
- Payments that are a spouse's part of community income
- Payments to maintain the payer's property
- Use of the payer's property

A payment to or for a spouse under a divorce or separation instrument is alimony if the spouses do not file a joint return with each other and all the following requirements are met:

- The payment is in cash (checks and money orders).
- The instrument cannot designate the payment as not alimony.
- The spouses are not members of the same household at the time the taxpayer makes the payments.
- There is no liability to make any payment (cash or property) after the death of the recipient spouse.
- The payment is not treated as child support.

Cash payments, checks, or money orders to a third party on behalf of a spouse under the terms of a divorce or separation instrument can be alimony, if they otherwise qualify. These include payments for a spouse's medical expenses, housing costs (rent, utilities, etc.), taxes, tuition, etc. The payments are treated as received by the spouse and then paid to the third party. In addition, cash payments made to a third party at the written request of a taxpayer's spouse may qualify as alimony if they meet all of the following requirements:

- The payments are in lieu of payments of alimony directly to the spouse.

- The written request states that both spouses intend to treat the payments as alimony.
- The taxpayer receives the written request from a spouse before filing the return.

If a divorce or separation instrument requires a taxpayer to pay mortgage payments for a home jointly owned with a spouse or former spouse, one-half of the payments are alimony.

5.5 Lawrence pays his ex-wife $1,200 each month as part of a divorce settlement. He is also required to pay $2,000 a month in child support. His ex-wife and children live in his house, but he pays the monthly mortgage of $2,500 and $200 monthly lawn and pool service. He does not live with them in the house. How much of these payments can Lawrence exclude from his income as alimony?

Recapture Rule

The recapture provision prevents a taxpayer from disguising nondeductible property settlements as deductible alimony. If alimony payments decrease or terminate during the first three calendar years, the taxpayer may have to include in the third year part of the alimony payments previously deducted from income as alimony received on Form 1040. The receiving spouse can deduct as an adjustment to gross income part of the alimony payments he previously included in income. A taxpayer is subject to the recapture rule in the third year if one of the following conditions exists:

- Alimony paid in the third year (Y_3) decreases by more than $15,000 from the second year (Y_2).
- The average alimony paid in Y_2 and Y_3 decreases by more than $15,000 from Y_1.

Calculate recapture in each of the first two years:

- Recapture amount for second year $(R_2) = (Y_2 - Y_3) - \$15{,}000$
- Recapture amount for first year $(R_1) = Y_1 - \frac{(Y_2+Y_3-R_2)}{2} - \$15{,}000$

The calculation for a decrease in alimony does not include the following amounts:

- Payments made under a temporary support order
- Payments required over a period of at least three calendar years that vary because they are a percentage of income from a business or property, or from compensation for employment
- Payments that decrease because of the death of either spouse or the remarriage of the spouse receiving the payments before the end of the third year

Child Support

A payment that is ***specifically designated as child support*** or treated as specifically designated as child support under a divorce or separation instrument is not alimony. Child support payments are not deductible by the payer and are not taxable to the recipient. The IRS will treat a payment as child support to the extent that the payment declines under either of the following conditions:

- On the happening of a contingency relating to a child, such as becoming employed, dying, leaving the household, leaving school, married, or reaching a specified age or income level
- At a time that can be clearly associated with the contingency

Education Related Adjustments

Educator Expenses

An ***eligible educator*** may deduct up to $250 of ***qualified expenses*** as an adjustment to gross income, rather than as a miscellaneous itemized deduction. If filing jointly and both are eligible educators, the maximum deduction is $500. Neither spouse can deduct more than $250 of qualified expenses.

- **Eligible educator** – An eligible educator is a kindergarten through grade 12 teacher, instructor, counselor, principal, or aide who worked in a school for at least 900 hours during a school year.
- **Qualified expenses** – Qualified expenses include ordinary and necessary expenses paid in connection with books, supplies, equipment (including computer equipment, software, and services), and other materials used in the classroom. Qualified expenses do not include costs for home schooling or nonathletic supplies for courses in health or physical education.

Student Loan Interest Deduction

Individuals may deduct up to $2,500 of the interest paid on a ***qualified student loan*** used for higher education. The loan cannot be from a related person or a qualified employer plan and must be for qualified educational expenses that are as follows:

- For the taxpayer, a spouse, or a dependent at time of the loan, who is enrolled at least half time in a program leading to a degree, certificate, or other recognized educational credential
- Paid or incurred within a reasonable period of time before or after obtaining the loan
- For education provided during an academic period for an eligible student.

Generally, the deduction is available if all of the following apply:

- The taxpayer paid interest on a qualified student loan.
- Filing status is not married filing separately.
- Modified adjusted gross income (MAGI) is less than $75,000 ($150,000 MFJ) for 2011.
- The taxpayer and spouse, if filing jointly, cannot be claimed as a dependent on another return.

Tuition and Fees Deduction

A taxpayer may deduct up to $4,000 of qualified education expenses paid during the year. A taxpayer may be able to take a credit for education expenses instead of a deduction, but not both. An individual can choose the one providing the lower tax. A taxpayer cannot claim a deduction for qualified education expenses paid with certain tax-free funds. He must reduce the qualified education expenses by the amount of any tax-free educational assistance and refunds received.

- Generally, a taxpayer can claim the deduction if all three of the following requirements are met:
    1) He paid qualified education expenses of higher education.
    2) He paid the education expenses for an eligible student.
    3) The eligible student is the taxpayer, his spouse, or a dependent for which he claims an exemption on his tax return.

- A taxpayer cannot claim the tuition and fees deduction if any of the following apply:
  1) Filing status is married filing separately.
  2) Another person can claim an exemption for the taxpayer as a dependent on his tax return, regardless if actually claimed.
  3) Modified adjusted gross income (MAGI) for 2011 is more than $80,000 ($160,000 MFJ).
  4) The taxpayer is a nonresident alien for any part of the year and did not elect treatment as a resident alien for tax purposes.
  5) The taxpayer or anyone else claims an American Opportunity or Lifetime Learning credit for the student for whom the taxpayer paid the qualified education expenses.

Other Adjustments to Income

- **Deductible Part of Self-employment Taxes** – Self-employed taxpayers other than S corporation shareholders may deduct a portion of the self-employment taxes reported on schedule SE. For 2011, the self-employment tax rate is reduced from 15.3% to 13.3%, accordingly, in determining net earnings from self-employment, a taxpayer must take account of the deduction for the "deductible part" of self-employment tax (rather than "one-half"). The deductible part is 6.2% Social Security and 1.45% Medicare.
- **Penalty on Early Withdrawal of Savings** – The penalty levied upon an early withdrawal of savings is an adjustment to (reduction) gross income.
- **Domestic Production Activities** – If a taxpayer builds, manufactures, or produces goods in the United States, he may be engaged in domestic production activities. For 2011, the deduction can be as much as **9%** of income.

Tax Return Preparer Competency Exam – Chapter 5 Quiz

Circle the letter next to the best answer. Remember to read the question carefully.

1) All of the following types of accounts are permitted for Individual Retirement Arrangements except:
   a. A trust or custodial account at an IRS approved entity.
   b. An individual retirement annuity.
   c. An employer and employee association trust account.
   d. Individual savings bonds clearly designated as an IRA.

2) Which of the following are examples of prohibited transactions with a traditional IRA?
   a. Selling property to it.
   b. Using it as security for a loan.
   c. Buying property for personal use with your IRA funds.
   d. All of the above.

3) Which of the following is correct regarding contributions to a Roth IRA?
   a. Contributions may be made regardless of age provided other requirements are met.
   b. Contributions may be deducted if you are within certain income limits.
   c. Contributions may be deducted if you are not covered under a retirement plan.
   d. Contributions may not be deducted, but earnings are taxable when distributed.

4) John failed to take required minimum distributions from his traditional IRA. The excess accumulation is subject to a penalty of:
   a. 6%
   b. 10%
   c. 15%
   d. 50%

5) Which of the following is compensation for the purpose of contributions to an IRA?

a. Deferred compensation received.

b. Foreign earned income excluded from income.

c. Pension or annuity income.

d. Taxable alimony and separate maintenance.

6) Which of the following is not allowed as a deductible moving expense?

a. Moving your household goods and personal effects.

b. In transit storage expenses for household goods and personal effects.

c. Meal expense incurred in traveling to your new home.

d. Traveling, including lodging, to your new home.

7) Mr. West must pay his former spouse $20,000 annually under a divorce decree in the following amounts:

- $1,000 a month for mortgage payments (including principle and interest) on a jointly owned home
- $200 a month for tuition fees paid to a private school until their son attains the age of 18 or leaves the school prior to age 18.
- $5,000 a year cash payment to former Mrs. West
- In addition to the above amounts, the former Mrs. West also received a lump-sum amount of $150,000 from the sale of their other marital assets.

The parties did not file a joint return and were not members of the same household. There were no written statements between the parties as to how the amounts should be treated. What is the amount of Mr. West's alimony deductions?

a. $20,000

b. $155,000

c. $17,600

d. $11,000

8) Sally, age 38, converted $14,000 from her traditional IRA to a Roth IRA in 2011. At the time of the conversion her income was $300,000. If she does not do a re-characterization by April 15, 2012 what are her consequences?

a. She can report 100% of the income in 2011

b. Pay a 6% penalty only on the full $14,000.

c. Pay tax and a 10% penalty on all of the $14,000 conversion, plus a 6% penalty on $14,000.

d. Pay tax and a 10% penalty on $11,000.

Tax Return Preparer Competency Exam – Chapter 5 Quiz Rationale

For more practice questions, visit fastforwardacademy.com and access our FREE online question bank.

1) **d** The sale of individual retirement bonds issued by the federal government was suspended after April 30, 1982.

2) **d** These are ALL specifically listed prohibited transactions. Generally, if there is a prohibited transaction in connection with a traditional IRA account at any time during the year, the account stops being an IRA as of the first day of that year. At that time, the entire account balance is considered a distribution. If someone other than the owner or beneficiary of a traditional IRA engages in a prohibited transaction, that person may be liable for certain taxes. There is a 15% tax on the amount of the prohibited transaction and a 100% additional tax if not corrected.

3) **a** Roth IRA contributions are never deductible, eliminating B and C. Qualified distributions from Roth IRAs are tax-exempt.

4) **d** Distributions must begin by April 1 of the year following the year the taxpayer reaches age 70½. The amount of the distribution is referred to as the *required minimum distribution (RMD).* The RMD for any year after the year attaining age 70½ must be made by December 31 of that later year. If distributions are less than the RMD for the year, taxpayers may have to pay a 50% excise tax on the amount not distributed as required. The penalty on early withdrawals (pre 59 ½) is 10%. The tax on excess contributions is 6%.

5) **d** For IRAs, consider the term "compensation" as direct payment received for active effort. The most common form of compensation is wages. Taxable alimony is specifically included as compensation for purposes of calculating IRA contributions. Income such as earning from property, interest and dividends, and pensions are not payment for services rendered.

6) **c** Meals are specifically excluded as a deductible moving expense.

7) **d** If a divorce or separation instrument requires a taxpayer to pay mortgage payments for a home jointly owned with a spouse or former spouse, one-half of the payments are alimony. Since it is a jointly owned home, half of the mortgage payments are includable in alimony, as is the $5,000 onetime payment, for a total of $11,000. The tuition is considered child support because of the contingency relating to the child (age and/or staying in school). $150,000 payment is not alimony as it is a transfer of property.

8) **a** The IRS removed income limitations for Roth IRA conversions in 2010. The taxpayer includes the entire amount in income in 2011. This is different from 2010, when the IRS allowed taxpayers to recognize taxable distributions equally over the following two years.

6 Standard and Itemized Deductions

Standard Deduction · Itemized Deductions · Medical and Dental Expenses · Taxes · Interest Expense · Charitable Contributions · Casualty and Theft Losses · Employee Business Expenses · Work-related Education · Miscellaneous Deductions · Limit on Itemized Deductions.

This chapter summarizes information contained in Pub 17 Chapters 21 through 29, and Pub 529.

Standard Deduction

The standard deduction reduces the amount of income subject to tax. Taxpayers benefit from a standard deduction if it is more than the allowable ***itemized deductions***.

The following taxpayers are not eligible for the standard deduction:

- Married filing a separate return (MFS), and the other spouse itemizes deductions.
- Tax return is for a **short tax year** because of a change in annual accounting period.
- ***Nonresident*** or ***dual-status alien*** during the year. A dual-status alien is both a nonresident and resident alien during the year. A nonresident alien who is married to a U.S. citizen or resident alien at the end of the year can choose tax treatment as a U.S. resident and claim the standard deduction.

Standard Deduction Amount

The standard deduction amount depends on filing status:

- $5,800 if filing as single (S) or married filing separately (MFS)
- $8,500 if filing as head of household (HH)
- $11,600 is filing as married filing jointly (MFJ) or qualifying widow(er) (QW)

The standard deduction is higher for taxpayers who are **65 or older** at the end of the year **and/or blind** (less than 20/200 vision). This extra deduction applies to both the taxpayer AND to a spouse if married.

- Increase the standard deduction by the following for each occurrence of the conditions above.
- $1,150 if MFJ, MFS or QW
- $1,450 if S or HOH

A blind taxpayer and spouse, both age 66, may add $3,450 ($1,150 x 3) to the basic standard deduction of $11,600 for a total deduction of $15,050.

Standard Deduction for Dependents

The standard deduction for a dependent cannot exceed the regular standard deduction, based on filing status. The basic standard deduction for an individual for whom an exemption can be claimed on another person's tax return (dependent) is generally limited to the greater of:

- $950
- The individual's earned income for the year, plus $300

6.1 Jill is age 23 and a full-time student at Purdue. She has $6,500 in wages from a modeling job during the year. Her only other income is $5,000 from CD's she inherited from her grandmother. Jill is single, and her parents provide more than half of her support. What is the amount of Jill's standard deduction?

Itemized Deductions

A taxpayer with more deductions than the standard deduction amount, or one who does not qualify for the standard deduction, may wish to itemize on ***Schedule A*** if it has a greater benefit. The phase-out of itemized deductions is eliminated for a second year in 2011. Common deductions include medical expenses, certain taxes, interest expense, charitable contributions, and certain miscellaneous deductions.

Medical and Dental Expenses

Medical expenses are the costs of diagnosis, cure, mitigation, treatment, or prevention of disease, and the costs for treatments affecting any part or function of the body. They include the costs of equipment, supplies, and diagnostic devices needed for these purposes. Medical expenses also include dental care, and the cost of insurance. Medical expenses must be primarily to alleviate or prevent a physical or mental defect or illness.

1) Do not include expenses for procedures that are purely cosmetic or those that are merely beneficial to general health, such as vitamins or a vacation.

- Include only the expenses paid this tax year, regardless of when the services were provided.
- A taxpayer can generally deduct medical expenses paid for himself, and someone who was a spouse or dependent when the services are provided or when the taxpayer paid for them.
- Only the amount of medical and dental expenses that **is more than 7.5%** of AGI is deductible.

TIP Employees who contribute through payroll deductions towards their medical insurance premiums –or any other benefits–cannot claim a deduction on their personal tax returns for amounts not included in wages, as doing so would provide a double benefit.

Deductible Medical Expenses

- **Medical insurance premiums,** (including Medicare parts B and D) for policies that cover:

  1) Hospitalization, surgical services, X-rays
  2) Prescription drugs and insulin

3) Dental care
4) Replacement of lost or damaged contact lenses
5) Long-term care (limited)

TIP The cost of insurance paid by an employee is not deductible unless the payments are part of wages on Form W-2 (box 1). Certain self-employed taxpayers or S corportation shareholders with a qualifying plan established under the business may benefit more by deducting the cost of insurance as an adjustment to gross income.

- Meals and lodging
    1) Include the cost of meals and lodging at a hospital or similar institution if a principal reason for being there is to get medical care.
    2) The cost of such lodging not provided in a hospital or similar institution while away from home if all of the following requirements are met:
        A) The lodging is primarily for and essential to medical care.
        B) A doctor in a licensed hospital or in a medical care facility related to, or the equivalent of, a licensed hospital provided the services.
        C) The lodging is not lavish or extravagant under the circumstances.
        D) There is no significant element of personal pleasure, recreation, or vacation in the travel away from home.
        E) The deduction for lodging cannot be more than $50 for each night for each person. Also, include lodging for a person traveling with the person receiving the medical care. For example, if a parent is traveling with a sick child, up to $100 per night can be included as a medical expense for lodging. Meals are not included.
- **Nursing home** – Costs of medical care in nursing home, home for the aged, or similar institution.
- **Transportation** – Amounts paid for transportation primarily for, and essential to, medical care:
    1) Bus, taxi, train, or plane fares, or ambulance service
    2) Transportation expenses of a parent who must go with a child who needs medical care
    3) Transportation expenses of a nurse or other person who can give injections, medications, or other treatment required by a patient who is traveling to get medical care and is unable to travel alone
    4) Transportation expenses for regular visits to see a mentally ill dependent, if the medical provider recommended these visits as a part of treatment
- **Car expenses** – Out-of-pocket expenses, such as the cost of gas and oil, when using a car for medical reasons. Individuals cannot include depreciation, insurance, general repair, or maintenance expenses. If preferred, the taxpayer may use a standard mileage rate of 19 cents per mile (23 1/2 cents after June 30, 2011) instead of actual expenses incurred.

6.2 Andrew has unpaid medical expenses from a 2005 car accident of $5,000. When he marries Jasmine in 2011, she pays off his hospital bills. Jasmine's employer has a cafeteria plan and she uses it to purchase health insurance using pre-tax dollars. Her total payments for health insurance total $6,000 for the year. Her AGI is $50,000. How much can she claim as a medical expense deduction on Schedule A.

Taxes

Deductible Taxes

A taxpayer receives a deduction for taxes he is legally liable to pay:

- State and local income taxes, if applicable, or general sales taxes, but not both.
- Foreign income taxes paid. Generally, one may take either a deduction or a credit for income taxes imposed by a foreign country or a U.S. possession.
- Real estate taxes on real property levied for the general public welfare. Deduct only the taxes that are based on the ***assessed value*** of the real property and charged uniformly against all property under the jurisdiction of the taxing authority.
  1) If property was bought or sold during the year, divide the current real estate taxes between buyer and seller according to the number of days owned, pro-rata. The seller pays the taxes up to, but not including, the date of sale.
  2) If mortgage payments include taxes placed in escrow, no tax is deductible until paid by the mortgage servicing company.
- Personal property taxes that meet the following criteria:
  1) Based only on the value of the personal property
  2) Charged on a yearly basis, even if they are collected more or less than once a year

Nondeductible Taxes

- Real estate items individuals generally cannot deduct include the following:
  1) Taxes for local benefits that increase the value of property, such as sidewalks or sewer
  2) Itemized charges for services (such as trash and garbage pickup fees)
     A) Service charges used to maintain or improve services (such as trash collection or police and fire protection) are deductible as real estate taxes if the following conditions exist:
        (a) Fees or charges are imposed at a like rate against all property in the taxing jurisdiction.
        (b) The funds collected are not earmarked; and are part of general revenue funds.
        (c) Funds used to maintain or improve services are not limited to or determined by the amount of these fees or charges collected.
  3) Transfer taxes (or stamp taxes)
  4) Rent increases due to higher real estate taxes

5) Homeowners' association charges

- Employment taxes, including Social Security and Medicare
- Estate, inheritance, legacy, or succession taxes
- Federal income taxes
- Fines and penalties
- Gift taxes
- License fees
- Per capita taxes

6.3 Marcus loves his mom. When he realizes she is going to lose her home for failure to pay her property taxes, he springs into action paying the $2,500 owed. Who is entitled to deduct the payment?

Interest Expense

Home Mortgage Interest

A person (or organization) engaged in a trade or business that receives at least $600 of mortgage interest (including certain points) on any one mortgage in the calendar year must report the mortgage interest on ***Form 1098, Mortgage Interest Statement*** to the payor and the IRS. The taxpayer may deduct interest paid on ***home acquisition debt*** to buy, build, or improve a ***qualified home*** (main home or second home). To receive a full deduction, the mortgages must total $1 million or less. Interest on ***home equity debt*** (mortgages taken other than to buy, build, or improve a home) is also deductible, but only on amounts of up to $100,000.

Mortgage interest is deductible if all the following conditions exist:

- File Form 1040 and itemize deductions on Schedule A
- The taxpayer is legally liable for the loan
- There is a true debtor-creditor relationship between the taxpayer and the lender
- The taxpayer has an ownership interest in the qualified home that secures the mortgage

Points

The term "points" describes certain charges paid, or treated as paid, by a borrower to obtain a home mortgage. In general, taxpayers amortize points (deduct ratably over the life of the mortgage). A taxpayer may fully deduct points in the year paid if the following conditions exist:

- The taxpayer must use the loan proceeds to buy or build a main home. Amortize points on a second home, or to refinance an existing loan, over the life of the loan
- Paying points is an established business practice in the area where the loan was made
- The points paid were not more than the points generally charged in that area

- The taxpayer uses the cash method of accounting
- The points are not in place of amounts that ordinarily are stated separately on the settlement statement, such as appraisal fees, inspection fees, title fees, attorney fees, and property taxes
- The points are not financed into the mortgage amount
- The points were computed as a percentage of the principal amount of the mortgage
- The amount clearly appears on the settlement statement as points charged for the mortgage

---

Lamont purchased a new home to use as his primary residence. He pays $5,000 in points to improve the rate on his 15-year loan. On Schedule A, he deducts the points as interest in the year paid. If this were an investment property, he would amortize the points over a period of 15 years.

Mortgage Insurance Premiums

Treat the amount paid during the year for ***qualified mortgage insurance*** as home mortgage interest. This deduction begins to phase out when AGI exceeds $100,000.

Investment Interest

Interest on a loan to buy property held for investment is ***investment interest***.

The deduction for investment interest is limited to the taxpayer's ***net investment income***. If the taxpayer does not use the deduction, he may carry it forward into the next year. Interest incurred to produce tax-exempt income is not deductible.

An individual, estate, or trust must use ***Form 4952*** to claim a deduction for investment interest expenses. Form 4952 is not necessary if a taxpayer meets both the following conditions:

- Income from interest and ordinary dividends (minus any qualified dividends) exceeds the amount of investment interest expenses
- The taxpayer does not have any other deductible investment expenses or carryover of disallowed prior year investment interest expense.

Charitable Contributions

Deductions for contributions to a ***qualified organization*** are generally limited to 50% of adjusted gross income, but in some cases, 20% and 30% limits may apply. Qualified organizations include:

- Churches, association of churches, temples, synagogues, mosques, and other religious organizations
- Most nonprofit charitable organizations such as the Red Cross and the United Way
- Most nonprofit educational organizations (Boy and Girl Scouts of America, colleges and museums)
- Nonprofit hospitals and medical research organizations
- Utility company emergency energy programs, if the utility company is an agent for a charitable organization that assists individuals with emergency energy needs

- Nonprofit volunteer fire companies
- Public parks and recreation facilities
- Civil defense organizations

Nondeductible Contributions

- Contributions to **specific individuals**, including the following:
    1) Contributions to fraternal societies for paying medical or burial expenses of deceased members
    2) Contributions to individuals who are needy or worthy
    3) Payments to a member of the clergy that the member may spend as he wishes
    4) Expenses paid for another person who provided services to a qualified organization
    5) Payments to a hospital for a specific patient's care or for services for a specific patient
- Contributions to nonqualified organizations:
    1) Groups that are run for a profit
    2) Certain state bar associations
    3) Chambers of commerce and other business leagues or organizations
    4) Civic leagues and associations
    5) Country clubs and other social clubs
    6) Foreign organizations except certain Canadian, Israeli, or Mexican charitable organizations
    7) Homeowners' associations
    8) Labor unions
    9) Political organizations and candidates

6.4 John donated $100 to the United Way, $200 to Veterans of Foreign Wars, and $300 to his neighbor whose home was destroyed by a tornado. How much is John's deduction for charitable contributions?

Contributions of Property

A taxpayer claiming a deduction for noncash gifts of more than $500 must file ***Form 8283***. The deductible amount for ***capital gain property*** is generally the fair market value of the property at the time of the contribution. The deduction for ***ordinary income property*** is limited to the gifts fair market value minus the amount that would be ordinary income or short-term capital gain if the taxpayer sold the property for its fair market value. Ordinary income property includes short-term gain property, inventory, works of art created by taxpayer, property subject to depreciation recapture, etc.

Donated clothing or household items must be in good used condition or better in order to qualify for a deduction. A good measure of value might be the price that buyers of these used items actually pay in consignment or thrift shops. However, a taxpayer may take a deduction for items in poorer condition if the deduction is more than $500 and the taxpayer includes a qualified appraisal with the return. The IRS requires an appraisal for any single item or group of related items with a value exceeding $5,000.

A taxpayer looking to deduct more than $500 resulting from a donation of a qualified vehicle must attach a copy of the contemporaneous written acknowledgment. In general, a contemporaneous acknowledgement must be issued within 30 days of the contribution or later sale. The organization receiving property may use Copy B of Form 1098-C as the acknowledgment. The deduction is limited to the smaller of the vehicle's FMV on the date of the contribution or the gross proceeds received from a later sale of the vehicle. An acceptable measure of the FMV of a donated vehicle is an amount not in excess of the price listed in a used vehicle-pricing guide for a private party sale of a similar vehicle.

Limits on Charitable Deductions

If a taxpayer receives a benefit because of a contribution to a qualified organization, reduce the charitable deduction by the FMV of the benefit received.

The deduction for charitable contributions is limited to 50% of adjusted gross income. This limit applies to the total of all charitable contributions made during the year. If a taxpayer makes gifts of appreciated property or gifts to certain types of organizations, those gifts may be limited to a lesser amount.

- **50% limit organizations** – The following is a partial list of the types of organizations that are 50% limit organizations:

  1) Churches and conventions or associations of churches
  2) Educational organizations with a regular faculty and curriculum that normally have a regularly enrolled student body attending classes on site
  3) Hospitals and certain medical research organizations associated with these hospitals
  4) Publicly supported charities

- **30% limit** – A 30% limit applies to the following gifts:

  1) Gifts to all qualified organizations other than 50% limit organizations. This includes gifts to veterans' organizations, fraternal societies, nonprofit cemeteries, and certain private non-operating foundations.
  2) Gifts for the use of any organization.

- Limit for capital gain property:

  1) A **special 30% limit** applies to gifts of capital gain property to 50% limit organizations. However, the special 30% limit does not apply when using the taxpayers' cost in place of FMV as the amount of the gift. Instead, only the 50% limit applies.

     A) This special 30% limit for capital gain property is separate from the other 30% limit. Therefore, the deduction of a contribution subject to one 30% limit does not reduce the amount taxpayers can deduct for contributions subject to the other 30% limit. However, the total cannot be more than 50% of adjusted gross income.

2) A **20% limit** applies to all gifts of capital gain property to or for the use of qualified organizations (other than gifts of capital gain property to 50% limit organizations).

Your adjusted gross income is $50,000. During the year, you gave capital gain property with a fair market value of $15,000 to a 50% limit organization. You do not choose to reduce the property's fair market value by its appreciation in value. You also gave $10,000 cash to a qualified organization that is not a 50% limit organization. The $15,000 gift of property is subject to the special 30% limit. The $10,000 cash gift is subject to the other 30% limit. Both gifts are fully deductible because neither is more than the 30% limit that applies ($15,000 in each case) and together they are not more than the 50% limit ($25,000).

Records for Cash Contributions

Cash contributions include those paid by cash, check, electronic funds transfer, credit card, or payroll deduction. To claim a cash contribution, taxpayers must have one of the following:

- Bank records (canceled check or statement)
- A receipt (or other written communication) from the qualified organization showing the name of the organization, the date of the contribution, and the amount of the contribution
- Payroll deduction records

To deduct a cash contribution of **$250 or more**, the taxpayer must receive an acknowledgment of the contribution from the qualified organization or have certain payroll deduction records.

Out-of-pocket Expenses in Giving Services

The value of taxpayer-provided services given to a qualified organization is not deductible; however, costs (automobile or travel expenses, etc.) associated with providing the services may be. The standard mileage rate is 14 cents per mile for charitable miles driven. Taxpayers cannot deduct personal expenses for sightseeing, fishing parties, theater tickets, nightclubs, or expenses for family members. To receive a deduction, the expenses must be as follows:

- Unreimbursed
- Directly connected with the services
- Expenses incurred only because of the services provided
- Not personal, living, or family expenses

Conventions

If a taxpayer is a chosen representative attending a convention of a qualified charitable organization, he may deduct actual unreimbursed expenses for travel and transportation, including a reasonable amount for meals and lodging, while away from home overnight in connection with the convention. Expenses are not deductible if attending as a member of the organization rather than as a chosen representative.

Miscellaneous Deductions Subject to the 2% Limit

A non-business taxpayer may deduct certain expenses as ***miscellaneous itemized deductions*** when they exceed 2% of adjusted gross income. Calculate the deductible amount by subtracting 2% of AGI from the total of these expenses. Generally, the 2% limit applies after any other deduction limit. There are three categories of deductions that are subject to the 2% limit:

- Unreimbursed employee expenses
- Tax preparation fees
- Other expenses

Unreimbursed Employee Expenses

A taxpayer can file ***Form 2106*** to claim certain expenses where they do not receive a complete reimbursement for costs incurred as an employee. Employees who do not receive any reimbursements from an employer may file ***Form 2106-EZ***, but only if they do not claim actual vehicle expenses. A taxpayer should not file this form unless the total expenses exceed the 2% limit on miscellaneous itemized deductions. Unreimbursed employee expenses are deductible provided they meet all the following conditions:

- Paid or incurred during the taxpayer's tax year
- For carrying on the taxpayer's trade or business of being an employee
- Ordinary and necessary – An expense is ordinary if it is common and accepted in the taxpayer's trade, business, or profession. An expense is necessary if it is appropriate and helpful to the business. An expense does not need to be required to be considered necessary.

Individuals may be able to deduct the following items as unreimbursed employee expenses:

- **Business bad debt** – Losses from a debt created or acquired in a trade or business are deductible. Any other worthless debt is a business bad debt only if there is a very close relationship between the debt and the taxpayer's trade or business when the debt becomes worthless.
    1) Example – A taxpayer makes a bona fide loan to the corporation he works for. The company fails to pay him back. The taxpayer had to make the loan in order to keep his job. He has a business bad debt as an employee.
- **Business liability insurance** – Insurance premiums paid for protection against personal liability for wrongful acts on the job are deductible.
- **Damages for breach of employment contract** – Damages paid to a former employer are deductible if the damages are attributable to the pay received from that employer.
- **Depreciation on computers**– Individuals may claim a depreciation deduction for a computer used at work as an employee if its use meets both the following conditions:
    1) For the convenience of the employer
    2) Required as a condition of employment
- **Dues to chambers of commerce and professional societies** – Deduct dues paid to professional organizations (such as bar associations and medical associations) and to chambers of commerce and

similar organizations, if membership helps taxpayer carry out his job duties. Dues related to lobbying and political activities may not be deductible. Similar organizations include the following:

1) Boards of trade
2) Business leagues
3) Civic or public service organizations
4) Real estate boards
5) Trade associations

- **Educator expenses** – ***Eligible educators*** may deduct up to $250 of qualified expenses paid in 2011 as an adjustment to gross income on Form 1040 rather than as a miscellaneous itemized deduction. If filing jointly and both are eligible educators, the maximum deduction is $500. However, neither spouse can deduct more than $250 of his qualified expenses. Eligible educators may deduct qualified expenses not taken as an adjustment to gross income as an itemized deduction subject to the 2% limit.

  1) **Eligible educator** – A kindergarten through grade 12 teacher, instructor, counselor, principal, or aide in a school for at least 900 hours during a school year
  2) **Qualified expenses** – Ordinary and necessary expenses paid in connection with books, supplies, equipment (including computer equipment, software, and services), and other materials used in the classroom

- **Home office** – Deduct a part of the operating expenses and depreciation of the home if the taxpayer uses that part of the home regularly and exclusively for one of the following:

  1) As a principal place of business for any trade or business
  2) As a place to meet or deal with patients, clients, or customers
  3) In connection with a trade or business, if a separate structure not attached to the home

- **Job search expenses** – Deduct expenses connected with looking for a new job, even if not hired. Examples of these are employment and outplacement agency fees, and the cost of preparing and mailing copies of a résumé. A taxpayer cannot deduct these expenses if one of the following is true:

  1) He is looking for a job in a new occupation.
  2) There was a substantial break between the ending of the last job and looking for a new one.
  3) He is looking for a job for the first time.

- **Legal fees** – Deduct legal fees related to doing or keeping a job.

- **Licenses and regulatory fees** – Deduct amounts paid to state or local governments for licenses and regulatory fees for the taxpayer's trade, business, or profession.

- **Occupational taxes** – A taxpayer may deduct an occupational tax charged at a flat rate by a locality for the privilege of working or conducting a business in the locality.

- **Repayment of income aid payment** – An "income aid payment" is one that the taxpayer received under an employer's plan to aid employees who lose their jobs because of lack of work. If the taxpayer repays an aid payment included as income in an earlier year, he can deduct the repayment.

- **Research expenses of a college professor** – A college professor may deduct research expenses, including travel expenses, for teaching, lecturing, or writing and publishing on subjects that relate directly to teaching duties. There can be no expectation of profit apart from salary.

- **Rural mail carriers' vehicle expenses** – Expenses while performing services as a rural mail carrier.

- **Tools used in work** – Generally, employees can deduct amounts spent for tools used in work if the tools wore out and the taxpayer threw them away within one year from the date of purchase. He can depreciate the cost of tools that have a useful life substantially beyond the tax year.

- **Gift expenses** – Taxpayers can deduct **up to $25** for business gifts given to each person during a tax year. The IRS considers a gift to a member of a customer's family an indirect gift to the customer, unless a bona fide business relationship exists with the family member. The following items do not count toward the $25 limit:

    1) Identical, widely distributed items costing $4 or less with the taxpayer's name imprinted

    2) Signs, racks, and promotional materials to display on the business premises of the recipient

- **Union dues and expenses** – Deduct dues and initiation fees for union membership and assessments for benefit payments to unemployed union members. Any part of the payment for sick, accident, or death benefits is not deductible. Contributions to a pension fund are not deductible. Amounts related to certain lobbying and political activities may not be deductible.

- **Work clothes and uniforms** – The cost and upkeep of work clothes is deductible if the following two requirements are met:

    1) The taxpayer is required to wear them as a condition of employment.

    2) The clothes are not suitable for everyday wear.

A judge required to purchase a robe may deduct his cost and dry cleaning expenses since the robe is not suitable for wear outside of his work. An attorney, required to wear suits cannot deduct the cost.

- **Military uniforms** – Individuals generally cannot deduct the cost of uniforms if on full-time active duty in the armed forces. However, an armed forces reservist may deduct the unreimbursed cost of uniforms if military regulations restrict him from wearing it except while on duty.

- **Qualifying work-related education** – A deduction is unavailable if the education is necessary to meet the minimum requirements of the present trade or business, or is part of a program of study that will qualify the taxpayer for a new trade or business. The IRS does not allow a deduction for the cost of travel that in itself constitutes a form of education. For example, a French teacher who travels to France to maintain general familiarity with the French language and culture cannot deduct the cost of the trip as an educational expense. For the costs (tuition, books, supplies, laboratory fees, and similar items) of work-related education to qualify as a business expenses, at least one of the following two tests must be met:

    1) An employer or the law requires the education to maintain present salary, status, or job. The required education must serve a bona fide business purpose of the employer.

    2) The education maintains or improves skills needed in the taxpayer's present work.

Unreimbursed Employee Meals and Entertainment Expenses

Generally, entertainment expenses (including entertainment-related meals) are deductible only if they ***directly relate*** to the active conduct of the taxpayer's trade or business. However, the expense only needs to be ***associated*** with the active conduct of the taxpayer's trade or business if it directly precedes or follows a substantial and bona fide business-related discussion. Only **50%** of business-related meal and entertainment expenses are deductible (**80%** of meals if consumed during any period subject to the Department of Transportation's "hours of service" limits). These limits apply before considering the 2% of adjusted gross income limit. To deduct an entertainment-related meal, the taxpayer or his employees must be present when provided.

A taxpayer may deduct entertainment expenses only if they are both ordinary and necessary and meet one of the following tests:

- **Directly related test** – Taxpayers must show that the following conditions exist:
  1) The main purpose of the combined business and entertainment is the active conduct of business. Business is generally not considered the main purpose when on hunting or fishing trips, or on yachts or other pleasure boats.
  2) Taxpayers engaged in business with the person during the entertainment period and had more than a general expectation of getting income or some other specific business benefit at some future time.
- **Associated test** – If the taxpayer's expenses do not meet the directly related test, they may meet the associated test. The taxpayer must show that the entertainment is as follows:
  1) Associated with the active conduct of his trade or business
  2) Directly before or after a substantial business discussion

Expenses a taxpayer may not deduct include the following:

- **Lavish or extravagant entertainment** – Expenses that are reasonable considering the facts and circumstances will not be disallowed simply because they are more than a fixed dollar amount or take place at deluxe restaurants, hotels, nightclubs, or resorts.
- **If a taxpayer rents a private luxury box** for more than one event at the same sports arena, the taxpayer generally may not deduct more than the price of a non-luxury box seat ticket.
- **Membership dues** (including initiation fees) for any club organized for business, pleasure, recreation, or other social purpose.
- **Cost for the use of an entertainment facility** or any property he owns, rents, or uses for entertainment. Examples include a yacht, hunting lodge, fishing camp, swimming pool, tennis court, bowling alley, car, airplane, apartment, hotel suite, or home in a vacation resort.

Unreimbursed Employee Travel Expenses

Employee travel expenses are those incurred while traveling away from home for an employer. An employee can deduct travel expenses paid or incurred in connection with a temporary work assignment (lasting less than one year). Generally, expenses paid or incurred in connection with an indefinite work assignment are not deductible. Travel expenses may include the following:

- The cost of getting to and from the business destination (air, rail, bus, car, etc.)
- Meals and lodging while away from home
- Taxi fares
- Baggage charges
- Cleaning and laundry expenses

An individual is traveling away from home if duties require the individual to be away from the general area of the individual's ***tax home*** for a period substantially longer than an ordinary day's work, requiring sleep or rest to meet the demands of work while away. Generally, a tax home is the entire city or general area where the main place of business or work is located, regardless of where the individual maintains the family home.

A person lives with family in Florida but works in Boston where that person stays in a hotel and eats in restaurants. That person returns to Florida every weekend. The taxpayer may not deduct any of the travel, meals, or lodging in Boston because that is the taxpayer's tax home. The travel on weekends to family home in Florida is not for work, so these expenses are also not deductible.

If a person regularly works in more than one place, the person's tax home is the general area where main place of business or work is located. Deductible travel expenses while away from home include, but are not limited to, the costs of the following:

- Travel by airplane, train, bus, or car between home and business destination.
- Using personal car while at a business destination.
- Fares for taxis or other transportation between an airport or train station and a hotel, a hotel and a work location, and from one customer to another or from a place of business to another.
- Meals and lodging.
- Tips paid for services related to any of these expenses.
- Dry cleaning and laundry.
- Business calls while on business trip. This includes business communications by fax machine or other communication devices.
- Other similar ordinary and necessary expenses related to business travel. These expenses might include transportation to and from a business meal, public stenographer's fees, computer rental fees, and operating and maintaining a house trailer.

In addition to the deductions described below, a taxpayer may deduct **50% of meals** when traveling if it is necessary for the taxpayer to stop for substantial sleep or rest while traveling away from home on business. The taxpayer may not deduct expenses for meals that are lavish or extravagant. Expenses are not lavish or extravagant if reasonable based on the following facts and circumstances:

- Travel in the United States:

    1) Taxpayers may deduct all travel expenses if the trip was entirely business related.

2) If the trip was primarily for business, and while at the business destination, the taxpayer extended his stay for a vacation, made a personal side trip, or had other personal activities, the taxpayer may deduct business-related travel expenses.

3) If the trip was primarily for personal reasons, such as a vacation, the entire cost of the trip is a nondeductible personal expense. However, a taxpayer may deduct any expenses he had while at a destination directly related to business.

- Travel outside the United States:

    1) If a taxpayer travels outside the United States and spends the entire time on business activities, he may deduct all of the travel expenses:

        A) Even if he did not spend the entire time on business activities, the trip is considered entirely for business if the taxpayer meets any of the following exceptions:

            (a) Did not have substantial control over arranging the trip

            (b) Taxpayer was outside the United States for a week or less, combining business and non-business activities

            (c) The taxpayer spent less than 25% of the total time the taxpayer was outside the United States on non-business activities

            (d) The taxpayer can establish that a personal vacation was not a major consideration, even if the taxpayer has substantial control over arranging the trip

    2) If the trip is primarily for business but the taxpayer spends some time on other activities, he generally may not deduct all of the travel expenses. The taxpayer may deduct only the business portion of the cost of getting to and from the destination. Individuals must allocate the costs between business and other activities to determine the deductible amount.

    3) If the trip is primarily for vacation or for investment purposes, the entire cost of the trip is a non-deductible personal expense. If a taxpayer spends some time attending brief professional seminars or a continuing education program, the taxpayer may deduct registration fees and other expenses directly related to business.

Travel expenses to attend a convention are deductible so long as conference attendance benefits the taxpayer's trade or business. If the convention is for investment, political, social, or other purposes unrelated to the taxpayer's trade or business, he cannot deduct the expenses.

- A taxpayer cannot deduct the travel expenses for his family.
- A taxpayer may deduct expenses of up to $2,000 per year for attending conventions on a ***cruise ship*** that directly relate to his trade or business. The taxpayer must attach a statement of agenda and attendance by the taxpayer and an officer of the organization sponsoring the trip to the tax return.

Unreimbursed Employee Local Transportation and Lodging

Transportation expenses do not include expenses while traveling away from home overnight. Those expenses are travel expenses. Transportation expenses include the ordinary and necessary costs of all of the following:

- Getting from one workplace to another within the area of an individual's tax home
- Visiting clients or customers

- Going to a business meeting away from a regular workplace
- Getting from home to a temporary (lasting less than a year) workplace
    1) Deduct the expenses of the daily round-trip transportation between the taxpayer's home and the temporary location, regardless of distance.
    2) Driving from home to a permanent (more than 1 year) location is not deductible.

Transportation expenses include the cost of transportation by air, rail, bus, and taxi, and the cost of using a taxpayer's vehicle. A deduction for ***car expenses*** is available if using the taxpayer's vehicle.

- **Business and personal use** – If the taxpayer uses the vehicle for business <u>and</u> personal purposes, divide the expenses between business and personal use based on the miles driven for each purpose. Only the business use portion is deductible. Taxpayers may deduct all business-related parking fees and tolls, regardless of method used.
- Use one of the two following methods to figure deductible car expenses:
    1) **Standard mileage rate** – For 2011, the rate is **<u>51 cents per mile</u>** (55 1/2 cents after June 30, 2011) on business miles driven. To qualify, the taxpayer must use this method for the first year placing the vehicle in service. A taxpayer may not use the business standard mileage rate for a vehicle after using any depreciation method other than straight-line, or after claiming a Section 179 deduction for that vehicle. The taxpayer cannot claim the business standard mileage rate for more than four vehicles used simultaneously. Beginning in 2011, a taxpayer may use the business standard mileage rate for vehicles used for hire, such as taxicabs.
    2) **Actual car expenses** – Depreciation, garage rent, gas, insurance, lease payments, licenses, oil, parking fees, registration fees, repairs, tires, and tolls are deductible expenses.
- In general, commuting between a residence and normal place of business is not deductible.
    1) ***Work at two places in a day*** – When working at two places in a day, whether or not for the same employer, the expenses of traveling from one workplace to the other are deductible.
    2) ***Temporary work location*** – Deduct expenses incurred in traveling between the taxpayer's home and a temporary work location if at least one of the following applies:
        A) The work location is outside the area where the taxpayer lives and normally works.
        B) At least one regular work location exists (not in home) for the same trade or business.
    3) ***Home office*** – Expenses incurred in traveling between home and a workplace if the home is the taxpayer's principal place of business for the same trade or business.

If an employer provides or requires a taxpayer to obtain ***lodging*** while <u>not</u> traveling away from home, the taxpayer can deduct the cost of the lodging if it meets all the following criteria:

- It is on a temporary basis.
- It is necessary for the taxpayer to be available for a business meeting or employer function.
- The costs are ordinary and necessary, but not lavish or extravagant.

If the employer provides the lodging or reimburses the cost of the lodging, deduct the cost only if the value is included in the taxpayer's gross income as wages on Form W-2.

Tax Preparation Fees

Deduct tax preparation fees in the year paid. These fees include the cost of tax software programs, tax publications, and electronic filing.

Other Expenses

"Other Expenses" include certain miscellaneous itemized deductions subject to the 2% of adjusted gross income limit. A taxpayer may deduct expenses paid for the following:

- To produce or collect income that must be included in gross income
- To manage, conserve, or maintain property held for producing such income
- To determine, contest, pay, or claim a refund of any tax

These other expenses include the following items:

- Appraisal fees for a casualty loss or charitable contribution
- Casualty and theft losses from property used in performing services as an employee
- Clerical help and office rent in caring for investments
- Depreciation on home computers used for investments
- Excess deductions (including administrative expenses) allowed a beneficiary on termination of an estate or trust
- Fees to collect interest and dividends
- Hobby expenses, but generally not more than hobby income
- Indirect miscellaneous deductions of pass-through entities
- Investment fees and expenses
- Legal fees related to producing or collecting taxable income or getting tax advice
- Loss on deposits in an insolvent or bankrupt financial institution
- Loss on traditional IRAs or Roth IRAs, when all amounts have been distributed
- Repayments of income
- Repayments of Social Security benefits
- Safe deposit box rental
- Service charges on dividend reinvestment plans
- Tax advice fees
- Trustee's fees for IRA, if separately billed and paid

Deductions NOT Subject to the 2% Limit

The items listed below are miscellaneous itemized deductions that are not subject to the 2% limit:

- Amortizable premium on taxable bonds
- Casualty and theft losses from income-producing property
- Federal estate tax on income in respect of a decedent
- Gambling losses up to the amount of gambling winnings
- Impairment-related work expenses of persons with disabilities
- Loss from other activities from Schedule K-1 (Form 1065-B), box 2
- Losses from Ponzi-type investment schemes
- Repayments of more than $3,000 under a claim of right
- Unrecovered investment in an annuity

Nondeductible Expenses

A deduction is not available for the following expenses:

- Adoption expenses (may claim credit)
- Broker's commissions that paid in connection with IRA
- Burial or funeral expenses, including the cost of a cemetery lot
- Campaign expenses
- Capital expenses
- Check-writing fees
- Club dues
- Commuting expenses
- Fees and licenses, such as car licenses, marriage licenses, and dog tags
- Fines and penalties, such as parking tickets
- Health spa expenses
- Hobby losses (but see *Hobby expenses,* earlier)
- Home repairs, insurance, and rent
- Home security system
- Illegal bribes and kickbacks
- Investment-related seminars

- Life insurance premiums
- Lobbying expenses
- Losses from the sale of taxpayer's home, furniture, personal car, etc.
- Lost or misplaced cash or property
- Lunches with co-workers
- Meals while working late
- Medical expenses as business expenses
- Personal disability insurance premiums
- Personal legal expenses
- Personal, living, or family expenses
- Political contributions
- Professional accreditation fees
- Professional reputation, expenses to improve
- Relief fund contributions
- Residential telephone line
- Stockholders' meeting, expenses of attending
- Tax-exempt income, expenses of earning or collecting
- The value of wages never received or lost vacation time
- Travel expenses for another individual
- Voluntary unemployment benefit fund contributions
- Wristwatches

6.5 Rhonda is the principal at Oak Park Elementary. She was driving fast in order to not be late on the first day of school. The officer did not think that was a good reason and gave her a $285 ticket for speeding. She made a payment of $300 to a lawyer to contest the charges in court, which she won. What is her miscellaneous deduction on Schedule A, before the 2% limitation?

Tax Return Preparer Competency Exam – Chapter 6 Quiz

Circle the letter next to the best answer. Remember to read the question carefully.

1) All of the following capital improvements may be itemized and deducted as medical expenses except:

   a. Cost of constructing wheelchair accessible ramps for your home.

   b. Cost of modifying a car with special hand controls.

   c. Lowering or modifying kitchen cabinets and equipment.

   d. An elevator costing $8,000 that adds $8,000 to the appraised value of your home.

2) Taxes deductible as an itemized deduction include all of the following except:

   a. Real estate taxes based on the assessed value of the property and charged uniformly against all property.

   b. State and local income taxes.

   c. Taxes you paid on property owned by your parents or children.

   d. Personal property taxes based on the value of the personal property.

3) Heather spent $2,500 for lottery tickets during the year. She saved all her tickets. She won $2,000 in November on a $1 ticket. Heather's adjusted gross income is $50,000. How much of her lottery ticket costs can she deduct as an itemized deduction?

   a. $1

   b. $0

   c. $2,500

   d. $2,000

4) Rosa purchased a home in Quogue, NY, in 1990 but she lives in Brooklyn with her sister. She lets her son Bob and his wife Samantha live in the Quogue house. Astoria Bank holds the mortgage with only Rosa's name on the property, as she did not add her son's name to the property deed. Since Bob lives in the Quogue house, he makes the monthly mortgage payments to Astoria Bank. Who can deduct the mortgage interest expense for the year 2011?

   a. Bob, since he makes the payments

   b. Rosa, since she owns the property and is liable for the payments

   c. Both, since they are related

   d. Neither, since Rosa is not paying her liability and Bob is paying for what he is not liable

5) Lisa traveled from Philadelphia to New York on a business trip for her employer. She is not reimbursed for the travel expenses. Lisa spends two days in business meetings and one day on vacation. Lisa's meals cost $90 ($30 per day), lodging costs $360 ($120 per day), and train fare costs $102. What is the total amount of Lisa's business related travel expense?

a. $366

b. $372

c. $507

d. $552

6) Money or property given to the following is deductible as charitable contributions except:

a. Nonprofit schools or hospitals.

b. Civic leagues and chambers of commerce.

c. Churches, synagogues, temples, mosques, and other religious organizations.

d. War veterans' groups.

7) During the year, Ron paid $85 to have his tax return prepared. He also paid a lawyer $215 to prepare his will. At work, he paid union dues of $650, bought safety boots for $200, and contributed $75 to collections for sick co-workers. What is Ron's miscellaneous deduction on his Schedule A, before the 2% limitation?

a. $935

b. $1,010

c. $1,150

d. $1,225

8) Robin, an employee, had the following unreimbursed employee expenses: $100 professional license renewal, $75 subscription to professional journal, and $500 business liability insurance. Her adjusted gross income was $40,000. What net amount can Robin deduct?

a. $675

b. $0

c. $575

d. $175

For more practice questions, visit fastforwardacademy.com and access our FREE online question bank.

1) **d** Adding an elevator is one of the very few modifications to the home made for medical reasons that might increase the value of the property. Any increase in property value must be deducted from the cost before taking the item as a medical expense. Since the cost of the improvement is equal to the increase in property value, there is no allowable medical deduction for this elevator.

2) **c** You cannot deduct the payment of any taxes that you are not legally liable to pay. Since your parents or your children own the taxed property, they are legally liable for those taxes, and they can deduct them only if they pay them.

3) **d** Gambling losses up to the amount of gambling winnings are not subject to the 2% of AGI limitation, so she can itemize $2,000 (the amount of her winnings).

4) **b** Since Rosa is the only one on the property and the mortgage, she is the only person legally liable for the debt. Rosa is the only person who may take the deduction. A payment by Bob of Rosa's mortgage is income constructively received by Rosa. The payments are rental income to Rosa. She may deduct all rental expenses, including interest on schedule E. Bob is not entitled to take the deduction because he is not a beneficial owner of the property, nor legally liable to make payments.

Additional comment:

If Bob is a part owner (but not on the mortgage) he may claim a deduction for interest as a "beneficial owner" under the rules established in 26 C.F.R. §1.163-1(b). Under these rules, interest paid by a taxpayer on a mortgage is deductible if the taxpayer is a legal or "equitable" owner, even if the taxpayer is not directly liable for the mortgage.

5) **b** Train cost fully allowed $102. Two of the three days were for business, so two days lodging allowed $240. Only 50% of the meals expense for the two business days are allowable $30. $102 + $240 + $30 = $372.

6) **b** Contributions to the following Nonqualified Organizations are not deductible: 1) Groups that are run for a profit. 2) Certain state bar associations. 3) Chambers of commerce and other business leagues or organizations. 4) Civic leagues and associations. 5) Country clubs and other social clubs. 6) Foreign organizations except certain Canadian, Israeli, or Mexican charitable organizations. 7) Homeowners' associations. 8) Labor unions. 9) Political organizations and candidates.

7) **a** Preparation of a will is not deductible (only legal fees relevant to generating or collecting taxable income are deductible). Voluntary gifts to collections for sick co-workers are not deductible. Only the union dues, safety clothes and tax return preparation fees qualify.

8) **b** Her total unreimbursed expenses are $675, and all of them are subject to the 2% of AGI limit. That amount is $800. Since her expenses are less than the $800, she has no deduction.

7 Taxes and Credits

Tax Calculations · AMT · Kiddie Tax · Taxes for Household Employees · Additional Taxes Estimated Tax · Child and Dependent Care Credit · Adoption Credit · Education Credits· Earned Income Credit · First-time Homebuyer Credit · Credit for Elderly or the Disabled Child Tax Credit · Other Credits · General Business Credit

This chapter summarizes IRS Forms 5329, 3800, 8839 and Publications 15-A, 15-B, 17, 334, 536, 501, 503, 596, 926, 970, and 972.

Tax Calculations

Calculate income tax as a percentage of ***taxable income***. Tax rates vary according to the amount of taxable income. U.S. income tax is a ***progressive tax***, whereby rates increase as taxable income increases. The IRS has established ***tax brackets*** at various income levels. Taxable income within each bracket is taxed at the corresponding tax rate. The ***marginal tax rate*** is the rate at which the last dollar of income is taxed. After income tax and any ***alternative minimum tax (AMT)***, subtract any non-refundable ***tax credits*** and add any other taxes owed. The result is the taxpayer's ***total tax.*** Compare the total tax with total payments (including refundable credits) to determine whether a refund or additional tax is due. Most taxpayers use either the Tax Table or the Tax Computation Worksheet to figure their income taxes. However, there are special methods if income includes any of the following items:

- A net capital gain
- Qualified dividends taxed at the same rates as a net capital gain
- Lump-sum distributions
- Farming or fishing income
- Investment income more than $1,900 for certain children
- Parents' election to report child's interest and dividends
- Foreign earned income exclusion or the housing exclusion

After income tax and any AMT (discussed later), determine any ***tax credits***. Subtract the tax credits and determine if any other taxes are due. These taxes include, but are not limited to the following:

- Additional taxes on qualified retirement plans and IRAs
- Advance earned income credit payments
- Household employment taxes
- Social Security and Medicare tax on wages and tips
- Uncollected Social Security and Medicare taxes on tips

Alternative Minimum Tax

Taxpayers with income or expenses that receive special treatment under the regular tax system may be subject to an additional tax known as the ***alternative minimum tax*** (AMT). Figure AMT separately, after eliminating certain deductions and credits, to arrive at ***alternative minimum taxable income (AMTI)***. AMT liability exists if taxable income for regular tax purposes, combined with these ***adjustments*** and ***tax preference items***, is more than the 2011 ***AMT exemption*** amount as follows:

- $74,450 if filing status is MFJ or QW
- $48,450 if filing status is single or HOH
- $37,225 if filing status is MFS

The exemption amounts above reduce by 25% of AMTI in excess of the following:

- $150,000 if filing status is MFJ or QW
- $112,500 if filing status is single or HOH
- $75,000 if filing status is MFS

The exemption reduces AMTI; apply a flat tax rate of 26% (up to $175,000, 28% thereafter) to arrive at the ***tentative minimum tax***. If the tentative minimum tax exceeds normal income tax liability, the excess is the AMT amount to include on the return.

Adjustments and Tax Preference Items

AMT is caused by two types of adjustments and preferences—deferral items and exclusion items. Deferral items (for example, depreciation) generally do not cause a permanent difference in taxable income over time. Exclusion items (for example, the standard deduction) do cause a permanent difference. The more common adjustments and tax preference items include the following:

- **Adjustments** – The first step to determine AMTI is adjusting the taxpayer's taxable income:
  1) Add the amount claimed for personal or dependency exemptions.
  2) Add the amount claimed for the standard deduction, or itemized deductions for state and local taxes, certain interest (not eligible mortgage on main home), most miscellaneous deductions, and part of medical expenses not greater than 10% of AGI.
  3) Subtract any refund of state and local taxes included in gross income.
- **Preference Items** – The tax code provides preferential treatment to certain income and deduction items. Under AMT rules, these items do not receive special treatment, thus increasing tax liability for an individual who would otherwise pay less tax. Add the following items to arrive at AMTI:
  1) Tax exempt interest from specified private activity municipal bonds
  2) The excess of accelerated depreciation claimed when compared to a hypothetical straight-line amount on property placed in service before 1987
  3) Addition of certain income from incentive stock options
  4) Change in certain passive activity loss deductions
  5) Depletion that is more than the adjusted basis (not applicable to independent producers)

6) Deduction for excess intangible drilling costs not amortized over a 60-month period

7) Difference between the gain or loss on the sale of property reported for regular tax purposes and the gain or loss reported for AMT purposes

---

7.1 Landon is married and has five children who are dependents. His taxable income is $137,300. He claims a standard deduction of $11,600. The 2011 amount for personal or dependency exemptions is $3,700. The tax due shown on his return without considering AMT is $26,688. Does Landon have AMT liability?

Credit for Prior Year's Minimum Tax

A taxpayer with AMT liability in the current year may recapture that amount in future years in the form of a credit. This non-refundable credit can offset future tax liability only to the extent prior AMT tax paid was due to deferral items. The credit cannot reduce tax below the *tentative minimum tax* for the year. The credit may become refundable if a taxpayer cannot use it for a period of three years. At that time, the refundable amount for the long-term unused minimum tax credit is the larger of 50% of long-term unused minimum tax credit or the amount (if any) of the AMT refundable credit amount for the taxpayer's preceding taxable year.

7.2 Luis has tax due in the current year of $35,000. Last year he paid $6,000 in AMT because of an incentive stock option exercise. His tentative minimum tax this year is $33,500. What amount of credit for prior year's minimum tax can he claim on his return this year?

Tax on Investment Income of Certain Children

When a child has more than $1,900 in income from interest, dividends, or other investments, part of that income may be taxed at the parent's tax rate instead of the child's tax rate. If the child's interest and dividend income (including capital gain distributions) is less than $9,500, the parent may elect to include that income on the parent's return rather than file a return for the child.

The parent can make that election on ***Form 8814*** only if all the following conditions are met:

- The child was under age 19 (or under age 24 if a full-time student) at the end of the year.
- The child had income only from interest and dividends (including capital gain distributions and Alaska Permanent Fund dividends).
- The child's gross income was less than $9,500.
- The child is required to file a return unless the parent makes this election.
- The child does not file a joint return for the year.
- There is no estimated tax payment or prior year overpayment applied to this year under the child's name and Social Security number.
- No federal income tax was taken out of the child's income under the backup withholding rules.
- The taxpayer cannot file Form 1040A or Form 1040EZ.

7.3 Julianna is 12 and has $800 in interest income in 2011. She has no other income in 2011. Her father, who claims her as a dependent is in the 35% tax bracket. Who must report the interest?

Taxes for Household Employees

A taxpayer has a household employee if he hires someone to do household work and that worker is his ***employee***. The worker is an employee if the taxpayer controls the work performed and how the worker performs the duties. If the worker controls how duties are performed, he is considered ***self-employed***.

While popularly referred to as a "Nanny Tax," other household employees are also subject to these rules. Other examples of workers who do household work are babysitters, cleaning people, drivers, domestic workers, private nurses, yard workers, etc.

A worker who performs childcare services in his home generally is not an employee of the taxpayer. If an agency provides the worker and controls the work performed and how duties are performed, the worker is not an employee of the taxpayer. Other individuals specifically excluded are the taxpayer's parents (unless caring for the taxpayers child under age 18 and the taxpayer is divorced or widowed), spouse, child under age 21, or anyone under age 18 whose principal occupation is not household employment (for example, a student).

Withholding

A taxpayer is not responsible for withholding federal income tax for household employees unless the employee asks and he agrees; however, he must withhold and pay the following taxes when applicable:

- **Social Security and Medicare taxes** – If a household employee is paid cash wages more than $1,700 in 2011, the employer must pay 7.65% of wages. The employer may either pay or withhold the employee share, which in 2011 is 5.65%.
- **Federal unemployment** – If the combined cash wages of all household employees is $1,000 or more in any calendar quarter, the employer must pay FUTA tax. Before July 1, 2011, the, the FUTA tax rate was 6.2% and afterwards decreased to 6.0%. The tax applies to the first $7,000 in wages paid to each employee during the year. The $7,000 is the federal wage base. The state wage base may be different. Wages more than $7,000 a year per employee are not taxed. The employer may also owe state unemployment tax. Generally, the employer takes a credit against FUTA tax for amounts paid into state unemployment funds. The credit may be as much as 5.4% of FUTA taxable wages. If entitled to the maximum 5.4% credit, the FUTA tax rate after credit is 0.8% (0.6% after June 30, 2011). Only the employer pays FUTA tax; it is not withheld from the employee's wages.

7.4 Meg is single and hires a nanny through a placement agency. Meg's nanny watches Meg's daughter in Meg's home while Meg works as the CEO of a Fortune 500 company. The nanny is paid $2,000 cash per week. Meg provides instructions to the nanny about the daughter's schedule for sleeping, playing, and eating. How much should Meg withhold from the nanny's weekly wages for Social Security and Medicare taxes?

Reporting

A taxpayer with household employees files ***Schedule H*** to report the taxes with his personal tax return by the due date plus extensions. In general, the amount of tax attributed to household employees increases the tax due on the taxpayer's personal return (1040). A household employer needs an employer identification number (EIN), and all household employees with cash wages more than $1,700 or withheld taxes must receive a W-2 by February 1.

Additional Tax on IRAs, Other Qualified Retirement Plans, etc.

A taxpayer may need to file ***Form 5329*** to calculate the following additional taxes:

1) 10% additional tax (25% for a SIMPLE IRA held less than two years) if the taxpayer receives an early distribution and the total distribution was not rolled over in a qualified rollover contribution from the following types of accounts:

   A) IRA or other qualified retirement plan

   B) Annuity

   C) Modified endowment contract entered into after June 20, 1988

2) 6% additional tax for excess contributions made to IRAs, Coverdell education savings accounts (ESAs), Archer MSAs, or health savings accounts (HSAs)

3) 10% additional tax on taxable distributions from Coverdell ESAs or qualified tuition programs

4) 50% additional tax on excess accumulation (taxpayer does not take the minimum required distribution) in Qualified Retirement Plans (Including IRAs)

If only item (1) applies and the taxpayer's Form 1099-R reflects distribution code 1 (early distribution, no known exception) in box 7, the taxpayer does not have to file Form 5329. Instead, multiply the taxable amount of the distribution by 10% and enter the result directly on form 1040. The taxpayer must file Form 5329 if the distribution code is not correct, or the taxpayer is eligible for an exception for qualified medical expenses, qualified higher education expenses, qualified first-time homebuyer distributions, or a qualified reservist distribution.

7.5 Jason needs money to buy a new car. He has no savings other than his IRA, so he decides to withdraw $10,000. Does Jason need to file Form 5329?

Underpayment of Estimated Tax

Certain taxpayers with estimated tax liability may face a penalty when they do not make sufficient payments on time. When applicable, individuals, estates, and trust taxpayers file ***Form 2210*** to calculate the penalty. The IRS may issue a penalty even if a refund is due when a sufficient amount of tax is unpaid by the due date for each payment. The IRS can figure the penalty for underpayment of estimated tax and send a bill the taxpayer. To elect this method the taxpayer leaves the penalty line on the return blank and does not file Form 2210. The IRS will not charge interest on the penalty if the taxpayer makes payment by the date shown on the bill. A taxpayer must use form 2210 to calculate the penalty in the following circumstances:

- The taxpayer requests a partial waiver of the penalty

- The taxpayer has variable income throughout the year and will calculate the penalty using the ***annualized income installment method***
- The penalty is lower when figured by treating the federal income tax withheld from income as paid on the dates it was actually withheld, instead of in equal amounts on the payment due dates

Certain taxpayers may request a waiver from the penalty. A taxpayer requesting a complete waiver can elect to have the IRS calculate the penalty, while a taxpayer requesting a partial waiver must calculate the penalty on Form 2210. The taxpayer must attach Form 2210 and a statement to their tax return explaining the reasons for not meeting the estimated tax requirements and the period for the waiver request. All or part of the penalty for an underpayment is waived if the IRS determines that:

- In 2010 or 2011, the taxpayer retired after reaching age 62 or became disabled, and the underpayment was due to reasonable cause, or
- The underpayment was due to a casualty, disaster, or other unusual circumstance, and it would be inequitable to impose the penalty.

If the waiver request is due to retirement or disability, the taxpayer must attach documentation that shows the retirement date (and age on that date) or the date of disability. For a waiver due to a casualty, disaster (other than a federally declared disaster, which the IRS automatically identifies) or other unusual circumstance, attach documentation such as copies of police and insurance reports.

7.6 Lee owes a penalty for underpayment of estimated taxes. He feels he qualifies for an exception to the entire penalty and requests a waiver. Can he elect to have the IRS calculate the penalty?

Child and Dependent Care Credit (Non-refundable)

To qualify for this credit, a taxpayer must meet all the following tests:

- The taxpayer cannot file Form 1040EZ.
- The filing status must be single, head of household, qualifying widow(er) with dependent child, or married filing jointly. Married couples must file a joint return, unless an exception exists.
- The care must be for one or more ***qualifying person(s)***.
- The taxpayer (and spouse if married) must have earned income during the year.
- The taxpayer must pay the expenses so taxpayer (and spouse if married) can work or look for work.
- Payments cannot go to the following individuals:
    1) A spouse
    2) Person who is a dependent of taxpayer, or the taxpayer's child if under age 19 at the end of the year (even if not a dependent)
    3) The parent of the qualifying person if the qualifying person is the taxpayer's child (under age 13)
- Taxpayer must identify the care provider on the tax return (name, address, TIN).

- If taxpayers exclude dependent care benefits provided by a dependent care benefits plan, the total exclusion must be less than the dollar limit for qualifying expenses (generally, $3,000 if one qualifying person was cared for or $6,000 if two or more qualifying persons were cared for).

7.7 ? Nasir works for NASA and earns $180,000 in wages. His wife Camilla cares for their 2-year old daughter Emily while he works 80 hours a week. Needing a break, Camilla places Emily in day care three days a week at a cost of $300 per month. Do they qualify for the child and dependent care credit?

Qualifying Person Test

For purposes of the *child and dependent care credit*, a qualifying person is:

- A dependent who was **under age 13** when the care was provided
- An individual living with a taxpayer for more than half of a year who is physically or mentally unable to care for himself, if he is:
  1) A spouse
  2) A dependent
  3) Would have been a dependent except for one of the following:
     A) He received gross income of $3,700 or more
     B) He filed a joint return
     C) Another person could claim the taxpayer or the taxpayer's spouse as a dependent

In determining whether a person is a qualifying person, treat a person who is born or dies as living with the taxpayer for the entire year if he lived in the taxpayer's home the entire time he was alive.

TIP A qualifying person for this credit must meet different requirements than a qualifying person for purposes of a dependency exemption or the EIC. All three are important topics on the exam.

Joint Return Test

Generally, married couples must file a joint return to take the credit. Those legally separated or living apart from a spouse may be able to file a separate return and still take the credit. Only the custodial parent can claim the credit. A married taxpayer living apart from a spouse is not considered married, and he can take the credit if all the following apply:

- Taxpayer files a separate return.
- Taxpayer's home is the home of a qualifying person for more than half the year.
- Taxpayer paid more than half of the cost of keeping up a home for the year.
- Spouse did not live in the taxpayer's home for the last six months of the year.

How to Figure the Credit

The credit is a percentage of ***work-related expenses,*** which allow the taxpayer to work or look for work. The amount of expenses used to figure the credit cannot be more than one of the following:

- $3,000 if one qualifying person, or $6,000 if more than one qualifying person
- Taxpayer's earned income for the year if single at the end of the year
- If married at end of year, the smaller of taxpayer or a spouse's earned income for the year

---

TIP A spouse who is a full-time student or incapable of self-care is treated as having earned income of at least $250/m if there is one qualifying person in the taxpayer's home, or at least $500 for two or more.

To determine the credit amount, multiply work-related expenses (after applying the earned income and dollar limits) by a percentage (based on AGI). The applicable percentage begins at 35% for taxpayers with AGI less than $15,000 and decreases by 1% for each $2,000 increase in AGI. Taxpayers with AGI more than $43,000 receive the minimum percentage of 20%. The maximum amount of this credit is $1,050 (one qualifying person) or $2,100 (more than one qualifying person).

Adoption Credit (Refundable)

A credit is available for ***qualified expenses*** paid to adopt an ***eligible child*** (under age 18 or with special needs). This credit was not refundable for tax year 2009 and was set to expire at the end of 2010. Recent changes make the credit refundable and available for tax years through 2012. For 2011, the maximum adoption credit is $13,360 per child (minus any qualified adoption expenses claimed for the same child in a prior year). The full credit may be allowed for the adoption of a child with special needs even if there are no qualified expenses. For 2011, the adoption credit phases out ratably for taxpayers with MAGI between $185,210 and $225,210.

- **Qualified adoption expenses** are reasonable and necessary expenses directly related to, and whose principal purpose is for, the legal adoption of an eligible child. These expenses include the following:
  1) Adoption fees
  2) Court costs
  3) Attorney fees
  4) Travel expenses (including meals and lodging) while away from home
  5) Re-adoption expenses to adopt a foreign child
- **Nonqualified expenses** are expenses that meet the following criteria:
  1) Expenses that violate state or federal law
  2) Expenses for carrying out any surrogate parenting arrangement
  3) Expenses for the adoption of spouse's child
  4) Expenses for which the taxpayer received funds under any federal, state, or local program
  5) Expenses allowed as a credit or deduction under any other federal income tax rule
  6) Expenses paid or reimbursed by employer or any other person or organization
  7) Expenses paid before 1997

When to Claim the Credit

If the eligible child is a U.S. citizen or resident, a taxpayer may claim the adoption credit even if the adoption never became final. A taxpayer may claim expenses paid prior to finalization in the year following the year of payment. Expenses paid in the year the adoption becomes final are included in that year. A taxpayer may claim expenses paid after the adoption becomes final in the year of payment. If the eligible child is <u>not</u> a U.S. citizen or resident, a taxpayer cannot take the adoption credit or exclusion unless the adoption becomes final.

7.8 Vijay is a U.S citizen. In 2011, he incurs expenses to adopt a child from India. The adoption does not become final until the following year. When can Vijay claim a credit for his adoption expenses?

Substantiation Requirements

To claim the credit a taxpayer must include a copy of one or more adoption-related documents and ***Form 8839*** along with his tax return.

- **Domestic or foreign adoption finalized in the United States** – copy of an adoption order or decree.
- **Domestic adoptions that are not final** – include an adoption taxpayer identification number, obtained for the child, or provide a copy of one of the following documents:
    1) A home study completed by an authorized placement agency
    2) A placement agreement with an authorized placement agency
    3) A document signed by a hospital official authorizing the release of a newborn child from the hospital to the taxpayer for legal adoption
    4) A court document ordering or approving the placement of the child for legal adoption
    5) An original affidavit or notarized statement, from an adoption attorney, government official, or other person, stating that he (a) placed or is placing a child with the taxpayer for legal adoption or (b) is facilitating the adoption process for the taxpayer in an official capacity
- **Adoptions of special needs children** – a copy of the state determination of special needs.

Education Credits (Non-refundable)

For 2011, there are two tax credits for higher (postsecondary) education expenses. They are as follows:

- The Lifetime Learning credit
- The American Opportunity credit

Generally, a taxpayer may claim a credit if he meets all of the following three requirements:

- He pays *qualified education expenses* of higher education.
- He pays the education expenses for an *eligible student*.
- The student is the taxpayer, a spouse, or a dependent (must claim an exemption).

A taxpayer <u>cannot</u> claim a credit if any of the following applies:

- Filing status is married filing separately (MFS).
- Someone else claims a dependency exemption for the taxpayer on his tax return.
- Modified adjusted gross income (MAGI) is above the phase-out limit.
- Taxpayer (or spouse) is a nonresident alien for any part of the year and did not elect to be treated as a resident alien for tax purposes.
- The student claims another education credit, or tuition and fees deduction for the same year.

For each student, the taxpayer can choose only one of the credits each year. If a taxpayer claims the *American Opportunity credit* for a child on his 2011 tax return, he cannot, for that same child, also claim the Lifetime Learning credit for 2011. A taxpayer who is eligible for more than one credit can choose to claim either credit, but not both. When a taxpayer pays qualified education expenses for more than one student in the same year, he can choose to take the credits on a per-student, per-year basis.

For example, a taxpayer can claim the *American Opportunity credit* for one student and the *Lifetime Learning credit* for another student in the same year. A taxpayer can claim both the *American Opportunity credit* and the *Lifetime Learning credit*—but not for the same student.

Qualified Education Expenses

For purposes of the education credits, consider only ***qualified education expenses*** in determining the credit amount. The expenses must be required for enrollment or attendance at an ***eligible educational institution*** and include tuition and required enrollment fees. Qualified education expenses include required amounts paid to the institution for course-related books, supplies, and equipment.

- Only certain expenses for course-related books, supplies, and equipment qualify:
  1) **American Opportunity credit** – Qualified education expenses include amounts spent on books, supplies, and equipment needed for a course of study, whether or not the taxpayer purchases materials from the educational institution as a condition of enrollment or attendance.
  2) **Lifetime Learning credits** – Qualified education expenses include **only** amounts for books, supplies, and equipment required to be paid to the institution as a condition of enrollment or attendance.
- Qualified education expenses **do not** include amounts paid for:
  1) Room and board, insurance, medical expenses (including student health fees), transportation, or other similar personal, living, or family expenses
  2) Any course or other education involving sports, games, or hobbies, or any noncredit course, unless such course or other education is part of the student's degree program or (for the Lifetime Learning credit only) helps the student acquire or improve job skills
  3) Nonacademic fees, such as student activity fees, athletic fees, insurance expenses, or other expenses unrelated to the academic course of instruction

TIP Expenses paid or deemed paid by a dependent are considered paid by the taxpayer. Someone other than the taxpayer, spouse, or dependent (such as a relative or former spouse) may make a payment directly to an eligible educational institution to pay for an eligible student's qualified education expenses. In this case, treat the student as receiving the payment from the other person and, in turn, paying the institution. If the taxpayer claims an exemption on his tax return for the student, he is considered to have paid the expenses.

Table 7-1. 2011 Education Credits

	American Opportunity Credit	**Lifetime Learning Credit**
Maximum credit	$2,500 credit per **eligible student**	$2,000 credit per **return**
Limit on (MAGI)	$180,000 MFJ, $90,000 S, HH, or QW	$122,000 if MFJ, $61,000 if S, HH, or QW
Refundable	**40% refundable**	Non-refundable credit limited to the amount of tax liability.
Availability	Available **ONLY** for the first **4 years.**	Available **ALL years AND** for courses to acquire or improve job skills
Number of tax years credit available	Available **ONLY** for **4** tax years per eligible student	Available for an **UNLIMITED** number of years
Type of degree required	Student must be pursuing an undergraduate degree or other recognized education credential	Student does not need to be pursuing a degree or other recognized education credential
Number of courses	Student enrolled at least half time for at least one academic period beginning in the tax year	Available for one or more courses
Felony drug conviction	No felony drug convictions on student's records	Felony drug convictions permitted
Qualified expenses	Books, supplies, and equipment **do not** need to be purchased from the institution in order to qualify.	Tuition and required enrollment fees, including required amounts paid to the institution for course-related books, supplies, and equipment.

American Opportunity Credit (Partially Refundable)

The American Opportunity credit replaces the Hope credit and is available through 2012. Students must attend at least half time for one academic period.

- The credit is available for the first **four years** of postsecondary education, and **40% of the credit is refundable** for most taxpayers.
- The maximum credit per student is $2,500 (100% of first $2,000 and 25% of the next $2,000).
- The threshold before the reduction of the credit is more than that for the Lifetime Learning credit. The phase out begins if MAGI is between $80,000 and $90,000 ($160,000 and $180,000 MFJ). A taxpayer cannot claim a credit if MAGI is $90,000 or more ($180,000 MFJ).

Lifetime Learning Credit (Non-refundable)

A Lifetime Learning credit of up to $2,000 is available for *qualified education expenses* paid for students enrolled in *eligible educational institutions*. The credit is 20% of the first $10,000 of qualified education expenses paid for all eligible students. Differences from other credits include the following:

- Student does not need to pursue a degree or other credentials
- Available for unlimited number of years

- Used for courses to acquire or improve job skills and all years of postsecondary education
- No half-year requirement for eligible students, available for one or more courses
- Felony drug conviction rule does not apply

The amount of the Lifetime Learning credit phases out (gradually declines) if modified adjusted gross income (MAGI) is between $51,000 and $61,000 ($102,000 and $122,000 MFJ). No credits are available when (MAGI) exceeds $61,000 ($122,000 MFJ).

7.9 Josie pays $20,000 in tuition for law school. Of the two credits available for education, which provides her with the greatest benefit? What is the amount of her credit?

Earned Income Credit (Refundable)

The ***earned income tax credit*** *(EITC or EIC)* is a tax credit for certain people who work and have ***earned income*** under $49,078. For 2011, the maximum credit is 40% (45% if three or more children) of the first $12,570 of earned income. The EITC is a refundable credit. Receiving the payments in advance was not very popular and is repealed beginning in 2011. A taxpayer looking to claim the credit must file a return. Earned income includes all of the following:

- Wages, salaries, and tips
- Union strike benefits
- Long-term disability benefits received prior to minimum retirement age
- Net earnings from self-employment
- Non-taxable combat pay (only if elected and included in taxable income)

Earned Income does not include:

- Interest and dividends
- Pensions
- Social Security
- Unemployment benefits
- Alimony
- Child support

Who May Claim the EITC?

To claim the EITC, taxpayers must meet all of the following rules:

- Investment income must be $3,150 or less for the year.
- If married, the taxpayers cannot file separately; they must file a joint return (MFJ).

- Taxpayer(s) and all qualifying children must have a valid Social Security number.
- Taxpayer must be a U.S. citizen or a nonresident alien married to a U.S. citizen or resident alien and filing a joint return.
- Taxpayer cannot file Form 2555 related to foreign-earned income.
- Taxpayer cannot be the ***qualifying child*** of another person.
- Taxpayer must have earned income; however, earned income <u>and</u> AGI cannot be more than:
    1) $43,998 ($49,078 MFJ) with three or more qualifying children
    2) $40,964 ($46,044 MFJ) with two qualifying children
    3) $36,052 ($41,132 MFJ) with one qualifying child
    4) $13,660 ($18,740 MFJ) with no qualifying children

Taxpayers with <u>no</u> qualifying children must meet the following criteria:

- Be age 25 but younger than 65 at the end of the year
- Live in the United States for more than half of the year
- Not qualify as a dependent of another person

Taxpayers <u>with</u> a qualifying child <u>must</u> meet the ***relationship***, ***age***, and ***residency tests***:

- **Relationship Test** – To be a qualifying child, a child must fall into one of the following categories:
    1) Son, daughter, stepchild, foster child, adopted child, or a descendant of any of them (for example, a grandchild)
    2) Brother, sister, half brother, half sister, stepbrother, stepsister, or a descendant of any of them (for example, a niece or nephew)
- **Age Test** – A qualifying child must be as follows:
    1) Younger than the taxpayer or taxpayer's spouse if filing a joint return, and
        A) Under age 19 at the end of the year, or
        B) A full-time (five months or more) student under age 24 at the end of the year
    2) Permanently and totally disabled at any time during the year, regardless of age
- **Residency Test** – Child must have lived with taxpayer in the U.S. for more than half of the tax year.

Sometimes a child meets the rules to be a qualifying child of more than one person. However, only one person can treat that child as a qualifying child and claim the EITC using that child. Taxpayers can choose which person will claim the EITC. If the taxpayers do not reach an agreement and more than one person claims the EITC using the same child, the tiebreaker rule applies, and the parent with whom the child lived the longest during the year receives the credit. If the child lived with each parent the same amount of time, the parent with the higher AGI receives the credit.

7.10 Gloria and her son Jake lived with her mother all year. Gloria is 25 years old. Her only income was $9,300 from a part-time job. Her mother's adjusted gross income was $15,000. All her mother's income was from her job. Who may claim Jake as a qualifying child for the earned income tax credit?

Paid preparers of federal income tax returns or claims for refund involving the earned income credit must meet the due diligence requirements in determining if the taxpayer is eligible for, and the amount of, the EITC. Failure to do so could result in a $100 penalty for each failure. See IRC section 6695(g). A tax preparer can use ***Form 8867*** to document due diligence.

Disallowance of the EITC

Certain errors may cause the IRS to deny a taxpayer the EITC. If the denial is because of taxpayer error due to reckless or intentional disregard of the rules, the taxpayer cannot claim the EIC for the next two years. If the error is due to fraud, the taxpayer cannot claim the EITC for the next 10 years. A taxpayer who wants (and meets the requirements) to claim the EITC must attach ***Form 8862*** to his return if the EITC was reduced or disallowed for any reason other than a math or clerical error for a year after 1996.

A taxpayer can claim the EITC without filing Form 8862 if he meets all the EITC eligibility requirements and either of the following applies:

- After the EIC was reduced or disallowed in an earlier year:
    1) The taxpayer filed Form 8862 (or other documents) and the EIC was then allowed, and
    2) EITC was not reduced or disallowed again for any reason other than a math or clerical error.
- The taxpayer is taking the EITC without a qualifying child and the only reason the EITC was disallowed in the earlier year was that a child listed on Schedule EIC was not his qualifying child.

First-time Homebuyer Credit (Refundable)

To qualify as a first-time homebuyer, a taxpayer (and spouse, if married) cannot own any other main home during the three-year period ending on the date of purchase. Certain first-time homebuyers who bought a home in the United States may claim a refundable credit that is the smaller of **$8,000** ($4,000 MFS), or **10% of the purchase price**. The credit begins to phase-out when MAGI is more than $125,000 ($225,000 MFJ). Most taxpayers can no longer claim this credit. To claim the first-time homebuyer credit for 2011, the taxpayer (or spouse if married) must have been a member of the uniformed services or Foreign Service or an employee of the intelligence community on qualified official extended duty outside the United States for at least 90 days during the period beginning after December 31, 2008, and ending before May 1, 2010. The taxpayer must have bought a main home in 2011 before May 1. The credit is not available for the following cases:

- Nonresident aliens cannot take the credit.
- The home is located outside the United States.
- The taxpayer sells the home or it stops being his main home before the end of 2011.
- The taxpayer acquires the home by a gift or inheritance.
- MAGI is $145,000 or more ($245,000 MFJ).

- The purchase price is more than $800,000.
- Taxpayer can be claimed as a dependent on someone else's return.
- Taxpayer (and spouse, if married) were younger than 18 when they bought the home.
- Taxpayer acquired the home from a related person.

Special Rule for Long-time Residents of Same Main Home

Taxpayers who owned and used the same home as a main home for any period of five consecutive years during the eight-year period ending on the date of purchase may claim a reduced credit of up to $6,500.

Repayment

In general, a taxpayer must repay the credit if he disposes of the home or the home stops being his main home within the 36-month period beginning on the purchase date. This includes if he sells the home; converts it to business or rental property; the home is destroyed, condemned, or disposed of under threat of condemnation; or the lender forecloses on the mortgage. The taxpayer can repay the credit by including it as additional tax on the return for the year the home stops being his main home. The following are exceptions to the repayment rule:

- If the sale is not to a related party, the repayment is limited to the amount of gain on the sale. When figuring the gain, reduce the adjusted basis of the home by the amount of the credit.
- If a home is destroyed, condemned, or disposed of under threat of condemnation, and the taxpayer acquires a new main home within two years of the event, he does not have to repay the credit.
- If, as part of a divorce settlement, the taxpayer transfers the home to a spouse or former spouse, the spouse who receives the home is responsible for repaying the credit if required.
- If the taxpayer dies, repayment of the credit is not required. For joint filers, the surviving spouse must repay his or her half of the credit if required.
- In some cases, there is an exception for members of the uniformed services or Foreign Service and for intelligence community employees.

Home Purchased in 2008

For homes purchased in 2008, a different credit was available that generally requires taxpayers begin repaying it on their 2010 return. In addition, taxpayers generally must repay any credit they claimed for a home they bought in 2008 if during the repayment period they sold the home, or the home stopped being their main. If the taxpayer dies, any remaining annual installments are not due. If a spouse dies (files a joint return), the IRS requires the survivor to continue payments for his or her half of the credit.

Credit for Elderly or the Disabled (Non-refundable)

To take the credit for the elderly or the disabled, taxpayers must meet all of the following:

- Must be a qualified individual:
    1) A U.S. citizen or resident alien age 65 or older at the end of the year, or
    2) Younger than age 65 at the end of the year and all of the following statements are true:

A) Retired on permanent and total disability (expected to result in death or last 12 months or more)

B) Received taxable disability income in the tax year

C) On January 1 of the tax year, had not reached mandatory retirement age

- Income no more than certain limits
- Cannot file 1040EZ

TIP An individual is considered to be age 65 on the day before his 65th birthday. If the taxpayer is younger than age 65, he must maintain records containing a statement of permanent and total disability on the date he retired, certified by a physician or the Dept. of Veterans Affairs (VA).

Income Limits

The credit is 15% of the applicable base amount (reduced by excess AGI and any nontaxable Social Security or other nontaxable pensions received). Nontaxable benefits reduce the base amount dollar for dollar while excess AGI (above the AGI limit) reduces the base amount by $1 for every $2 excess. Due to these reductions, only taxpayers with modest income will qualify for this credit.

- **Example:** A married couple files a joint return, and only one spouse qualifies for the credit. They received $11,500 in taxable IRA distributions and $4,000 in nontaxable Social Security benefits.
    1) Subtract $4,000 of nontaxable Social Security benefits from the base amount of $5,000.
    2) Determine excess AGI ($11,500 AGI minus $10,000 threshold equals $1,500 excess AGI).
    3) Reduce the remaining base amount by $750 (one-half of the excess AGI).
    4) Multiply the resulting base amount of $250 ($5,000 minus $4,000 minus $750) by 15% to arrive at the credit of $37.50.

Table 7-2. Credit for Elderly or Disabled

IF filing status is . . .	**AGI Phase-out Begins**	**THEN, you CANNOT take the credit if . . .**	
		AGI is equal to or more than . . .	**OR the total of nontaxable Social Security and pension(s) is equal to or more than the BASE AMOUNT**
single, head of household, or qualifying widow(er)	$7,500	$17,500	$5,000
married filing a joint return and both spouses qualify	$10,000	$25,000	$7,500
married filing a joint return and only one spouse qualifies	$10,000	$20,000	$5,000
married filing a separate return*	$5,000	$12,500	$3,750

*Married taxpayers must file jointly to claim the credit if living together at any time during the year.

Child Tax Credit (Non-refundable)

For each ***qualifying child***, a maximum non-refundable ***child tax credit*** of $1,000 is available, subject to certain income limits. A qualifying child for purposes of the child tax credit is a child who meets the following criteria:

- Is the taxpayer's son, daughter, stepchild, foster child, adopted child, brother, sister, stepbrother, stepsister, or a descendant of any of them (a grandchild, niece, or nephew)
- Was younger than age 17 at the end of the tax year and younger than the taxpayer (and spouse)
- Did not provide more than half of his own support for the year
- Lived with the taxpayer for more than half of the year
- Is claimed as a dependent on the return
- Is a U.S. citizen, a U.S. national, or a resident of the United States

In determining whether a person is a qualifying child, treat a person who was born or died as having lived with the taxpayer for the entire tax year if the taxpayer's home was the person's home the entire time he was alive. Temporary absences for special circumstances, such as school, vacation, business, medical care, military service, or detention in a juvenile facility, count as time the child lived with the taxpayer.

Limits on the Credit

This credit is reduced (phased-out) when ***modified adjusted gross income (MAGI)*** (AGI plus foreign income that was excluded from AGI) is above the amount shown below the following:

- Married filing jointly – $110,000
- Single, head of household, or qualifying widow(er) – $75,000
- Married filing separately – $55,000

Round income above these levels up to the nearest thousand and multiply by 5% ($50 per $1,000). Subtract the result from the maximum child tax credit. This credit is not refundable and cannot be more than the amount of tax due.

The "child tax credit" is not refundable. If a taxpayer cannot claim the full amount of the child tax credit, a refundable ***additional child tax credit*** may be available. For 2011, the portion refundable as the additional child tax credit is up to 15% of earned income (including tax-free combat pay) that exceeds $3,000. To claim this credit, the taxpayer must attach ***Form 8812*** to his tax return.

Other Non-refundable Credits

Non-refundable credits only reduce tax. The taxpayer does not receive a refund of any excess.

Foreign Tax Credit

If a taxpayer paid income tax to a foreign country, he can choose to take a credit against his U.S. income tax or an itemized deduction. He cannot take a credit (or deduction) for foreign income taxes paid on income if it was excluded from U.S. tax under any of the following:

- Foreign earned income exclusion
- Foreign housing exclusion
- Income from Puerto Rico exempt from U.S. tax
- Possession exclusion

The taxpayer must file Form 1116 to take the credit unless all of the following apply:

- All of the foreign source income is passive income, which generally includes interest and dividends.
- The taxpayer reported all of his foreign source income and the foreign tax paid on it on a qualified payee statement, which includes Form 1099-INT and Form 1099-DIV.
- The total of creditable foreign taxes was not more than $300 ($600 if married filing jointly).
- The taxpayer elects this procedure for the tax year.

Savers Credit

A taxpayer may claim the savers credit (formerly Retirement Savings Contributions Credit) for qualified contributions or deferrals made to certain retirement plans. The credit amount begins at 50% of the taxpayer's contributions to the plan and is reduced depending on income levels and filing status. The maximum credit is $1,000 ($2,000 MFJ).

- A taxpayer may not take the credit if one of the following is true:
    1) Year 2011 AGI is more than $28,250 ($42,375 HH, $56,500 MFJ).
    2) Someone else claimed him as a dependent.
    3) He is younger than age 17.
    4) He is a student.

Plug-in Electric Vehicle Credit (IRC 30)

A taxpayer may claim this credit if he acquired a new qualified plug-in electric vehicle in 2011. A qualified vehicle can have two, three, or four wheels.

- The credit is 10% of the cost of the vehicle, limited to $2,500 per vehicle.
- A qualified plug-in electric vehicle is a new motor vehicle meeting all the following requirements:
    1) Is acquired for the taxpayer's use or lease and not for resale
    2) Is made by a manufacturer
    3) Is manufactured primarily for use on public streets, roads, and highways

4) Has a gross vehicle weight rating of less than 3,000 pounds if it has four wheels, and less than 14,000 pounds if it has two or three wheels

5) Is a low-speed vehicle if it has four wheels

6) Is propelled to a significant extent by an electric motor drawing electricity from a battery that has a capacity of at least 4 kilowatt hours (2.5 kwh for vehicle with two or three wheels) and can recharge from an external source of electricity

Qualified Plug-in Electric Drive Motor Vehicles (IRC 30D)

Dubbed the "golf cart credit," this credit is no longer available for low-speed vehicles. The credit applies to four-wheel vehicles only and varies according to battery capacity, from $2,500 to $7,500 per vehicle.

Other Non-refundable Credits

- **Alternative motor vehicle credit** – A credit may be available if a taxpayer places a qualified fuel cell vehicle in service in 2011, or converts a vehicle to a qualified plug-in electric drive vehicle.
- **Residential energy efficient property credit** – For costs related to taxpayer's home located in the United States involving qualified solar electric, solar water heating, fuel cell, small wind energy, or geothermal heat pump property. The credit is limited to 30% of costs.
- **Mortgage interest credit** – Lower income individuals who own a home may be eligible for the credit if issued a qualified mortgage credit certificate (MCC) from their state or local government. Generally, an MCC issues only in connection with a new mortgage for the purchase of a main home.
- **Credit to holders of tax credit bonds** – The issuers do not pay interest on these types of bonds (except build America bonds). Instead of receiving interest, the bondholders qualify to claim a tax credit. The amount of any tax credit allowed must be included as interest income on the taxpayer's return. Tax credit bonds include:

    1) Clean renewable energy bonds
    2) Gulf tax credit bonds
    3) Qualified energy conservation bonds
    4) Midwestern tax credit bonds
    5) Qualified forestry conservation bonds
    6) Qualified school construction bonds
    7) Qualified zone academy bonds
    8) Build America bonds

Other Refundable Credits

The IRS treats the credits discussed below as payments of tax. If the total of these credits, withheld federal income tax, and estimated tax payments is more than the total tax, the taxpayer can receive a refund of the excess:

- Credit for tax on undistributed capital gain

- Health coverage tax credit
- Refundable credit for prior year minimum tax
- Credit for excess Social Security tax or railroad retirement tax withheld

General Business Credit

A business taxpayer groups most available business credits into a ***general business credit***, and reports on ***Form 3800***. The general business credit for the year consists of any carry forward of business credits from prior years plus the total current year business credits. In addition, the general business credit for the current year may increase later by the carry-back of business credits from later years.

The general business credit is not a refundable credit; a taxpayer can only subtract the credit directly from tax liability. The general business credit cannot reduce tax liability <u>below</u> the *tentative minimum tax* <u>or</u> 25% of regular tax in excess of $25,000, whichever is greater. Any unused credit may be carried back one year <u>or</u> forward for up to 20 years. Under the ***Small Business Jobs Act of 2010***, an ***eligible small business*** (50 million or less average gross receipts over the past three years) may carry back 2011 general business credits five years and use the general business credit against their regular tax or AMT.

The following credits are part of the general business credit:

- **Agricultural chemicals security credit** – This credit applies to qualified agricultural chemical security expenses paid or incurred by eligible agricultural businesses. The credit cannot exceed $100,000 per facility or $2 million for all such facilities.
- **Alcohol and cellulosic biofuel fuels credit** – This credit consists of the alcohol mixture credit, alcohol credit, small ethanol producer credit, and cellulosic biofuel producer credit. The credit amount will vary based on the number of gallons and type(s) of fuels involved.
- **Alternative fuel vehicle refueling property** – This credit applies to the cost of any qualified fuel vehicle refueling property placed in service during the business's tax year.
- **Alternative motor vehicle credit** – Unless otherwise indicated, the maximum tentative credit is based on year, make, model, and type of <u>new</u> qualifying alternative motor vehicle purchased, which may be one of the following:
  1) Qualified fuel cell vehicle
  2) Qualified plug-in electric drive motor vehicle (<u>10%</u> of cost up to <u>$2,500</u>)
- **Biodiesel and renewable diesel fuels credit** – This credit applies to certain fuels sold or used in a business. The amount of credit that the taxpayer can claim depends on the type of eligible fuels involved and how many gallons of each the taxpayer sold or used.
- **Carbon dioxide sequestration credit** – This credit is for carbon dioxide, which is captured at a qualified facility and disposed of in a secure geological storage or used in a qualified enhanced oil or natural gas recovery project.
- **Credit for employer Social Security and Medicare taxes paid on certain employee tips** – This credit is generally equal to the employer's portion of Social Security and Medicare taxes paid on tips received by employees of a food and beverage establishment where tipping is customary.

- **Credit for employer differential wage payments** – This credit provides certain small businesses with an incentive to continue to pay wages to an employee performing services on active duty in the uniformed services of the United States for a period of more than 30 days.

- **Credit for employer-provided childcare facilities and services** – The credit is 25% of the qualified childcare facility expenditures *plus* 10% of the qualified childcare resource and referral expenditures paid or incurred during the tax year. The credit limit is $150,000 per year.

- **Credit for increasing research activities** – This credit is designed to encourage businesses to increase the amounts they spend on research and experimental activities, including energy research. The regular credit is 20% of the <u>increase</u> in research activities.

- **Credit for small employer pension plan start-up costs** – This credit applies to pension plan start-up costs of a new qualified defined benefit or defined contribution plan (including a 401(k) plan), SIMPLE plan, or simplified employee pension. The credit equals 50% of the cost to establish and administer the plan and educate employees about the plan, up to a maximum of $500 per year for each of the first three years of the plan. Taxpayers can choose to start claiming the credit in the tax year prior to the tax year in which the plan becomes effective.

- **Disabled access credit** – This credit is for an eligible small business that pays or incurs expenses to provide access to persons who have disabilities. The credit is 50% of the first $10,000 spent.

- **Distilled spirits credit** – This credit is available to distillers and importers of distilled spirits and eligible wholesalers of distilled spirits.

- **Empowerment zone and renewal community employment credit** – This credit is for employers who have employees in and engage in business in an empowerment zone or renewal community for which the credit is available. For tax years that include December 31, 2011, the credit is:

    1) 20% of the employer's qualified wages (up to $15,000) paid or incurred during calendar year 2011 on behalf of qualified <u>empowerment zone</u> employees, *plus*

    2) 15% of the employer's qualified wages (up to $10,000) paid or incurred during calendar year 2011 on behalf of qualified <u>renewal community</u> employees

- **Energy efficient appliance credit** – For 2011, the maximum overall credit for manufactures of qualified energy efficient appliances (dishwashers, clothes washers, and refrigerators) is the smaller of 4% of average annual gross receipts for the three prior tax years or $25 million.

- **Energy efficient home credit** – This credit is available for eligible contractors of certain homes sold for use as a residence. For each home that meets the 50% energy efficient standard, the allowable credit is $2,000, or $1,000 for those that meet the 30% energy efficient standard.

- **Indian employment credit** – This credit applies to qualified wages and health insurance costs paid or incurred for qualified (American Indian) employees. Credit is up to 20% of expenses.

- **Investment credit** – The investment credit is the total of the following credits:

    1) Rehabilitation credit (<u>10%</u> for rehabilitation expenses of a pre-1936 building, or <u>20%</u> if a certified historic structure)

    2) Energy credit

    3) Qualifying advanced energy project credits

4) Qualifying advanced coal project
5) Qualifying gasification project

- **Low sulfur diesel fuel production credit** – This credit is for the production of low sulfur diesel by a qualified small business. The credit generally is 5 cents for every gallon of low sulfur diesel fuel produced by a qualified small business refiner during the tax year.
- **Low-income housing credit** – This credit generally applies to each new qualified low-income building placed in service after 1986. Generally, it is taken over a 10-year credit period.
- **Mine rescue team training credit** – This credit applies to training program costs paid or incurred for qualified mine rescue team employees for tax years beginning before January 1, 2012.
- **New markets credit** – This credit is for qualified equity investments made in qualified community development entities.
- **Nonconventional source fuel credit** – This credit is allowed for qualified coke or coke gas produced and sold to an unrelated person during the tax year.
- **Orphan drug credit** – This credit applies to qualified expenses incurred in testing certain drugs for rare diseases and conditions. The credit is 50% of qualified clinical testing expenses paid or incurred during the tax year.
- **Qualified railroad track maintenance credit** – This credit applies to certain regional and switching railroads that may be able to claim a credit for expenses made to upgrade their railroad tracks (including roadbed, bridges, and related track structures).
- **Renewable electricity, refined coal, and Indian coal production credit** – This credit is for the sale of electricity, refined coal, or Indian coal produced in the United States or U.S. possessions from qualified energy resources at a qualified facility.

Work opportunity credit – This credit is for qualified first- or second-year wages paid to targeted group employees during the tax year. In general, the amount of wages cannot exceed $6,000; however, it may for certain targeted groups. These employees have a high unemployment rate or other special employment needs. The business does not have to be in an empowerment zone, renewal community, or rural renewal county to qualify for this credit. The credit is 25% of qualified first-year wages of employees working more than 120 but less than 400 hours in the year, *plus* 40% of qualified first-year wages for employees working more than 400 hours in the year, *plus* 50% of qualified second-year wages of employees certified as long-term family assistance recipients.

Tax Return Preparer Competency Exam – Chapter 7 Quiz

Circle the letter next to the best answer. Remember to read the question carefully.

1) Consider the following expenditures and determine the total amount that would be deducted as adjustments to income in arriving at adjusted gross income (assuming no income limitations) on Form 1040, Individual Income Tax Return:

   - $1,000 interest paid on student loan
   - $2,000 paid to a SIMPLE retirement plan
   - $100 jury duty pay given to the employer
   - $500 expenses from the non-business rental of personal property

   a. $3,600

   b. $2,600

   c. $3,100

   d. $1,100

2) Michael had to pay $4,000 alternative minimum tax last year. This year, his regular income tax is $60,000 and alternative minimum tax on his income is $57,000, so he will pay only regular income tax. How much credit for prior year minimum tax can he take this year?

   a. $0

   b. $4,000

   c. $2,000

   d. $3,000

3) Which of the following statements is not true regarding tax benefits for education?

   a. The American Opportunity credit may be claimed for tuition expenses incurred in the first four years of post-secondary education.

   b. The dollar limitation for the American Opportunity credit is calculated on a per-student basis.

   c. The Lifetime Learning Credit is allowed for tuition paid for graduate program studies.

   d. Room and board are qualifying expenses for the American Opportunity Credit.

4) Which of the following are not considered earned income for the purposes of earned income credit?

   a. Amounts deducted from wages for insurance under a cafeteria plan.

   b. Disability benefits received at age 35 under a former employer's insurance plan.

   c. Unemployment compensation.

   d. Housing allowance for ministers.

5) Mary files as head of household and has three dependent children, ages 15, 16, and 17. Mary and the children are U.S. citizens. Her only income is a salary of $77,500. Her tax is $13,262. How much child tax credit is she allowed in 2011?

a. $2,000

b. $3,000

c. $1,500

d. $1,850

6) A taxpayer purchased two electric vehicles for personal use in 2011. He paid $45,000 for each vehicle. What is his qualified Electric Vehicle Credit for 2011 before the tax liability limit?

a. $ -0 -

b. $4,000

c. $5,000

d. $9,000

7) Mr. and Mrs. Rose are both older than 65. Their adjusted gross income is $100,000. During the year, their 35-year-old single son, Tom, lived with them while attending college and earned $4,000. Mr. Rose's mother, Ivy, lived with them until June 1 when she was placed in a nursing home for an indefinite period to receive medical care. Ivy received no income and was supported solely by Mr. and Mrs. Rose. Determine the number of exemptions Mr. and Mrs. Rose can claim on their joint return.

a. 2

b. 3

c. 4

d. 6

8) Minnie's tax return shows the following income:

- $800 wages
- $6,490 unemployment compensation
- $1,000 alimony
- $8,000 rental income from apartment buildings she owns

What is Minnie's earned income for determining how much she can contribute to an IRA?

a. $800

b. $7,290

c. $1,800

d. $16,290

9) Daniel and Lindsey recently adopted a little boy from Ethiopia. They incurred various expenses throughout this adoption process. Qualified adoption expenses for Daniel and Lindsey include expenses for all of the following, EXCEPT:

a. Adoption fees related to their new son

b. The former adoption of Daniel's step-son, from Lindsey's previous marriage

c. Travel expenses (including meals and lodging) while Daniel and Lindsey were away from home

d. Court costs involved in the adoption process

10) A taxpayer uses Form 5329 to calculate additional taxes. Which of the following taxes is not reported on Form 5329?

a. 10% additional tax on an early distribution from an IRA

b. Additional tax due to the Alternative Minimum Tax

c. 6% additional tax for excess contributions made to Coverdell education savings accounts

d. 50% additional tax on excess accumulation in Qualified Retirement Plans

11) Which of the following applies to the allowable credit for prior year minimum tax?

a. Any unused portion may not be carried forward

b. It is allowed in full against the current year's tax

c. It may only be carried forward for five years

d. The allowable credit cannot reduce the current year's tax below the current year's tentative minimum tax

12) Travis did not make his estimated tax payments on time due to a disability. He would like to request a waiver of the penalty for underpayment of estimated tax from the IRS. What should he do in this situation?

a. He should not enter the penalty on Form 1040, and must attach documentation that shows his date of disability

b. He should write DISABLED on Form 1040 instead of the penalty amount

c. He must allow the IRS to calculate his penalty, then request a refund using Form 2210

d. He should file Form 2210 with his tax return and include documentation that shows his date of disability

13) A company increased its research expenses by $3,600. What is the maximum credit it qualifies for on its tax return for tax year 2011?

a. $360

b. $900

c. $2,700

d. $720

14) The General Business Credit cannot lower your tax below:

a. The poverty level for the year.

b. The taxpayer's tax for the prior year.

c. A number IRS announces each year.

d. The taxpayer's alternative minimum tax for the tax year, unless an eligible small business.

15) Which of the following credits is not part of the General Business Credit?

a. Credit for employer provided childcare facilities

b. Credit for prior year minimum tax

c. Credit for small employer pension plan start-up costs

d. Welfare-to-work credit

16) Margaret Michelson began the process of adopting Sahara in 2011. She incurred over $20,000 in qualified expensed, including airfare to Sahara's native country of Kenya. Margaret did not finalize the adoption until 2012. She did not incur any expenses in 2012. When can Margaret claim the credit for her qualified adoption expenses?

a. She can claim the credit in 2011 since that is when she incurs the expenses

b. She can claim the credit in 2011 only if she files Form 8839 along with a court document ordering or approving the placement of the child for legal adoption

c. Since Sahara was not a U.S. citizen, Margaret cannot claim the credit until the adoption becomes final

d. She cannot claim the credit because Sahara is not a U.S. citizen

For more practice questions, visit fastforwardacademy.com and access our FREE online question bank.

1) **a** If modified adjusted gross income (MAGI) is less than $75,000 ($150,000 MFJ) for 2011 there is deduction allowed for paying up to $2,500 in interest on a student loan used for higher education. The $1,000 in student loan interest is taken as an adjustment to income. The $2,000 Simple IRA contribution is also an adjustment to gross income. Compensation for jury duty is included in income on Form 1040. If the taxpayer must give the pay to an employer because the employer continues to pay a salary while serving on the jury, he may deduct the amount turned over to the employer as an adjustment to income. If a rental activity is not a business, report rental income as other income on Form 1040 and include any expenses as an adjustment to gross income.

2) **d** The credit for prior year minimum tax paid reduces the present year tax liability, but not below the *tentative minimum tax* for the year.

3) **d** The American Opportunity credit is restricted to the first four years of post-secondary education. The American Opportunity credit is calculated per student (and not per return like the Lifetime Learning credit). The Lifetime Learning credit covers ALL post-secondary education as well as courses to acquire or improve job skills. Room and board do not qualify as educational expenses for either the American Opportunity or Lifetime Learning credits. The American Opportunity Credit replaces the Hope credit through 2012.

4) **c** Unemployment benefits are not earned income and are specifically listed as "Income That Is Not Earned Income." A trick by the IRS is to include the cafeteria plan information. Under normal circumstances, amounts contributed to a cafeteria plan are not included in wages (not earned income). There is an exception. If the benefits under the plan are cash or an amount of life insurance more than $50,000 in face value, then the amount is included in wages and, therefore, earned income.

5) **d** A child must be younger than the age of 17 at the end of the tax year to qualify for the $1,000 child tax credit. Only the 15- and 16-year-olds qualify. The maximum total credit of $2,000 declines when AGI exceeds the $75,000 limit for HH filing status. Round up the excess AGI to the nearest thousandth and multiply by 5% ($50 per $1,000 excess). This reduces her credit by $150.

6) **c** The credit is 10% of the cost of the vehicle, limited to $2,500 per vehicle. This credit cannot be claimed on vehicles purchased for resale.

7) **b** Exemptions can be claimed for Mr. and Mrs. Rose, and for Ivy, as she is a qualifying relative for whom they provide more than half support. A parent does not need to live with the taxpayer to qualify. Tom is not a qualifying person for purposes of the dependency exemption, as he does not pass the age test to be a qualifying child or the income test to be a qualifying relative.

8) **c** Generally, compensation is the amount earned from working. Compensation includes wages, salaries, tips, professional fees, bonuses, and other amounts individuals receive for providing personal services. For IRA purposes, compensation includes amounts considered taxable alimony and nontaxable combat pay. Only the wages and alimony count as compensation, so they set the limit for the allowable contribution amounts.

9) **b** Qualified adoption expenses are reasonable and necessary expenses directly related to, and whose principal purpose is for, the legal adoption of an eligible child. A taxpayer cannot deduct costs associated with adopting the child of a spouse.

10) **b** Individuals use Form 6251 to calculate their AMT liability.

11) **d** A taxpayer with AMT liability in the current year may recapture that amount in future years in the form of a credit. This non-refundable credit can offset future AMT liability only to the extent prior AMT tax paid was due to deferral items. If unused after three years, the credit may become refundable

12) **d** Certain taxpayers may request a waiver from the penalty. A taxpayer requesting a complete waiver can elect to have the IRS calculate the penalty, while a taxpayer requesting a partial waiver must calculate the penalty on Form 2210. The taxpayer must attach Form 2210 and a statement to their tax return explaining the reasons for not meeting the estimated tax requirements and the period for the waiver request.

13) **d** This credit is designed to encourage businesses to increase the amounts they spend on research and experimental activities, including energy research. The regular credit is 20% of the increase in research activities.

14) **d** The general business credit is not refundable and cannot be more than the AMT. Although you may not owe AMT, you generally must still compute the tentative minimum tax (TMT) to figure your general business credit. Under the *Small Business Jobs Act of 2010*, an *eligible small business* (50 million or less average gross receipts over the past three years) may carry back 2011 general business credits five years and use the general business credit against their regular tax or AMT.

15) **b** A taxpayer calculates the credit for prior year minimum tax on Form 8801. All of the other credits mentioned are part of the general business credit, calculated on Form 3800.

16) **c** If the eligible child is not a U.S. citizen or resident, a taxpayer cannot take the adoption credit or exclusion unless the adoption becomes final. A taxpayer may claim expenses paid after the adoption becomes final in the year of payment.

8 Withholding and Reporting

Employees · Tax Withholding and Reporting · Informational Returns
Taxpayer Supporting Documentation · The E-file Process

This chapter summarizes the various requirements placed upon employers with respect to withholding, reporting, and payment of taxes.

Employees

Who Are Employees?

Before an employer can know how to treat payments made to workers for services, the employer must first know the business relationship that exists between the employer and worker. The person performing the services may be one of the following:

- **Independent contractor** – People such as lawyers, contractors, subcontractors, and auctioneers who follow an independent trade, business, or profession in which they offer their services to the public, are typically not employees. An individual is usually an independent contractor if the employer, the person for whom the individual performs the services, has the right to control or direct only the result of the work and not the means and methods of accomplishing the result.
- **Common-law employees** – Under common-law rules, anyone who performs services for a person is an employee of that person if the employer has the right to control what will be done and how it will be done. This is true even when an employer gives the employee freedom of action. What matters is the right to control the details of how the employee performs the services.
    1) It does not matter whether the individual is employed full time or part time.
    2) An ***officer*** of a corporation is generally an employee; however, an officer who performs no services or only minor services, and neither receives nor is entitled to receive any pay, is not considered an employee.
    3) A corporate ***director*** is not an employee with respect to services performed as a director.
    4) Employers generally must withhold and pay income, Social Security, and Medicare taxes on wages paid to common-law employees.
- **Statutory employees** – If a person is not an employee under the common law rules discussed above, the employer must not withhold federal income tax from pay unless backup withholding applies. Although the following persons may not be common law employees, they may be considered employees by statute for Social Security, Medicare, and FUTA tax purposes under certain conditions:
    1) A commission (or agent) driver who delivers beverages (not milk), food, laundry, or dry cleaning.
    2) A full-time life insurance sales agent who sells primarily for one life insurance company.

3) A home worker who works by guidelines of the person for whom the work is done, with materials furnished by and returned to that person or to someone that person designates.

4) A full-time traveling or city salesperson that works on an individual's behalf and turns in orders to the latter from wholesalers, retailers, contractors, or operators of hotels, restaurants, or other similar establishments. The goods sold must be merchandise for resale or supplies for use in the buyer's business operation. The work performed must be the salesperson's principal business activity.

- **Statutory nonemployees** – Direct sellers, qualified real estate agents, and certain companion sitters are, by law, considered nonemployees. They are treated generally as self-employed for all federal tax purposes, including income and employment taxes.

Tax Withholding and Reporting

Self-employment Tax

Self-employment tax (SE tax) is a Social Security and Medicare tax primarily for individuals who work for themselves. Payments of SE tax contribute to coverage under the Social Security system. Social Security coverage provides the taxpayer with retirement benefits, disability benefits, survivor benefits, and hospital insurance (Medicare) benefits. An individual may deduct one-half of the SE tax as an adjustment to income on Form 1040. The self-employed <u>must</u> pay SE tax and file Schedule SE (Form 1040) if either of the following applies:

- Net earnings from self-employment were $400 or more
- Had church employee income of $108.28 or more

In 2011, a tax rate of 13.3% applies to the first $106,800 of income from self-employment. A tax rate of 2.9% applies to the excess. Before applying the tax rates, a self-employed taxpayer reduces income from self-employment by the percentage of tax that employers normally pay for their employees.

Peter has $100,000 income from self-employment. If Peter were an employee, his employer would pay 7.65% or $7,650. His SE tax is $12,282.55 ($92,350 x 13.3%).

Payroll Taxes

Employment taxes include Social Security, Medicare, federal income tax withholding, and ***federal unemployment (FUTA)*** tax. Generally, taxpayers do <u>not</u> pay or withhold tax on payments to independent contractors. The general rule is that an individual is an independent contractor if the person for whom the services are performed has the right to control or direct only the result of the work and <u>not</u> the means and methods of accomplishing the result.

- **Income tax** – Employers generally must withhold federal income tax from wages. They use Form W-4 to figure how much federal income tax to withhold from each wage payment.

- **FICA taxes** – Social Security and Medicare taxes pay for benefits that workers and their families receive under the ***Federal Insurance Contributions Act (FICA)***. Social Security tax pays for benefits under the old age, survivors, and disability insurance part of FICA. Medicare tax pays for benefits under the hospital insurance part of FICA. Employers must withhold part of these taxes from their employee's wages and must pay a matching amount. The employee tax rate for social security is

4.2%. The employer tax rate for social security remains unchanged at 6.2%. The Medicare tax rate is 1.45% each (2.9% total) for employers and employees. The social security wage base limit to which this applies is $106,800 for 2011. There is no wage base limit for Medicare tax; all covered wages are subject to Medicare tax. Report these taxes on Form 941, Employer's Quarterly Federal Tax Return.

- **FUTA taxes** – This tax is part of the federal and state program under the ***Federal Unemployment Tax Act (FUTA)*** that pays unemployment compensation to workers who lose their jobs. Individuals must report and pay FUTA tax separately from Social Security and Medicare taxes and withheld income tax. The employer must pay FUTA tax only from separate funds. Employees do not pay this tax or have it withheld from their pay. Employers must report federal unemployment tax on Form 940, Employer's Annual Federal Unemployment (FUTA) Tax Return.

Under the ***Hiring Incentives to Restore Employment (HIRE) Act***, enacted March 18, 2010, employers (other than household employers) who hire certain previously unemployed workers may receive a credit up to $1,000 for each qualified employee retained for at least 52 consecutive weeks. This new hire retention credit is 6.2% of wages paid to the qualified employee over the 52-week period, up to a maximum credit of $1,000 per worker. The employer claims the credit on his 2011 income tax return. Each eligible employee must sign a statement certifying unemployment during the prior 60 days or, alternatively, worked no more than 40 hours for anyone during the 60-day period.

Uncollected Social Security and Medicare Tax on Wages

An employee who performs services for a firm, and the firm does not withhold social security and Medicare taxes from pay is required to file ***Form 8919*** to figure and report his share of the uncollected social security and Medicare taxes due on compensation. This applies if he is an employee but his employer treats him as an independent contractor. By filing this form, the social security and Medicare taxes are credited to his social security record.

Estimated Taxes

Generally, employers make estimated tax payments during the year to pay employment tax obligations.

- **Sole proprietors, partners, and S corporation shareholders** – When the owner(s) of such a business expect to owe $1,000 or more in taxes, those individuals generally make estimated tax payments. Individual taxpayers use **Form 1040-ES** to figure and pay estimated tax.

- **Corporations** – Generally, a corporation must make estimated tax payments (Form 1120-W) if expecting to owe tax of $500 or more when filing a return.

- **When to pay estimated tax** – Installment payments are due by the 15th day of the 4th, 6th, 9th, and 12th months of the taxable year.

Electronic Deposit of Employment Taxes

Beginning January 1, 2011, taxpayers must use electronic funds transfer to make all federal tax deposits (such as deposits of employment tax, excise tax, and corporate income tax). Generally, electronic funds transfers are made using the ***Electronic Federal Tax Payment System (EFTPS).*** If EFTPS is not required, employers can make deposits at authorized financial institutions with Form 941. There are two deposit schedules—monthly and semi-weekly. Employers determine the required deposit schedule before the beginning of each calendar year by calculating prior employment tax liability within a look back period (begins July 1 and ends June 30).

- **Monthly deposit schedule** – tax liability during look back period was less than $50,000.

- **Semi-weekly deposit schedule** – tax liability during look back period was more than $50,000.

Required Forms for Employers

Employers are required to collect ***Form I-9*** and ***Form W-4*** from employees. Employees who receive advanced ***earned income credit (EIC)*** payments must give the employer a completed **Form W-5.**

- **Form I-9** – The employer must verify that each new employee is legally eligible to work in the United States. He must complete the U.S. Citizenship and Immigration Services *Form I-9, Employment Eligibility Verification* and maintain in records.
- **Form W-4** – Employers use the filing status and withholding allowances shown on this form to calculate the amount of income tax to withhold from the employee's wages.
- **Form W-5** – An eligible employee who has a qualifying child is entitled to receive advance EIC payments during the year. An employer is required to make advance EIC payments to employees who provide a completed and signed Form W-5.

Informational Returns

An information return is a tax document that businesses are required to file in order to report certain business transactions to the Internal Revenue Service. Any person, including a corporation, partnership, individual, estate, and trust, with reportable transactions during the calendar year must file information returns to report those transactions to the IRS. Persons required to file must also furnish statements to the recipients of the income. Filers who have 250 or more returns must file the returns electronically. *See Appendix in back of book for examples of some of the following informational returns.*

TIP The recipient of an informational return does not send copies to the IRS unless required. A taxpayer must attach Form W-2 to the front of their Form 1040 series tax return. A taxpayer should also attach Forms W-2G and 1099-R, but only if federal income tax was withheld.

- **Form W-2, Wage and Tax Statement** – After the calendar year is over, each employer must furnish copies of Form W-2 to each employee who earned wages during the year. The employer must also send a copy to the Social Security Administration.
- **Form W-2G, Certain Gambling Winnings** – An organization conducting gaming activities must report certain gambling transactions to taxpayers and the IRS. Form W-2G reflects winnings and federal tax withholding. In general, the gambling organization must use Form W-2G if any tax is withheld or the taxpayer has winnings equivalent to the following:

  1) Bingo or Slot machine – $1,200 or more (not reduced by wager)
  2) Keno –$1,500 (reduced by wager)
  3) Poker – More than $5,000 (reduced by wager)
  4) All others – $600 or more and at least 300 times the amount of the wager.

- **Form 1098, Mortgage Interest Statement** – A person (or organization) engaged in a trade or business that receives at least $600 of mortgage interest (including certain points) on any one mortgage in the calendar year must report the mortgage interest on Form 1098 to the payor and the IRS. Report prepaid interest (other than points) only in the year in which it properly accrues. The form is not filed if the interest is received from a corporation, partnership, trust, estate, association, or company other than a sole proprietor.

- **Form 1098-E , Student Loan Interest Statement** – A person (including a financial institution, a governmental unit, and an educational institution) that receives interest payments of $600 or more during the year on one or more qualified student loans must furnish this statement to each student.

- **Form 1098-T, Tuition Statement** – An eligible educational institution must provide each enrolled student with reportable transactions this form in order to report certain amounts billed or payments received by the institution for qualified tuition and related expenses. The institution also reports scholarships or grants using this form.

- **Form 1099-B, Proceeds From Broker and Barter Exchange Transactions** –In general, a securities broker must report and provide a Form 1099-B for each person for whom the broker has sold (including short sales) stocks, bonds, commodities, regulated futures contracts, foreign currency contracts, forward contracts, debt instruments, etc., for cash. Recent legislation now requires brokers to report cost basis in addition to proceeds from these transactions. Cost basis information makes the calculation of gains and losses easier for taxpayers.

- **Form 1099-C, Cancellation of Debt** – Certain entities must issue a Form 1099-C to each borrower for canceled debts in excess of $600 on secured property. Under certain circumstances, a borrower may recognize taxable income because of a debt that is canceled.

- **Form 1099-DIV,** – A corporation must generally send Forms 1099-DIV to the IRS with Form 1096 by February 28 of the year following the year of a distribution. Generally, a corporation must furnish Forms 1099-DIV to shareholders by January 31 of the year following the close of the calendar year during which the corporation made the distributions. It is necessary to file a ***Form 1099-DIV*** with the IRS for each person the corporation:

    1) Paid dividends (including capital gain dividends) and other distributions on stock of $10 or more,

    2) Withheld and paid any foreign tax on dividends and other distributions on stock,

    3) Withheld any federal income tax on dividends under the backup withholding rules, or

    4) Paid $600 or more as part of a liquidation

- **Form 1099-G, Certain Government Payments** – This form reports certain payments that exceed $10, such as unemployment compensation and state or local income tax refunds.

- **Form 1099-INT, Interest Income** – Financial institutions that pay interest must report details regarding those payments in the following circumstances:

    1) The interest payments are at least $10. Certain types of interest, such as interest on delayed death benefits paid by a life insurance company or interest on a state or federal tax refund have a higher threshold of $600.

    2) If the institution withheld and paid any foreign tax on interest

    3) If the institution withheld (and did not refund) any federal income tax under the backup withholding rules regardless of the amount of the payment

- **Form 1099-MISC, Miscellaneous Income** – A business taxpayer uses Form 1099-MISC to report certain business payments. These payments include the following items:

1) Payments of $600 or more for services performed for one's business by people <u>not treated as employees</u>, such as subcontractors, attorneys, accountants, or directors. Generally, payments to a corporation are excluded from this reporting requirement

2) Rent payments of $600 or more, other than rents paid to real estate agents

3) Prizes and awards of $600 or more (not for services), such as winnings on radio shows

4) Royalty payments of $10 or more

5) Payments to certain crew members by operators of fishing boats

- **Form 1099-OID** – Original issue discount (OID) is the difference between the purchase price of a debt instrument and its maturity value. Each year, a portion of the discount accrues as income to the recipient. A financial institution must report OID if it amounts to $10 or more.

- **Form 1099-R, Distributions From Pensions, Annuities, Retirement or Profit-Sharing Plans, IRAs, Insurance Contracts, etc.** – Form 1099-R communicates reportable distributions of $10 or more from retirement accounts, insurance contracts, and annuities. In addition to the amount distributed, a number or letter code in box 7 tells the taxpayer details about the type of distribution they received.

8.1 In 2011, Julia receives income from the following sources: $250 interest from her brokerage account, $8 interest from her bank account, $35,000 salary from her job at the local bank, $800 for designing a website for her neighbor's dog. What forms should she receive as a result of each payment?

Backup Withholding

A business taxpayer reporting payments made to a U.S. person must withhold 28% (backup withholding rate) from certain payments that are subject to reporting if one of the following conditions exists:

- The person does not provide its ***taxpayer identification number (TIN)*** in the manner required. Generally, a person provides a TIN on ***Form W-9***
- The IRS provides notification that the TIN furnished by the payee is incorrect
- There has been a notified payee underreporting
- There has been a payee certification failure

Regular Gambling Withholding

Regular gambling withholding is 25% (33.33% for certain noncash payments) for 2011. Regular gambling withholding is applicable when gambling winnings exceed $5,000 for sweepstakes, wagering pools, or lotteries. Poker tournaments are "wagering pools" according to IRS Rev. Proc. 2007-57. For other wagering transactions (for example: blackjack, or similar table games), regular gambling withholding does not apply unless winnings are at least $600 <u>and</u> 300 times the amount wagered. If withholding applies, a taxpayer who does not provide a SSN or TIN is subject to backup withholding.

Table 8-1. Certain Informational Returns

Form	Title	What to Report	Amounts to Report	Due Date To IRS	Due Date To Recipient
1098	Mortgage Interest Statement	Mortgage interest (including points) and certain mortgage insurance premiums you received in the course of your trade or business from individuals and reimbursements of overpaid interest.	$600 or more	February 28*	January 31
1098-E	Student Loan Interest Statement	Student loan interest received in the course of your trade or business.	$600 or more	February 28*	January 31
1098-T	Tuition Statement	Qualified tuition and related expenses, reimbursements or refunds, and scholarships or grants (optional).	See form instructions	February 28*	January 31
1099-B	Proceeds From Broker and Barter Exchange Transactions	Sales or redemptions of securities, futures transactions, commodities, and barter exchange transactions.	All amounts	February 28*	February 15
1099-C	Cancellation of Debt	Cancellation of a debt owed to a financial institution, the Federal Government, a credit union, RTC, FDIC, NCUA, a military department, the U.S. Postal Service, the Postal Rate Commission, or any organization having a significant trade or business of lending money.	$600 or more	February 28*	January 31
1099-DIV	Dividends and Distributions	Distributions, such as dividends, capital gain distributions, or nontaxable distributions, that were paid on stock and liquidation distributions.	$10 or more, except $600 or more for liquidations	February 28*	January 31
1099-G	Certain Government Payments	Unemployment compensation, state and local income tax refunds, agricultural payments, and taxable grants.	$10 or more for refunds and unemployment	February 28*	January 31
1099-INT	Interest Income	Interest income.	$10 or more ($600 or more in some cases)	February 28*	January 31
1099-MISC	Miscellaneous Income (Also for direct sales of $5,000 or more of consumer goods for resale.)	Rent or royalty payments; prizes and awards that are not for services, such as winnings on TV or radio shows.	$600 or more, except $10 or more for royalties	February 28*	January 31
1099-OID	Original Issue Discount	Original issue discount.	$10 or more	February 28*	January 31
1099-R	Distributions From Pensions, Annuities, Retirement or Profit-Sharing Plans, IRAs, Insurance Contracts, etc.	Distributions from retirement or profit-sharing plans, any IRA, insurance contracts, and IRA recharacterization.	$10 or more	February 28*	January 31
W-2G	Certain Gambling Winnings	Gambling winnings from horse racing, dog racing, jai alai, lotteries, keno, bingo, slot machines, sweepstakes, wagering pools, poker tournaments, etc.	Generally, $600 or more; $1,200 or more from bingo or slot machines; $1,500 or more from keno	February 28*	January 31
W-2	Wage and Tax Statement	Wages, tips, other compensation; social security, Medicare, withheld income taxes; and advance earned income credit (EIC) payments. Include bonuses, vacation allowances, severance pay, certain moving expense payments, some kinds of travel allowances, and third-party payments of sick pay.	See form instructions	To SSA Last day of February*	January 31

*The due date is March 31 if filed electronically

Taxpayer Supporting Documentation

A taxpayer must keep records as long as needed for the administration of any provision of the Internal Revenue Code. Generally, this means keeping records that support items shown on the return until the ***period of limitations*** for that return expires. The period of limitations is the period of time in which the taxpayer can amend a return to claim a credit or refund, or the Internal Revenue Service can assess additional tax. This is generally the later of **three years** from the due date of the return or the date the taxpayer filed the return.

Table 8-2. Period of Limitations

	IF you...	**THEN the period is...**
1	Owe additional tax and (2), (3), and (4) do not apply	3 years
2	Do not report income and it is more than 25% of the gross income shown on return	6 years
3	File a fraudulent return	No limit
4	Do not file a return	No limit
5	File a claim for credit or refund after filing return	Later of 3 years or 2 years after tax was paid
6	File a claim for a loss from worthless securities	7 years

TIP It is good practice for taxpayers to maintain records, both basic and specific. Records do not need to be required to be of benefit. For example, a taxpayer who receives a Form W-2 should keep a copy until he begins receiving Social Security benefits. This will help protect his benefits in case there is a question about his work record or earnings in a particular year. The IRS does not require taxpayers to maintain records in a particular way. If using a computerized system, individuals must be able to produce legible records of the information needed to determine the correct tax liability and in addition, must keep proof of payment, receipts, and other documents to prove the amount shown.

8.2 ? David has not filed a tax return since 1998. Typically, his income consists only of partnership distributions. After subtracting his deductions, his income was not substantial enough to require filing. How long should he maintain records of his deductions?

Taxpayer Penalties and Interest

If the taxpayer does not file a return and pay the tax by the due date, he may have to pay a penalty. Substantially understated tax, understated reportable transactions, erroneous claims for refund or credit, frivolous tax submissions, or failure to supply a Social Security number or individual taxpayer identification number may also result in the IRS assessing a penalty. The IRS may assess a civil fraud penalty if the taxpayer provides fraudulent information on a return.

- **Filing late or *(failure-to-file)*** – If the taxpayer does not file a return by the due date (including extensions) the IRS may assess a failure-to-file penalty. The penalty is usually **5% for each month** or part of a month that a return is late, but **not more than 25%.** The penalty is based on the tax not paid by the due date (without regard to extensions).

1) ***Fraud*** – If the failure to file is due to fraud, the penalty is 15% for each month or part of a month that the return is late, up to a maximum of 75%.

2) ***Return more than 60 days late*** – If the return is filed more than 60 days after the due date or extended due date, the minimum penalty is the smaller of $135 or 100% of the unpaid tax.

8.3 Jessica paid her entire $10,000 tax liability for 2011 before the due date of her tax return. She was really busy and didn't file her tax return until December 2012. She did not request an extension. What is the amount of her failure to file penalty?

- **Paying tax late or *(failure-to-pay)*** – A taxpayer who does not pay all taxes by the due date is subject to the failure-to-pay penalty of **one-half of 1% (.50%)** of the unpaid taxes for each month, or part of a month, the tax is not paid. This penalty does not apply during the automatic six-month extension of time to file period if the taxpayer paid at least 90% of the actual tax liability on or before the due date of the return and paid the balance when he filed the return.

    1) The monthly rate of the failure-to-pay penalty is half the usual rate (.25% instead of .50%) if an installment agreement is in effect for that month. The taxpayer must file the return by the due date (including extensions) to qualify for this reduced penalty.

    2) If the IRS issues a notice of intent to levy, the rate will increase to 1% at the start of the first month beginning at least 10 days after the day the IRS issues the notice. If the IRS issues a notice and demand for immediate payment, the rate will increase to 1% at the start of the first month beginning after the day that the IRS issues the notice and demand.

    3) This penalty cannot be more than 25% of the unpaid tax.

- **Combined penalties** – If both the *failure-to-file penalty* and the *failure-to-pay* penalty apply in any month, the 5% (or 15%) failure-to-file penalty is reduced by the failure-to-pay penalty. However, if the return is filed more than 60 days after the due date or extended due date, the minimum penalty is the smaller of $135 or 100% of the unpaid tax.

- **Accuracy-related penalty** – An accuracy-related penalty (**20% of the underpayment)** may be due if the tax is underpaid due to:

    1) Negligence or disregard of the rules or regulations, or

    2) Substantial understatement of income tax. The understatement is substantial if it is more than the largest of 10% of the correct tax or $5,000.

The E-File Process

Tax preparers may file returns electronically through a system known as ***IRS e-file*** through ***electronic return originators*** who are authorized e-file providers.

- In prior years, IRS e-file did not accept returns with prescribed due dates that were not in the current year. Beginning January of 2011, Modernized E-File (MeF) accepts tax years 2009 and 2010 returns. In subsequent years, 1040 MeF will accept tax returns for the current year and two prior years. The IRS accepts an electronic version of Form 4868 for the current tax year.

- A taxpayer cannot electronically file an individual income tax return **after October 15**, even if the IRS has granted an extension to file a return beyond that date.

- All prescribed due dates for filing of returns apply to e-file returns. An electronically filed return is not considered filed until the IRS acknowledges acceptance of the electronic portion of the tax return for processing. The IRS accepts individual income tax returns electronically only if the taxpayer signs the return using a Personal Identification Number (PIN).

- The receipt of an electronic postmark provides taxpayers with confidence that they have filed their returns timely. The date of the postmark is considered the date of filing when the date of electronic postmark is on or before the prescribed due date and the return is received by the IRS after the prescribed due date for filing. All requirements for signing the return and completing a paper declaration, if required, as well as for timely resubmitting of a rejected timely filed return must be adhered to for the electronic postmark to be considered the date of filing.

New E-File Mandate

Starting January 1, 2011, paid preparers—or the preparer's firm in the aggregate—who prepare and expect to file 100 or more income tax returns for individuals, trusts, and estates in 2011 are required to file these returns electronically. Starting January 1, 2012, the 100-return threshold drops to 11 or more.

Electronic Return Originator (ERO)

An Electronic Return Originator (ERO) originates the electronic submission of returns for taxpayers who want to e-file their returns. An ERO originates the electronic submission of a return after the taxpayer authorizes (Form 8879) the filing of the return via IRS e-file. The ERO must have either prepared the return or collected it from a taxpayer. Duties of the ERO include the following:

- **Safeguarding IRS *e-file* from fraud and abuse** – An ERO who is also the paid preparer should exercise due diligence in the preparation of returns involving the Earned Income Tax Credit (EITC) because it is a popular target for fraud and abuse. EROs must not electronically file individual income tax returns prior to receiving Forms W-2, W-2G or 1099-R

- **Verifying Taxpayer Identification Numbers (TIN)** – Confirm identities on the return.

- **Be aware of non-standard information documents** – Look for suspicious or altered documents.

- **Be careful with addresses** – Verify the taxpayer's address has not changed.

- **Avoiding refund delays** – Recommend taxpayers supply current information, and check their return.

Returns Not Eligible for IRS E-File

Taxpayers may file both state and federal returns using the IRS e-file system. However, e-file is not available for the following individual income tax returns and related conditions:

- Returns that are not current year tax returns; however, beginning January of 2011, ***Modernized E-File* (MeF)** will accept tax years 2009 and 2010 returns. In subsequent years, 1040 MeF will accept tax returns for the current year and two prior years. Form 4868 will be accepted for the current tax year.

- Tax returns with fiscal year tax periods

- Amended tax returns

- Returns using a foreign or overseas address (other than Military APO or FPO)

- Returns containing forms or schedules that cannot be processed by RS e-file other than those forms and schedules that are required to be submitted with Form 8453
- Tax returns with a Taxpayer Identification Number (TIN) beginning with **9**. This does not apply to certain Adopted Taxpayer Identification Numbers (ATIN) and Individual Taxpayer Identification Numbers (ITIN).
- The IRS cannot electronically process tax returns with rare or unusual processing conditions or that exceed the specifications for returns allowable in IRS e-file.

Form 8453

IRS e-file returns must contain all of the same information as returns filed completely on paper. Not all forms are eligible to transmit electronically. In such cases, the ERO must submit to the IRS all paper documents required to complete the filing of returns by attaching them to the ***Form 8453*** and sending them to the IRS.

Length of Time to Keep Records

The ERO must retain the following material until the end of the calendar year at the business address from which it originated the return or at a location that allows the ERO access the material because it must be available at the time of IRS request. An ERO may retain the required records at the business address of the responsible official or at a location that allows the responsible official to access the material during any period of time the office is closed because it must be available at the time of IRS request through the end of the calendar year. The ERO must maintain the following records:

- A copy of ***Form 8453, U.S. Individual Income Tax Transmittal for an IRS e-file Return,*** and supporting documents that are not included in the electronic records submitted to the IRS
- Copies of Forms W-2, W-2G, and 1099-R
- A copy of signed IRS *e-file* consent to disclosure forms
- A complete copy of the electronic portion of the return that can be readily and accurately converted into an electronic transmission that the IRS can process
- The acknowledgement file for IRS accepted returns

IRS e-file Signature Authorization Forms 8879 and 8878 must be available to the IRS for three years from the due date of the return or the IRS received date, whichever is later.

EROs may electronically image and store all paper records they are required to retain for IRS e-file. This includes Forms 8453 and paper copies of Forms W-2, W-2G, and 1099-R, as well as any supporting documents not included in the electronic record and Forms 8879 and 8878. In brief, the electronic storage system must ensure an accurate and complete transfer of the hard copy to the electronic storage media. The ERO must be able to reproduce all records with a high degree of legibility and readability (including the taxpayers' signatures).

8.4 Juanita, a tax return preparer, prepares a 2011 Form 1040 tax return for Margaret on March 15, 2012. Margaret did not have her 1099-R reflecting an IRA distribution, so Juanita uses Margaret's brokerage records to determine the taxable amount of the distribution. Can Juanita e-file this return?

Providing Information to the Taxpayer

The ERO must provide a complete copy of the return to the taxpayer. EROs may provide this copy in any media, including electronic, that is acceptable to both the taxpayer and the ERO. A complete copy of a taxpayer's return includes Form 8453 and other documents that the ERO cannot electronically transmit, when applicable, as well as the electronic portion of the return. The ERO should also advise taxpayers that, if needed, they must file an amended return as a paper return and mail it to the processing center that would handle the taxpayer's paper return.

Rules for Returning Records

In general, at the request of a client, a practitioner must promptly return all records of the client that are necessary for the client to comply with his federal tax obligations. The practitioner may retain copies of the records returned to a client. The existence of a dispute over fees generally does not relieve the practitioner of his responsibility under this section. If applicable state law allows or permits the retention of a client's records in the case of a dispute over fees for services rendered, the practitioner need only return those records that must be attached to the taxpayer's return. The practitioner must provide the client with reasonable access to review and copy any additional records of the client retained by the practitioner that are necessary for the client to comply with his federal tax obligations.

Electronic Signature Requirements

As with an income tax return submitted to the IRS on paper, the taxpayer <u>and</u> paid preparer must sign an electronic income tax return. Electronic signatures are required for returns using e-file.

Taxpayers must sign and date the Declaration of Taxpayer to authorize the origination of the electronic submission of the return to the IRS prior to the transmission of the return to IRS. The Declaration of Taxpayer includes the taxpayer's declaration under penalties of perjury that the return is true, correct and complete, as well as the taxpayers' Consent to Disclosure. The Consent to Disclosure authorizes the IRS to disclose information to the taxpayers' Providers. Taxpayers authorize Intermediate Service Providers, Transmitters and EROs to receive from the IRS an acknowledgement of receipt or reason for rejection of the electronic return, an indication of any refund offset, and the reason for any delay in processing the return or refund and the date of the refund.

There are currently two methods for signing individual income tax returns electronically. Both methods allow taxpayers to use a Personal Identification Number (PIN) to sign the return and the *Declaration of Taxpayer*. The Declaration of Taxpayer includes the taxpayer's declaration under penalties of perjury that the return is true, correct and complete, as well as the taxpayers' Consent to Disclosure, authorizing the IRS to disclose information to the taxpayers' providers.

- The **Self-select PIN** method <u>requires</u> a taxpayer to provide his prior year Adjusted Gross Income (AGI) amount or prior year PIN for use by the IRS to authenticate the taxpayer. This method <u>may</u> be completely paperless if taxpayers enter their own PIN directly into the electronic return record using key strokes after reviewing the completed return. Taxpayers may also authorize the ERO to enter the PIN on their behalf, in which case the taxpayers must review and sign a completed signature authorization form (***Form 8879***) after reviewing the return.

- The **Practitioner PIN** method does <u>not</u> require the taxpayer to provide their prior year AGI amount or prior year PIN. When using the Practitioner PIN method, a taxpayer must always appropriately sign a completed signature authorization (Form 8879). A taxpayer, who uses the Practitioner PIN method and enters his own PIN in the electronic return record using keystrokes after reviewing the completed return, must still appropriately sign the signature authorization form.

- **IRS E-File Signature Authorization** – When a taxpayer is unable to enter his PIN directly in the electronic return, a taxpayer may authorize the ERO to enter his PIN in the electronic return record by signing the appropriate completed IRS e-file signature authorization form. ***Form 8879, IRS E-File Signature Authorization,*** authorizes an ERO to enter the taxpayer's PIN on Individual Income Tax Returns, and ***Form 8878, IRS E-File Authorization for Application of Extension of Time to File,*** authorizes an ERO to enter the taxpayer's PIN on Forms 4868 and 2350.

The ERO may enter the taxpayer's PIN in the electronic return record before the taxpayer signs Form 8879 or 8878, but the taxpayer must sign and date the appropriate form before the ERO originates the electronic submission of the return. The taxpayer must sign and date Form 8879 or Form 8878 after reviewing the return and ensuring the tax return information on the form matches the information on the return. The ERO may sign Forms 8879 and 8878 by rubber stamp, mechanical device (such as signature pen), or computer software program. This does not alter the requirement that taxpayers must sign Form 8879 and Form 8878 by handwritten signature.

8.5 Terrence uses the Self-select PIN method. He enters his own PIN directly into the electronic return record. Does his tax preparer need to obtain his signature on Form 8879 prior to submitting his return?

Electronic Signatures for EROs

The ERO must also sign with a PIN. The ERO should use the same PIN for the entire tax year. The ERO may manually input his PIN, or the software can generate the PIN in the electronic record in the location designated for the ERO Electronic Filing Identification Number (EFIN)/PIN. By entering a PIN in the ERO EFIN/PIN field, the ERO is attesting to the ERO Declaration. For returns prepared by the ERO firm, return preparers are declaring under the penalties of perjury that they reviewed the returns and they are true, correct, and complete. An ERO may authorize members of the firm or designated employees to sign for them, but the ERO is still responsible.

Rejected Returns and Resolution

The IRS electronically acknowledges the receipt of all transmissions. Returns in each transmission are either accepted or rejected for specific reasons. Accepted returns meet the processing criteria and IRS considers them "filed" as soon as the return is signed electronically or through the receipt by the IRS of a paper signature. Rejected returns fail to meet processing criteria and the IRS considers them "not filed."

If the IRS rejects the electronic portion of a taxpayer's individual income tax return for processing, and the ERO cannot rectify the reason for the rejection, the ERO must take reasonable steps to inform the taxpayer of the rejection **within 24 hours**.

The ERO may resubmit, without additional signatures, a return where the amounts do not differ by more than $50 to "Total Income" or "AGI," or $14 to "Total Tax," "Federal Income Tax Withheld," or "Amount You Owe." When the ERO advises the taxpayer of an unfiled return, the ERO must provide the taxpayer with the reject code(s) accompanied by an explanation. The taxpayer must file a paper return if the IRS cannot accept the return for processing, or if electing not to correct and retransmit the return. In order to timely file the return, the taxpayer must file the paper return by the later of the due date of the return or 10 calendar days after the date the IRS gives notification that it rejected the electronic portion of the return or that the return cannot be accepted for processing. A taxpayer should include an explanation in the paper return as to why he is filing the return after the due date.

Payments

Taxpayers who owe additional tax must pay their balances due by the original due date of the return or be subject to interest and penalties. An extension of time to file may be filed electronically by the original return due date, but it is an extension of time to file the return, not an extension of time to pay a balance due. Taxpayers can e-file and, at the same time, authorize an electronic funds withdrawal (EFW). Taxpayers who choose this option must provide account numbers and routing transit numbers for qualified savings, checking, or share draft accounts. In addition, taxpayers may make payments through the Electronic Federal Tax Payment System (EFTPS), by check, electronically using a credit or debit card, or by filing an installment agreement request.

Refunds

A provider must never charge a separate fee for direct deposit and must accept any direct deposit election by a taxpayer to any eligible financial institution designated by the taxpayer.

The taxpayer may designate refunds for direct deposit to qualified accounts in the taxpayer's name. Qualified accounts include savings, checking, share draft, or consumer asset accounts (for example, IRA or money market accounts). Providers should caution taxpayers that some financial institutions do not permit the deposit of joint income tax refunds into individual accounts. The IRS is not responsible if the financial institution refuses direct deposits for this reason. The provider must advise taxpayers that they cannot rescind a direct deposit election and they cannot make changes to routing transit numbers of financial institutions or to their account numbers after the IRS has accepted the return.

Refund Anticipation Loans (RAL)

A Refund Anticipation Loan (RAL) is money borrowed by a taxpayer from a lender based on the taxpayer's anticipated income tax refund. The IRS is in no way involved in or responsible for the RAL. Providers who offer RAL services have additional responsibilities. The IRS may sanction them if they fail to adhere to certain requirements. The provider must:

- Ensure taxpayers understand that by agreeing to a RAL they will not receive their refunds from the IRS because the IRS will send their refunds to the financial institution
- Advise taxpayers that a RAL is an interest-bearing loan and not a quicker way of receiving their refunds from the IRS
- Advise taxpayers that if a refund is not received within the expected time frame for whatever reason, the taxpayers may be liable to the lender for additional interest and other fees applicable for the RAL
- Advise taxpayers of all fees and other known deductions to be paid from their refund and the remaining amount the taxpayers will actually receive

Tax Return Preparer Competency Exam – Chapter 8 Quiz

Circle the letter next to the best answer. Remember to read the question carefully.

1) Ethel is 65 years old. She receives money from her two investment accounts to supplement her retirement income. She withdraws $25,000 from her IRA and $10,000 from her annuity. She received a 1099-R reflecting the amount of the distributions, including $2,500 withheld for taxes by the custodian of her IRA. What should Ethel do with the Form 1099-R's?

   a. Attach each 1099-R to her tax return to report both distributions

   b. Keep them for her records. The information is already reported to the IRS, so she does not need to turn anything in

   c. Attach only the 1099-R from her IRA as tax was withheld

   d. Attach only the annuity 1099-R because an IRA custodian already reports IRA distributions to the IRS on Form 1098

2) Wilma is an independent contractor for a real estate broker. Peter is Wilma's sales assistant, and he works in her office answering phones and filing paperwork. Wilma pays Peter's salary. She trusts Peter completely, and allows him do whatever he feels necessary to help her close more sales. Which of the following best describes Peter?

   a. Peter is a common law employee.

   b. Peter is a statutory employee.

   c. Peter is self-employed.

   d. Peter is an independent contractor.

3) Which fee arrangement described below is permissible for an electronic return originator (ERO)?

   a. Fees based on AGI from the tax return.

   b. Fees based on % of refund.

   c. Separate fees for direct deposits.

   d. None of the above.

4) Which of the following returns may be electronically filed?

   a. Tax returns with fiscal year periods.

   b. Amended tax returns.

   c. Current year Form 1040 with foreign address.

   d. Current year Form 1040 with APO address.

5) If a taxpayer's return is rejected by the IRS and the ERO cannot fix the problem and re-transmit the return in the time prescribed, the ERO must make reasonable attempts to notify the taxpayer of the reject. How long from the time the return is rejected does the ERO have to try to contact the taxpayer?

a. 12 hours

b. 24 hours

c. 48 hours

d. One week

6) A taxpayer calculates self-employment tax on which of the following forms or schedules:

a. Form 1040

b. Schedule K-1

c. Form 1099

d. Schedule SE

7) Who is required to sign form 8879 when the preparer enters a PIN for the taxpayer on an electronically filed return?

a. The taxpayer(s)

b. The electronic return originator (ERO)

c. Both the taxpayer(s) and the ERO

d. Neither

8) In 2011, Indian River Realty made a payment of $2,500 for attorney fees to Scott Free Legal Services LLP relating to a contract dispute with an employee. How does Indian River Report the payment to Scott Free?

a. Provide Form 1099-MISC by March 31, 2012

b. Provide Form 1099-MISC by Jan 31, 2012

c. Provide Form 1098 by February 28, 2012

d. No reporting is required for the payment

Tax Return Preparer Competency Exam – Chapter 8 Quiz Rationale

For more practice questions, visit fastforwardacademy.com and access our FREE online question bank.

1) **c** The recipient of an informational return does not send copies of to the IRS unless required. A taxpayer must attach Form W-2 the front of their Form 1040 series tax return. A taxpayer should also attach Forms W-2G and 1099-R, but only if federal income tax was withheld.

2) **a** Peter is a common law employee. Under common-law rules, anyone who performs services for a person is an employee of that person if the employer has the right to control <u>what</u> will be done and <u>how</u> it will be done. This is true even when an employer gives the employee freedom of action.

3) **d** Providers may not base their fees on a percentage of the refund amount or compute their fees using any figure from tax returns. A provider must never charge a separate fee for direct deposit.

4) **d** The only returns that can be e-filed are original returns for the current year (exceptions below) for calendar year filers. Beginning January of 2011, *Modernized E-File* (MeF) will accept tax years 2009 and 2010 returns. In subsequent years, 1040 MeF will accept tax returns for the current year and two prior years. Foreign addresses are also currently not accepted under the e-file program; however, military APO or FPO are considered domestic addresses.

5) **b** The ERO must take reasonable steps to inform the taxpayer of the rejection within 24 hours.

6) **d** A self-employed taxpayer with net earnings from self-employment of $400 or more, or church employee income of $108.28 or more, must file Schedule SE along with his tax return.

7) **c** When a taxpayer does not enter his own PIN, the taxpayer must sign and date Form 8879 after reviewing the return and ensuring the tax return information on the form matches the information on the return. The ERO may sign Forms 8879 by rubber stamp, mechanical device (such as signature pen), or computer software program.

8) **b** The taxpayer must send Form 1099-MISC to report payments of $600 or more for services performed for the business by people not treated as employees, such as subcontractors, attorneys, accountants, or directors. The taxpayer must provide the form by Jan 31 to the attorney and report the payment to the IRS by Feb 28. Generally, payments to a corporation are excluded from this reporting requirement.

9 Businesses

Schedule C · Farmers · Loss Limitations · Schedules K-1 · Business Property · Depreciation Section 179 Deduction · Installment Sales · Like-kind Exchanges · Abandonment Casualty and Theft Losses

This chapter summarizes the various return and reporting requirements for Small Businesses.

Schedule C

Certain taxpayers, such as statutory employees or those "self-employed" must file ***Schedule C*** along with Form 1040 to report income and deductions resulting from a trade or business. To file Schedule C the taxpayer must operate a trade or business as one of the following:

- **Statutory Employee** – If workers are independent contractors under the common law rules, such workers may nevertheless be treated as employees by statute (statutory employees) for certain employment tax purposes. Statutory employees report their wages, income, and allowable expenses on Schedule C (or Schedule C-EZ), Form 1040. A separate Schedule C is necessary when a statutory employee also has income from self-employment. The IRS requires an employer with statutory employees to withhold social security and Medicare tax from the statutory employee's earnings, but not federal income tax.

Statutory employees are not liable for self-employment tax because their employers must treat them as employees for social security tax purposes. Statutory employees include full-time life insurance agents, certain agent or commission drivers, traveling salespersons, and certain homeworkers. A taxpayer can alert the IRS to his status as a statutory employee by checking the appropriate box on Schedule C.

- **Sole Proprietor or Disregarded Entity** (single member LLC treated as a sole proprietor) – An unincorporated business that is owned by one individual.

    1) The business does not exist separately from the owner

    2) The owner personally accepts the risks of business to the extent of all the owner's assets, whether the owner uses them in the business or uses them personally

    3) The owner includes business income and expenses on his personal tax return (Schedule C)

- **Qualified Joint Venture** – An unincorporated business jointly owned by a married couple is generally classified as a partnership for federal tax purposes. A partnership is required to file an annual Form 1065 Partnership Return. For tax years after 2006, a *qualified joint venture* whose only members are a husband and a wife filing a joint return can elect <u>not</u> to be treated as a partnership. Spouses make the election on a jointly filed Form 1040 by dividing all items of income, gain, loss, deduction, and credit between them in accordance with each spouse's respective interest in the joint venture. Each spouse is treated as a sole proprietor and files a separate Schedule C.

1) A qualified joint venture conducts a trade or business where all the following exist:

   A) The only members of the joint venture are a husband and wife who file a joint return

   B) Both spouses materially participate in the trade or business (mere joint ownership of property is not enough)

   C) Both spouses elect not to be treated as a partnership

   D) The business is co-owned by both spouses (and not in the name of a state law entity, such as a partnership or LLC)

9.1 Sherri and her husband Manuel operate a local donut shop, which they jointly own. The business is not incorporated, and rather than file a Form 1065 partnership return they elect treatment as a qualified joint venture. Can they file a single Schedule C and report combined income on their joint return?

Schedule C Part I – Income

A taxpayer reports ***gross profit*** on Part I of Schedule C after deducting the ***cost of goods sold*** and any ***returns and allowances*** from ***gross receipts*** (including amounts on Forms 1099-MISC).

gross profit = gross receipts – cost of goods sold – returns

TIP ***Gross income*** of a business includes additional sources of income such as prizes and awards related to the trade or business, state gasoline or fuel tax refunds, and other kinds of miscellaneous business income.

Schedule C Part II – Expenses

A taxpayer groups deductible business related expenses by category on Schedule C. If Form 4562 is not required, a taxpayer may enter certain car or truck expenses directly on Schedule C as part total expenses. The taxpayer then reduces gross income by his total expenses and any expenses related to the business use of his home to arrive at the ***Net profit (or loss)*** of the business.

Schedule C Part III – Cost of Goods Sold (COGS)

The value of the inventory is a major factor in figuring taxable income. There are several inventory valuation methods. A common method is the ***cost method***. To properly value inventory at cost, include all associated direct and indirect costs. The following rules apply:

- For merchandise on hand at the beginning of the tax year, cost means the ending inventory price of the goods.
- For merchandise purchased during the year, cost means the invoice price less appropriate discounts plus transportation or other charges incurred in acquiring the goods. It can also include other costs that the business must capitalize under the uniform capitalization rules.
- For merchandise produced during the year, cost means all direct and indirect costs that the business must capitalize under the uniform capitalization rules.

If a business manufactures products or purchases them for resale, it generally must value inventory at the beginning and end of each tax year to determine the *cost of goods sold*. Selling or administrative salaries and office supplies do not directly relate to the cost of the manufactured product and are not part of the cost of goods sold. The following types of expenses figure into the cost of goods sold:

- The cost of products or raw materials, including freight
- Storage
- Direct labor (include contributions to retirement plans) for workers who produce the products
- Factory overhead

9.2 Giant Inflatable Ball Corp receives $150,000 worth of raw rubber in its initial year of business. The company pays $2,500,000 in executive salaries and $50,000 to factory line workers during the year. All of the rubber is used in the manufacturing process. Unfortunately, the business is not very successful and only 10% of the balls were sold during the year. What is the cost of goods sold?

Farmers

Schedule F

Farmers use ***Schedule F*** (Form 1040) to figure the net profit or loss from regular farming operations. This includes farm products raised for sale or products bought for resale. Income from farming includes amounts received from cultivating, operating, or managing a farm for gain or profit, as owner or tenant.

Schedule F includes income from operating a stock, dairy, poultry, fish, fruit, or truck (vegetable) farm and income from operating a plantation, ranch, range, or orchard. It also includes income from the sale of crop shares if the taxpayer materially participates in producing the crop. Income received from operating a nursery, which specializes in growing ornamental plants, is considered income from farming. Livestock held primarily for sale must be included in inventory. When a farmer sells farm products bought for resale, his profit or loss is the difference between the selling price and the basis in the item (usually the cost).

Income reported on Schedule F does not include gains or losses from sales or other dispositions of the following farm assets:

- Land
- Depreciable farm equipment (§1245 property)
- Buildings and structures (§1250 property)
- Livestock held for draft, breeding, sport, or dairy purposes (§1245 property)

Land and depreciable property (including not held for resale) used in farming are not capital assets. Farmers generally use Form 4797 to report these transactions as ordinary income or capital gain under the rules for §1231 transactions. A farmer who sells depreciable property (§1245 property or §1250 property) at a gain, may have to recognize all or part of the gain as ordinary income under the depreciation recapture rules. Any gain remaining after applying the depreciation recapture rules is a

§1231 gain, which may be taxed as a capital gain. Net §1231 gains are ordinary gains up to the amount of non-recaptured §1231 losses from the five prior years; the rest is long-term capital gain. Losses from §1231 property are ordinary losses. If the property is not held for the required holding period (generally 12 months), the transaction is not subject to §1231 treatment, and any gain or loss is ordinary income reported in Part II of Form 4797.

Livestock Used In Business

If the farmer holds livestock primarily for draft, breeding, dairy, or sporting purposes, it is used in the farm business and must either be depreciated or included in nventory. Sales of livestock used in the business may result in ordinary or capital gains or losses, depending on the circumstances. In either case, farmers should always report these sales on **Form 4797.** Since farmers usually deduct the cost of raising livestock (not added to basis) the animals usually do not have a depreciable basis.

- Sale or exchange of this livestock may qualify as a **Section 1231** gain or loss.
- For Section 1231 transactions, livestock includes cattle, hogs, horses, mules, donkeys, sheep, goats, fur-bearing animals, and other mammals. Livestock does not include chickens, turkeys, pigeons, geese, emus, ostriches, rheas, or other birds, fish, frogs, reptiles, etc.

Gain on the sale of ***raised livestock*** is generally the gross sales price reduced by any expenses of the sale. Expenses of sale include sales commissions, freight or hauling, and other similar expenses. The basis of the animal sold is zero if the taxpayer deducted the costs of raising it during the years the taxpayer raised the animal. Gain on the sale of ***purchased livestock*** is generally the gross sales price minus the adjusted basis and any expenses.

Table 9-1. Where to Report Sales of Farm Product

Item Sold	Schedule F	Form 4797
Farm products raised for sale, including crops and livestock	X	
Farm products bought for resale, including crops and livestock	X	
Farm products not held primarily for sale, such as livestock held for draft, breeding, sport, or dairy purposes (bought or raised)		X

9.3 Randal, a day trader during the dot com days, sold everything and moved to Iowa after the last stock market crash. Finding old habits hard to break, he decides trading cows could be a lucrative pastime. In 2011, he bought 800 cows for $400,000 and sold them for a profit. Does Randal have a capital gain?

Sales Caused by Weather-related Conditions

If a farmer sells or exchanges more livestock, including poultry, than he normally would in a year because of a drought, flood, or other weather-related condition, he may be able to postpone reporting the gain from the additional animals until the next year.

The farmer must meet all of the following conditions to qualify:

- Their principal trade or business is farming.
- They use the cash method of accounting.

- They can show that, under their usual business practices, they would not have sold or exchanged the additional animals this year except for the weather-related condition.
- The weather-related condition caused the federal government to designate an area as eligible for assistance.

Crop Insurance and Crop Disaster Payments

Farmers must include in income any crop insurance proceeds they receive as the result of crop damage. The income is generally recognized in the year received. Farmers treat the crop disaster payments received from the federal government as crop insurance proceeds. The government provides crop disaster payments to a farmer as the result of destruction or damage to crops, or the inability to plant crops, due to drought, flood, or any other natural disaster. Farmers can postpone reporting crop insurance proceeds as income until the year following the year the damage occurred if they meet all the following conditions:

- They use the cash method of accounting.
- They receive the crop insurance proceeds in the same tax year the crops are damaged.
- Under normal business practices, they would have included income from the damaged crops in any tax year following the year the damage occurred.

A December 2011 cold spell in Florida froze the entire Florida Citrus temple orange crop, scheduled for February harvest. The entire 2011 crop was declared a disaster, and Florida Citrus received a crop disaster payment in December 2011. Florida Citrus uses the accrual method of accounting and–unlike other citrus farmers using the cash method–cannot postpone reporting the payment.

Income Averaging for Farmers

Taxpayers who are engaged in a farming business may be able to average all or some of their farm income by allocating it to the three prior years (base years).

Only a taxpayer engaged in a farming business as an individual, a partner in a partnership, or a shareholder in an S corporation may use income averaging. Corporations, partnerships, S corporations, estates, and trusts cannot use income averaging.

Estimated Taxes

A taxpayer with at least two-thirds of gross income from farming who pays entire tax liability by March 1 following the tax year does not need to make estimated tax payments. Otherwise to avoid penalty, he must make one estimated tax payment by January 15 (following the tax year) equaling the lesser of 66 2/3% of the tax due, or 100% of the prior year tax liability.

Gross income from farming is the total of the following amounts from the tax return:

- Gross farm income from Schedule F (Form 1040)
- Gross farm rental income from Form 4835

- Gross farm income from Schedule E (Form 1040)
- Gains from the sale of livestock used for draft, breeding, sport, or dairy purposes (Form 4797)

Gross income from farming does not include wages as a farm employee, income from contract grain harvesting and hauling with workers and machines furnished by taxpayer, gains from the sale of farmland, and depreciable farm equipment.

Farm Rental Income

A landowner who receives rental payments based on crops or livestock produced by a tenant, but does not materially participate in operating the farm, reports his farm rental income and expenses on ***Form 4835*** and carries the net income or loss to Schedule E (Form 1040). The income is not included in self-employment income. A loss on the activity is subject to the passive activity loss limitations. The landowner does not use Form 4835 if basing rent for pasture or farmland on a flat charge.

Credit for Federal Tax Paid on Fuel (Refundable)

Certain taxpayers receive a tax credit based on nontaxable uses (or sales) of fuel during the year. A taxpayer must file ***Form 4136*** with his tax return in order to claim this refundable credit. To calculate the amount of the credit, a farmer multiplies the number of gallons he uses for farming by the rate on the form. The rate for fuel used on a farm for farming purposes is .183 for 2011. Other nontaxable uses include commercial fishing, off-highway business use and commercial aviation.

Loss Limitations

A taxpayer may not take a deduction against ordinary income for a loss if the amount is not ***at risk*** or if the loss is the result of a ***passive activity***.

At-risk Limits

Generally, any loss from an activity subject to the at risk rules is allowed only to the extent of the total amount at risk in the activity at the end of the tax year. A taxpayer must file ***Form 6198*** for activities that incur a loss, where he has any amounts not at risk. Losses disallowed because of the at risk limits are deductions from the same activity in the next tax year. A taxpayer is at risk in any activity for:

- The money and adjusted basis of property he contributes to the activity, and
- Amounts he borrows for use in the activity if:
  1) He is personally liable for repayment, or
  2) He pledges property (other than property used in the activity) as security for the loan.

Jim contributes $50,000 to a partnership that limits his liability. He also personally guarantees a recourse loan of $25,000 made to the partnership to purchase equipment. He is "at risk" for $75,000.

Passive Activities

Generally, losses from passive activities are not deductible unless income from other passive activities exists to offset them. Carry forward any excess ***passive activity loss (PAL)*** or credit to the next tax year and use to offset only passive income.

There are two kinds of passive activities:

- Business activities in which the taxpayer does not materially participate during the year
- Rental activities (even with material participation, unless the taxpayer is a real estate professional)

Material Participation

The IRS will consider participation to be material if the taxpayer can satisfy any of the following tests:

- The taxpayer participated in the activity for more than 500 hours during the tax year.
- The taxpayer's participation was substantially all the participation in the activity of all individuals for the tax year, including the participation of individuals who did not own any interest in the activity.
- The taxpayer participated in the activity for more than 100 hours during the tax year, and at least as much as any other individual for the year.

Rental Real Estate Professional Exception

A loss from rental real estate may offset ordinary income if under one of following exceptions:

- A ***Real Estate Professional*** may deduct losses against ordinary income, when:
    1) More than half of work is involved in real property trades or businesses in which the person ***materially participates***, and
    2) More than **750 hours** of material participation is in real property trades or businesses.
- If rental losses are ***less than $25,000*** and the taxpayer or spouse actively participates in the rental activity, the passive activity limits may not apply. ***Active participation*** is a less stringent standard than material participation. Active participation includes management decisions such as approving tenants, deciding rental terms, approving expenditures, etc.
    1) If a taxpayer (S or MFJ) has ***modified adjusted gross income (MAGI)*** more than $100,000, the $25,000 special allowance is limited to 50% of the difference between $150,000 and MAGI. There is no allowance when MAGI is more than $150,000.

9.4 Rene has income from 10 rental properties. After deducting depreciation, repairs, and other expenses, she has a loss of $45,000. Her property manager handles most tenant issues, but she is involved in most major decisions. Her MAGI is $110,000. How much of her loss is deductible against ordinary income?

Schedules K-1

A partner, S corporation shareholder, and beneficiary of an estate or trust should receive Schedule K-1 reflecting his share of income, credits, deductions, and certain other items. A taxpayer includes the information from the K-1 on his individual income tax return; however, he does not file Schedule K-1 with the tax return unless backup withholding applies.

Partnership Form 1065 K-1

A partnership is the relationship between two or more taxpayers who join to carry on a business. Each partner contributes money, property, labor, or skill, and expects to share in business profits and losses. Partners, other than limited partners are personally liable for company debts. Partners can be individuals, corporations, trusts, estates, or other partnerships. ***Form 1065*** is an information return used to report income, gains, losses, deductions, credits, etc., from the operation of a partnership. The partnership does not pay taxes; instead, income or loss items pass through to its partners. ***Schedule K-1*** states each partner's ***distributive share*** of these items for partners to include on their own tax returns:

- Income (loss) items
    1) Ordinary business income (loss)
    2) Net rental real estate income (loss)
    3) Other net rental income (loss)
    4) Guaranteed payments
- Portfolio income
    1) Interest income
    2) Ordinary and qualified dividends
    3) Royalties
    4) Net short-term and long-term capital gain (loss)
    5) Collectibles (28%) gain (loss)
    6) Unrecaptured Section 1250 gain
    7) Net Section 1231 gain (loss)
- Deductions
    1) Section 179 deduction
    2) Other deductions (charitable contributions, intangible drilling costs, pensions, etc.)
- Self-employment earnings (loss)
- Credits
- Foreign transactions
- Alternative Minimum Tax (AMT) items
- Tax-exempt income and nondeductible expenses
- Distributions

S Corporation Form 1120S K-1

An eligible domestic corporation can avoid double taxation by electing treatment as an ***S corporation (SCORP)***. Like a partnership, an SCORP is a flow through entity. Generally, an SCORP is exempt from federal income tax other than tax on certain capital gains and passive income. On their tax returns, the SCORP shareholders include their share of the corporation's separately stated items of income, deduction, loss, and credit, and their share of non-separately stated ordinary business income or loss reported to them on ***Schedule K-1 (Form 1120S).*** Unlike a partnership, the shareholders of an SCORP receive a share of income (or loss) and separately stated items in proportion to the percentage ownership of each shareholder. Ownership is determined for each day of the year.

Schedule K-1 (Form 1120S) is essentially the same as *Schedule K-1 (Form 1065)*. Some of the notable differences on the K-1 include:

- Unlike the partners in a partnership, an S corporation shareholder does not receive guaranteed payments.
- *Schedule K-1 (Form 1120S)* does not report self-employment income to shareholders. Except for certain instances (e.g. fringe benefits), an S corporation shareholder is not considered self-employed.

Beneficiary Form 1041 K-1

Unlike Partnerships and S corporations, income from an estate or trust (other than a grantor trust) is taxable to the estate/trust unless distributions are made (or required to be made) to beneficiaries. The estate/trust must pay tax on undistributed income, and the beneficiary will pay tax on actual (or required) distributions. The income distributed to the beneficiary retains the same character in the hands of the beneficiary as in the hands of the estate or trust. Beneficiaries of an estate or trust receive Schedule K-1 reflecting their share of applicable pass through items.

Some of the notable differences on the *Schedule K-1 (Form 1041)* include:

- Unlike the partners in a partnership, a beneficiary does not receive guaranteed payments.
- *Schedule K-1 (Form 1041)* does not report self-employment income to shareholders.
- Other Portfolio and Nonbusiness income – This box reflects the distributive share of royalties, annuities, and other income that is not subject to the passive activity rules. It also includes income in respect of a decedent (IRD).
- Estate tax deduction – The beneficiary is entitled to an income tax deduction equal to the estate taxes paid on income earned by the estate.
- Final-year deductions – An estate or trust with more fees than income in its final year may pass those expenses through to the beneficiaries.
- Credit for estimated taxes – Estates or trusts required to make estimated tax payments can file ***Form 1041-T, Allocation of Estimated Tax Payments to Beneficiaries,*** for the beneficiary to get the credit for an estimated tax payment. The estate or trust then reports the amount of the pass through credit to the beneficiary on a K-1.

9.5 Donna has a net long-term capital gain reported to her on Schedule K-1. How does she report this on her Form 1040 tax return?

Business Property

Generally, a sale or trade of an asset results in a ***capital gain*** or loss. A sale or trade of a non-capital asset results in ***ordinary gain*** or loss. In some situations, part of the gain or loss may be a capital gain or loss and part may be an ordinary gain or loss.

Capital Assets

Rather than defining capital assets, the law provides a list of properties that are not capital assets:

- Accounts or notes receivable acquired in the ordinary course of a trade or business for services rendered or from the sale of property held mainly for sale to customers
- Copyright, literary, musical, or artistic composition when created by the efforts of the taxpayer.
- Inventory or property held mainly for sale to customers or property that will physically become a part of the merchandise that is for sale to customers
- Depreciable property and real property (real estate) used in the taxpayer's trade or business
- Supplies regularly used or consumed in the ordinary course of a taxpayer's trade or business

In general, ordinary income tax rates apply when selling assets other than capital assets. Capital assets receive preferential tax treatment. Taxpayers generally hold capital assets for business or investment purposes (for example, stocks or copyrights acquired for investment).

Section 1231 Property

Some property held more than one year receives special treatment when sold. Net §1231 gains are ordinary gains up to the amount of non-recaptured §1231 losses from the five prior years; the rest is long-term capital gain. A loss from §1231 property is an ordinary loss.

Section 1231 property includes:

- Depreciable or amortizable property (personal or real) used in a business
- Leasehold interests
- Timber, coal, or iron ore
- Livestock or un-harvested crops
- Goodwill and other Section 197 intangibles
- Copyrights if acquired for investment

Section 1245 Recapture

Any property (other than depreciable real property) that is or has been subject to an allowance for depreciation or amortization is subject to ***Section 1245 recapture*** rules. The taxpayer recaptures a portion of the gain from the disposition of the property due to depreciation as ordinary income. Section 1245 property does not include buildings and structural components.

TIP The term "building" includes a house, barn, warehouse, or garage. The term "structural component" includes walls, floors, windows, doors, central air conditioning systems, light fixtures, etc.

Section 1250 Recapture

All real property that is subject to an allowance for depreciation and has never been Section 1245 property is subject to ***Section 1250 recapture*** rules. It includes leasehold of land or Section 1250 property subject to an allowance for depreciation. A fee simple interest in land is not included because it is not depreciable. A tax rate of 25% applies to depreciation up to the amount of straight-line depreciation. This portion is ***unrecaptured Section 1250 gain***. Any amount of ***additional depreciation*** is taxed at ordinary income rates and is recaptured as Section 1250 gain. Additional depreciation is the actual depreciation that is more than the depreciation figured using the straight-line method. If a taxpayer holds Section 1250 property for one year or less, all the depreciation is additional depreciation.

Christine is in the 35% tax bracket. She purchased a rental property several years ago for $100,000. She sells the property for $150,000. The depreciation taken under ACRS was $41,840, but if she had used the straight-line method, the depreciation would have been $37,970. Christine used a method of accelerated depreciation (ACRS) and has a Section 1250 gain. Section 1250 gain is $3,870, the difference between ACRS and the straight-line depreciation. Sec 1250 Gain is taxed at ordinary income rates. Unrecaptured Section 1250 gain is $37,970, the amount of straight-line depreciation taxed as a capital gain at a 25% rate. The remaining $50,000 gain is taxable as a long-term capital gain at a maximum rate of 15% in 2011.

Depreciation

There are two basic types of property:

- **Tangible property** – Is physical in nature. Includes land, structures, equipment, natural resources, etc. Tangible property is further divided into:
  1) **Real property** – Real estate including land, houses, buildings, etc.
  2) **Personal property** – Any tangible property other than real property
- **Intangible property** – Does not have a physical presence. Includes computer software, patents, goodwill, stocks, and bonds.

Expenditures that do not have a useful life beyond one year are ***expenses**, which are* generally deductible in the year incurred. Property acquired with a useful life greater than one year or ***improvements*** that increase the value of the property, lengthen its life, or adapt it to a different use are ***capital expenditures***. A capital expenditure is ***capitalized*** (added to capital), and the cost is systematically ***recovered*** (written off) each year, in various ways, depending on type of property. Depreciation reduces basis for figuring gain or loss on a later sale or exchange.

The methods for recovering the cost of an asset over its useful life include the following:

- **Depreciation** – For tangible income producing property, other than natural resources
- **Depletion** – For assets that diminish over time, such as oil, gas, and other natural resources
- **Amortization** – For intangible assets, such as patents and goodwill

The taxpayer recovers the cost of tangible income-producing property through yearly tax deductions by depreciating the property, that is, by deducting some of the cost each year on the tax return. Three basic factors determine how much depreciation the taxpayer may deduct:

- The basis in the property
- The recovery period for the property
- The depreciation method used

What Property Can Be Depreciated

- Property may be depreciated if it meets all the following requirements:
    1) The taxpayer owns the property.
    2) The taxpayer uses the property in business or income-producing activity (e.g., rental property).
    3) The property has a determinable useful life.
    4) The taxpayer expects the property to last more than one year.
- Certain property <u>cannot</u> be depreciated:
    1) Land (land preparation costs, such as landscaping costs are depreciable)
    2) Property placed in service and disposed of in the same year
    3) Equipment used to build capital improvements
    4) ***Section 197 intangibles*** – The following assets are Section 197 intangibles and must be amortized over 180 months:
        1. Goodwill
        2. Going concern value
        3. Workforce in place
        4. Business books and records, operating systems, or any other information base, including lists or other information concerning current or prospective customers
        5. A patent, copyright, formula, process, design, pattern, know-how, format, or similar item
        6. A customer-based intangible
        7. A supplier-based intangible
        8. Any item similar to items (3) through (7)
        9. A license, permit, or other right granted by a governmental unit or agency

10. A covenant not to compete in connection with the acquisition of a business

11. Any franchise, trademark, or trade name,

12. A contract for the use of, or a term interest in, any item in this list

A taxpayer cannot amortize any of the intangibles listed in items (1) through (8) that he created rather than acquired unless he created them in acquiring assets that make up a trade or business or a substantial part of a trade or business.

TIP A taxpayer cannot depreciate personal-use property. Deduct depreciation only on the part of property used for a business or income-producing activity.

Repairs and Improvements

If depreciable property is improved, the taxpayer must treat the improvement as separate depreciable property. Improvement means an addition to or partial replacement of property that adds to its value, appreciably lengthens its useful lifetime, or adapts it to a different use. Generally, a taxpayer deducts the cost of repairing business property in the same way as any other business expense. However, if a repair or replacement increases the value of the property, makes it more useful, or lengthens its life, it is an improvement and is added to capital and depreciated.

Depreciation Methods

- Generally, a taxpayer must use the ***Modified Accelerated Cost Recovery System (MACRS)*** to depreciate residential rental property placed in service after 1986. MACRS consists of two systems that determine how property may be depreciated:

    1) **General Depreciation System (GDS)** – Generally, taxpayers must use GDS for property used in most rental activities. Recovery periods generally are shorter than under ADS.

    2) **Alternative Depreciation System (ADS)** – ADS uses the straight-line method of depreciation. The taxpayer cannot change the election, which applies to all property in the same class that is placed in service during the tax year of the election. However, the election applies on a property-by-property basis for residential rental property and nonresidential real property.

- If rental property was in service before 1987, the taxpayer uses one of the following methods:

    1) ***ACRS (Accelerated Cost Recovery System)*** for property in service between 1980 and 1987

    2) ***Straight-line*** or ***declining balance method*** over the useful life of property placed in service before 1981

Taxpayers must continue to use the same depreciation method unless the IRS grants approval to change accounting methods. The methods under MACRS (GDS) for depreciating property are as follows:

- **Straight-line depreciation** – Deduct equal amounts throughout the recovery period.

    1) A taxpayer must use the straight-line method and a mid-month convention for residential rental property. In the first year of claiming depreciation for residential rental property, take depreciation only for the number of months the property is in use.

Saul purchases a $2,000 computer for his business that has a useful life of 5-years. He uses the computer exclusively for business. He can claim $400 in annual depreciation until he no longer has a basis in the computer. If he uses the half-year convention, he claims $200 in the first year.

- **200% or 150% declining balance** – Allows for greater depreciation percentages in early years. Use the straight-line method in place of accelerated depreciation in the first tax year it provides an equal or larger deduction than either the 200% or 150% declining balance method.

    1) Upon sale or other disposition, certain nonresidential real estate may be subject to recapture of excess depreciation ***(un-recaptured Section 1250 gain)*** if a method other than straight-line depreciation was used. The recaptured amount is the excess depreciation amount above what would have been claimed using the straight-line method.

Special Depreciation Allowance

A business taxpayer may take an additional 50% ***special depreciation allowance***, often referred to as "bonus depreciation" on certain qualified property. The *2010 Tax Relief Act* allows for 100% expensing of property placed in service after September 8, 2010, but before January 1, 2012. The special depreciation allowance applies only for the first year the property is in service. The allowance is an additional deduction taken after any ***Section 179 expense deduction*** and before the taxpayer figures regular depreciation under MACRS. Qualified property includes tangible property depreciated in 20 years or less under MACRS.

Recovery Periods

Under regular MACRS (GDS), rental property generally falls into one of the following classes:

- **Five-year property** – Computers and peripheral equipment, office machinery (typewriters, calculators, copiers, etc.), automobiles, light trucks, appliances, carpeting, furniture, etc., used in a residential rental real estate activity. Depreciation on automobiles and certain computers is limited. Taxpayers may use 200% or 150% DB.

- **Seven-year property** – Office furniture and equipment (desks, file cabinets, etc.). This class also includes any property that does not have a class life and that has not been designated by law as being in any other class. Taxpayers may use 200% or 150% DB.

- **Fifteen-year property** – Roads, fences, and shrubbery. Taxpayers may use 150% DB.

- **Twenty-year property** – Includes improvements such as utilities and sewers.

- **Residential rental property (27.5-year property)** – Real property that is a rental building or structure (including mobile homes) for which 80% or more of the gross rental income for the tax year is from dwelling units. It does not include a unit in a hotel, motel, inn, or other establishment where more than half of the units are used on a transient basis. Depreciate additions or improvements to the structure over the same period. In a case like this, the straight-line method is necessary along with a mid-month convention. For the first year, take depreciation only for the number of months the property was in use.

- **Non-residential rental property (39-year property)** – Commercial buildings and structures. Includes Section 1250 property. Must use straight-line method and mid-month convention.

Conventions

Depreciation begins when the taxpayer places the property in service for the production of income. Depreciation ends when either the taxpayer fully recovers the cost, or the property is retired from service, whichever happens first. Property is placed in service in a rental activity when it is ready and available for a specific use in that activity. Even if unused, it is in service when it is ready and available for its specific use. A ***convention*** is a method established under MACRS to set the beginning and end of the recovery period. The convention used determines the number of months that the taxpayer may claim as depreciation in the year the property was placed in service and in the year in which it was disposed. Use the mid-month convention for residential rental property and nonresidential real property. For all other property, use the half-year or mid-quarter convention, as appropriate.

- **Mid-month convention** – Use a mid-month convention for all residential rental property and nonresidential real property. Treat all property placed in service, or disposed of, during any month as placed in service, or disposed of, at the midpoint of that month.
- **Mid-quarter convention** – Use a mid-quarter convention if the mid-month convention does not apply and the total depreciable basis of MACRS property placed in service in the last three months of a tax year is more than 40% of the total basis of all such property placed into service during the year. For this convention, the MACRS property excludes nonresidential real property, residential rental property, and property placed in service and disposed of in the same year. Under this convention, treat all property placed in service, or disposed of, during any quarter of a tax year as placed in service, or disposed of, at the midpoint of the quarter.
- **Half-year convention** – Use the half-year convention if neither the mid-quarter convention nor the mid-month convention applies. Under this convention, treat all property placed into service, or disposed of, during a tax year as being placed into service, or disposed of, at the midpoint of that tax year. If this convention applies, the taxpayer may deduct a half year of depreciation for the first year and the last year that the taxpayer depreciates the property. The taxpayer may deduct a full year of depreciation for any other year during the recovery period.

TIP The half-year convention applies to most transactions. Under this convention all propery transactions are considered to occur at the midpoint of the year.

Section 179 Deduction

Use a Section 179 deduction to recover the cost of qualifying property used in a trade or business. If a taxpayer buys qualifying property with cash and a trade-in, its cost for purposes of the section 179 deduction includes only the cash paid. This deduction is not allowed for property held for the production of income, such as rental property. Instead of depreciating property over time, a taxpayer may elect to claim as an expense up to $500,000 in 2011. Section 179 deduction limits apply to both a partnership and its partners. The partnership determines its Section 179 deduction subject to the limits. It then allocates the deduction among its partners. The same is true for an S corporation and a shareholder. The property must be placed in service during the tax year, and must be one of the following types of depreciable property:

- Tangible personal property
- Machinery and equipment

- Property contained in or attached to a building (not structural components), such as office equipment, refrigerators, grocery store counters, printing presses, testing equipment, and signs
- Gasoline storage tanks and pumps at retail service stations
- Livestock, including horses, cattle, hogs, sheep, goats, and mink and other furbearing animals
- Other tangible property (except buildings and their structural components) used as:
    1) An integral part of manufacturing, production, or extraction; or as an integral part of furnishing transportation, communications, electricity, gas, water, or sewage disposal services,
    2) A research facility used in connection with any of the activities in (1) above, or
    3) A facility used in any of the activities in (1) for the bulk storage of fungible commodities
- Single purpose agricultural (livestock) or horticultural structures
- Petroleum storage or distribution facilities (except buildings and their structural components)
- Off-the-shelf computer software

Reduced Section 179 Deduction

Under certain conditions, the amount of the Section 179 deduction may be reduced or eliminated:

- If the cost of the qualifying Section 179 property placed in service in a year is more than $2 million, the taxpayer generally must reduce the dollar limit (but not below zero) by the amount of cost more than $2 million. If the cost of Section 179 property placed in service during 2011 is $2.5 million or more, the taxpayer cannot take a Section 179 deduction.
- Married taxpayers who file separately in 2011 must combine all purchases as if they were filing jointly to determine the allowable Section 179 deduction; otherwise, the deduction is $250,000 each.
- The taxpayer must use the property more than 50% for business in the year placed in service. The Section 179 deduction is allowed only for the business use portion of property. If the property is also for personal use, that part cannot receive a deduction. If the business use falls below 50% in future years, the taxpayer must include a portion of the Section 179 deduction in income.
- **Sport Utility and Certain Other Vehicles** – Taxpayers cannot elect to expense more than $25,000 of the cost of any heavy sport utility vehicle (SUV) and certain other vehicles placed in service during the tax year. This rule applies to any four-wheeled vehicle primarily designed or used to carry less than nine passengers over public streets, roads, or highways, rated at more than 6,000 pounds gross vehicle weight and not more than 14,000 pounds gross vehicle weight. In addition to the Section 179 deduction, a taxpayer may claim a special depreciation allowance and MACRS depreciation.
- **Passenger Vehicles** – The total depreciation deduction (including the Section 179 expense deduction) a taxpayer can take for a passenger automobile (not a truck or a van) first placed in service in 2011 is $3,060 ($11,060 if the depreciation allowance applies). The maximum deduction for a truck or van is $3,260 ($11,260 if the special depreciation allowance applies).

Installment Sale

Some sales involve arrangements that provide for part or the entire selling price to be paid in a later year. These sales are ***installment sales.*** The buyer's obligation to make future payments can be in the form of a deed of trust, note, land contract, mortgage, or other evidence of the buyer's debt. If a sale qualifies as an installment sale, the taxpayer must report the gain under the ***installment method*** unless the taxpayer elects to report the gain in the current year. If the sale results in a loss, a taxpayer may not use the installment method. The following conditions apply to an installment sale:

- Increase the adjusted basis for installment sale purposes by selling expenses (commissions, attorney fees, and any other expenses paid on the sale) and depreciation recapture.
- If a taxpayer sells property on which a depreciation deduction was claimed or could have been claimed, the taxpayer must report the amount of the deduction (or amount that could have been claimed) as ***depreciation recapture*** income in the year of sale, whether or not an installment payment was received that year. Report the recapture income in full as ordinary income in the year of sale; report only the gain greater than the recapture income on the installment method.
- Each payment on an installment sale usually consists of three parts—interest income, return of adjusted basis in the property, and gain on the sale.
- The method to determine the amount of gain recognized as installment income is as follows:
    1) **Determine gross profit** – Gross profit is the selling price less the adjusted basis for installment sale purposes. If the property sold was the main home, subtract any gain that the taxpayer can exclude from the gross profit.
    2) **Gross profit percentage** – A certain percentage of each payment (after subtracting interest) is reported as installment sale income. Calculate this ***gross profit percentage*** by dividing the gross profit from the sale by the contract price.
    3) **Installment sale income recognized** – To arrive at the amount recognized, multiply the payments received each year (less interest) by the gross profit percentage.

Jim and Jean purchased a vacation home in 1997 for $100,000. They sold the property for $500,000 and received a down payment of $200,000. They took a mortgage from the purchaser for the remaining $300,000. Gross profit is $400,000 ($500,000 selling price - $100,000 basis). Determine the gross profit percentage by dividing the gross profit from the sale by the contract price. Gross Profit Percentage is 80% ($400,000 gross profit divided by $500,000 selling price). Jim and Jean must report 80% of each payment (after subtracting interest) as installment sale income.

- In each year that a taxpayer receives an installment payment, the taxpayer must include in income both the interest part and the part that is the taxpayer's gain on the sale. If an installment sale contract does not provide for adequate stated interest (when compared to the ***applicable federal rate***), the taxpayer may reclassify part of the stated principal amount of the contract as interest. The taxpayer should not include in income the part that is the return of the basis in the property. Basis is the amount of the investment in the property for installment sale purposes.
- If the taxpayer sells depreciable property to certain ***related persons***, the taxpayer may not report the sale using the installment method. Instead, all payments due are considered received in the year of sale. However, the taxpayer may use the installment method in a related party transaction if he derives no significant tax deferral benefit from the sale. The taxpayer must show, to the satisfaction of the IRS, that avoidance of federal income tax was not a principal purpose of the sale.
- If the taxpayer sells property to a related person and, within two years, the related person disposes of the property before the taxpayer receives all payments with respect to the sale, the taxpayer may

have a reporting obligation. The taxpayer may have to treat part or all of the amount the related person realizes (or the FMV if the disposed property is not sold or exchanged) from the second disposition as if the taxpayer received it at the time of the second disposition.

- **Disposition of an installment obligation** – A disposition generally includes a sale, exchange, cancellation, bequest, distribution, or transmission of an installment obligation. An installment obligation is the buyer's note, deed of trust, or other evidence that the buyer will make future payments to the taxpayer.

  1) If a taxpayer is using the installment method and the installment obligation is disposed of, generally the taxpayer will have a gain or loss to report. The gain or loss applies to the sale of the property for which the taxpayer received the installment obligation. If the original installment sale produced ordinary income, the disposition of the obligation will result in ordinary income or loss. If the original sale resulted n a capital gain, the disposition of the obligation will result in a capital gain or loss.

  2) **Rules to figure gain or loss** – Use the following rules to figure gain or loss from the disposition of an installment obligation:

     A) If the taxpayer sells or exchanges the obligation, or accepts less than face value in satisfaction of the obligation, the gain or loss is the difference between the basis in the obligation and the amount realized.

     B) If the obligation is disposed of in any other way, the gain or loss is the difference between the basis in the obligation and FMV at the time of the disposition. This rule applies, for example, when the taxpayer gives the installment obligation to someone else or cancels the buyer's debt.

  3) Calculate the basis in an installment obligation by multiplying the unpaid balance on the obligation by the gross profit percentage. Subtract that amount from the unpaid balance. The result is the basis in the installment obligation.

In 2000, Sue sold an airplane on the installment method. She needed cash in 2011 so she sold the note for $110,000 when the balance due her was $140,000. Her gross profit percentage was 60%. Of the $140,000 still owed to Sue, $84,000 is profit owed to her on the obligation, and $56,000 is her basis. She receives $110,000 for the note so she has a profit of $54,000.

Like-kind Exchanges

If a taxpayer trades <u>business or investment</u> property for other business or investment property of a ***like kind***, the taxpayer does not pay tax on any gain or deduct any loss until he sells or disposes of the property received. Like-kind properties are properties of the same nature or character, even if they differ in grade or quality. The exchange of real estate for real estate and the exchange of personal property for similar personal property are exchanges of like-kind property. For example, the following transactions involve property of a like kind:

- Trade of land improved with an apartment house for land improved with a store building
- City property for farm property
- Improved property for unimproved property

- Real estate owned by a taxpayer for a real estate lease that runs 30 years
- A barge for a tugboat
- Office desk for an office file cabinet
- A panel truck for a pickup truck

An exchange of personal property for real property does not qualify as a like-kind exchange. The following transactions do not involve property of a like kind:

- Exchange of a piece of machinery for a store building
- Real property located in the United States and real property located outside the United States
- Exchange of livestock of different sexes

TIP In a like-kind exchange, the taxpayer must hold both the property transferred and the property received for investment or productive use in a trade or business. Machinery, buildings, land, trucks, and rental houses are examples of property that may qualify.

The rules for like-kind exchanges do not apply to exchanges of the following property:

- Personal use property, such as a home and family car
- Stock-in-trade or other property held primarily for sale, such as inventories, raw materials, and real estate held by dealers
- Stocks, bonds, notes, or other securities or evidences of indebtedness, such as accounts receivable
- Partnership interests
- Certificates of trust or beneficial interest
- Choses in action (a right to sue)
- Certain tax-exempt use property subject to a lease

The replacement property must be identified within 45 days and received by the earliest of the 180th day after the date on which the property given up in the exchange transfers, or the due date of the tax return, including extensions, for the tax year in which the transfer of the property given up occurs.

Gain Recognition

The amount ***realized*** from a sale or trade of property is everything received for the property. This includes the money, the fair market value of any property or services, and debt or other liabilities assumed by the buyer. The difference between the ***adjusted basis*** and the amount realized in a sale is the ***realized gain (or loss)*** on the transaction. The amount of income or loss ***recognized*** is the amount a taxpayer includes in taxable income for the tax year.

Transactions such as ***like-kind exchanges*** may defer or partially defer recognition of gain. A taxpayer may have a ***partially nontaxable*** exchange and could realize a gain if he receives property that is not like kind, known as ***boot***.

Boot is the total amount of the following:

- Any money received
- Net liabilities assumed by other party (after subtracting the liabilities assumed by taxpayer)
- The FMV of unlike property received

A taxpayer recognizes gain up to the amount of boot received or the amount of realized gain, whichever is less. The taxpayer cannot recognize a loss unless it is on a transfer of unlike property. The recognized (taxable) gain on the disposition of the like-kind property given up is the smaller of the following:

- The amount of gain realized
- The FMV of boot received *less* exchange expenses (closing costs) paid

Exchange Expenses

Exchange expenses are generally the closing costs paid by the taxpayer. They include such items as brokerage commissions, attorney fees, and deed preparation fees. Subtract exchange expenses from the total consideration received to figure the amount realized on the exchange. Exchange expenses increase the basis of the like-kind property received by the amount of exchange expenses incurred. Exchange expenses reduce boot before determining the recognized gain.

Assumption of Liabilities

To determine the amount of realized gain, increase the amount realized by any liabilities assumed by the other party. Subtract liabilities of the other party assumed by the taxpayer from the amount realized. For purposes of figuring the limit of recognized gain, if the other party assumes a net liability, treat the taxpayer as if he received money for the liability. The taxpayer can decrease (but not below zero) the amount of money he is treated as receiving by the amount of the other party's liabilities he assumes, by any cash he pays or unlike property he gives up.

Basis of Property Received

The basis of property a taxpayer acquires in a like-kind exchange is generally the same as the basis of the property he transfers, with the following adjustments:

- **Increase** basis by the total amount of:
    1) Additional money paid, including exchange expenses
    2) FMV of any non-like-kind property transferred to other party
    3) Net liabilities assumed by the taxpayer
    4) Any gain recognized on the exchange
- **Decrease** basis by the amount of:
    1) Boot received (money, FMV of non-like-kind property, net liabilities other party assumes)
    2) Any loss recognized on the exchange

Allocate basis first to non-like-kind property in an amount equivalent to its FMV at the date of the exchange. Allocate the remaining basis to the like-kind property. In situations where a taxpayer receives multiple like-kind replacement properties, the basis is allocated between the properties (other than money) received, in proportion to its relative FMV on the date of the exchange.

A taxpayer exchanges real estate held for investment with an adjusted basis of $8,000 for other real estate he now holds for investment. The fair market value (FMV) of the real estate received is $14,000. The taxpayer also receives $1,000 in cash and pays $500 in exchange expenses. The property the taxpayer gave up was subject to a $3,000 mortgage for which he was personally liable. The other party in the trade agreed to pay off the mortgage. The property received is subject to a $4,000 mortgage that the taxpayer assumes.

FMV of like-kind property received		$14,000
Cash		$1,000
Mortgage assumed by other party		$3,000
Total received		$18,000
less: Exchange expenses	$500	
Amount realized		$17,500
less: Adjusted basis of property transferred		$8,000
less: Mortgage taxpayer assumed		$4,000
Realized gain		**$5,500**

The realized gain is recognized (taxable) gain only up to $500, figured as follows:

Money received (cash)		$1,000
Net liability other party assumes ($3,000 – $4,000 not below $0)		$0
Total money and unlike property received		$1,000
less: Exchange expenses paid	$500	
Recognized gain		**$500**

The basis for the property received is increased by $1,000:

Basis of transferred property	$8,000	
Net liability taxpayer assumes ($4,000 – $3,000)		$1,000
Exchange expenses		$500
Recognized gain		$500
less: Boot received	$1,000	
Adjusted basis		**$9,000**

Related Party

If a taxpayer trades property with a ***related party*** in a like-kind exchange and either party disposes of the like property within two years after the trade, both parties must report any gain or loss not recognized on the original trade on the return for the year in which the later disposition occurs. A taxpayer may not deduct a loss, other than a distribution in complete liquidation of a corporation, if the transaction is directly or indirectly between the taxpayer and the following related parties:

- Members of taxpayer's family, which includes only brothers and sisters, half-brothers and half-sisters, spouse, ancestors (parents, grandparents, etc.), and lineal descendants (children, grandchildren, etc.)
- A partnership or corporation with more than 50% directly or indirectly owned by the taxpayer
- A tax-exempt charitable or educational organization controlled by taxpayer or family member

Acquisition or Abandonment of Secured Property

The abandonment of property is a disposition of property, whereby a taxpayer voluntarily and permanently gives up possession and use of the property with the intention of ending ownership, but without passing it on to anyone else. Certain lenders who acquire an interest in property that was security for a loan or who have reason to know that such property has been abandoned must provide the taxpayer with ***Form 1099-A***; however, a lender who cancels part of the taxpayer's debt may use Form 1099-C instead.

The taxpayer may have reportable income or loss because of such acquisition or abandonment. Gain or loss from an acquisition generally is measured by the difference between adjusted basis in the property and the amount of debt canceled in exchange for the property, or, if greater, the sale proceeds. The taxpayer may have income from the discharge of indebtedness in the amount of the unpaid balance of the canceled debt. The taxpayer may have a loss from abandonment up to the adjusted basis of the property at the time of abandonment. Losses on acquisitions or abandonments of property held for personal use are not deductible. Loss from abandonment of business or investment property is deductible as an ordinary loss (Form 4797), even if the property is a capital asset. The loss is the property's adjusted basis when abandoned. The deduction for an abandonment loss is made in the tax year in which the loss is sustained.

If the abandoned property secures a debt for which a taxpayer is personally liable and the debt is canceled, the taxpayer will realize ordinary income equal to the canceled debt. This income is separate from any loss realized from abandonment of the property. Report income from cancellation of a debt related to a business or rental activity as business or rental income. Report income from cancellation of a nonbusiness debt as miscellaneous income on Form 1040. However, income from cancellation of debt is not taxed if any of the following apply.

- The cancellation is intended as a gift
- The debt is qualified farm debt
- The debt is qualified real property business debt
- The taxpayer is insolvent or bankrupt
- The debt is qualified principal residence indebtedness

Casualty and Theft Losses

A casualty is the damage, destruction, or loss of property resulting from an identifiable event that is sudden, unexpected, or unusual. Deductible casualty losses include the following:

- Car accidents or shipwrecks
- Earthquakes, fires, floods, or volcanic eruptions
- Storms, including hurricanes and tornadoes
- Terrorist attacks
- Vandalism
- Government-ordered demolition or relocation of a home because of a disaster
- Mine cave-ins
- Sonic booms
- Damage from corrosive drywall

A casualty loss is <u>not</u> deductible if the damage or destruction is the result of any of the following causes:

- Accidentally breaking articles such as glassware or china under normal conditions
- A family pet
- A fire if the taxpayer willfully set it or paid someone else to set it
- A car accident if the taxpayer's willful negligence or willful act caused it
- Progressive deterioration:
    1) The steady weakening of a building due to normal wind and weather conditions.
    2) The deterioration and damage to a water heater that bursts. However, the rust and water damage to rugs caused by the bursting of a water heater does qualify as a casualty.
    3) Losses of property caused by droughts, other than business or investment property.
    4) Termite or moth damage.
    5) Damage to trees or other plants by a fungus, disease, insects, worms, or similar pests.

Gain or Loss

A casualty or theft of property usually results in a taxpayer realizing either a gain or loss. If the amount of insurance or other reimbursements is more than the cost or other basis of the property, the taxpayer has a gain. A taxpayer can generally choose to postpone all or part of a gain by using the reimbursement to restore the property or by purchasing similar property within two years of the <u>end</u> of the first tax year in which any part of the gain is realized. To postpone reporting the entire gain, the cost of the replacement property must be at least as much as the reimbursement. The taxpayer includes the amount of gain up to the amount of unspent reimbursement in income.

The loss is the smaller of the adjusted basis in the property before the casualty or theft, or the decrease in FMV of the property because of the casualty or theft, minus any insurance or other reimbursement. Taxpayers generally must deduct a casualty loss in the year it occurs. However, if there is a casualty loss from a federally declared disaster, a taxpayer may deduct that loss on his return or amended return for the tax year immediately preceding the tax year of the disaster. If an individual makes this choice, treat the loss as having occurred in the preceding year. Claiming the loss on the previous year's return may result in a lower tax for that year, often producing or increasing a cash refund.

A taxpayer must use ***Form 4684*** to report each casualty or theft and complete the appropriate section(s) of the form.

- **Section A: Personal Use Property** – Report casualties and thefts of property not used in a trade or business or for income-producing purposes in Section A. If the result is a gain, the taxpayer may elect to account for it is as a capital gain on schedule D (Form 8949), or postpone reporting the gain (must acquire related replacement property within two tax years). A taxpayer can report a loss on Schedule A, subject to 2% of AGI limitation. There are two limits on the deductible amount for non-business casualty or theft loss on personal use property:

  1) For 2011, reduce each casualty or theft loss by $100 ($100 rule).

  2) The total of all casualty or theft losses is further reduced by 10% of AGI (10% rule).

- **Section B: Business and Income-Producing Property** – The $100 and 10% limitations do not apply to business and income-producing property. A taxpayer can use Form 4684 to account for multiple properties resulting from the same event; however, he must use a separate Form 4684 for each separate casualty or theft. The method for reporting gain or loss on business and income producing property depends on the holding period.

- **Held One Year or Less** – Generally, a taxpayer uses ***Form 4797*** to report these transactions as ordinary gain or loss. Depending on the circumstances, an individual taxpayer then reports the resulting gain (loss) on Form 1040 as other income (loss), or deducts the loss on Schedule A.

- **Held More Than One Year** – Business or income-producing property held more than one year (i.e., §1231 property) will receive special treatment. Net §1231 gains are ordinary gains up to the amount of non-recaptured §1231 losses from the five prior years; the rest is long-term capital gain. Losses from §1231 property are ordinary losses. If the damaged or stolen property was depreciable property, the taxpayer may have to treat all or part of the gain as ordinary income to the extent of depreciation allowed or allowable.

Tax Return Preparer Competency Exam – Chapter 9 Quiz

Circle the letter next to the best answer. Remember to read the question carefully.

1) Qualified farmers have the following choices to file their tax return without incurring any penalties:
   a. File and pay 100% of the tax due by March 1 each year
   b. File one estimated payment for two-thirds of the tax by January 15 and file and pay the balance by April 15
   c. File and pay the tax due by April 15 each year
   d. Both A and B

2) Which of the following taxpayers is not eligible to file a schedule C?
   a. Statutory employee
   b. Sole Proprietor
   c. Partnership
   d. Qualified Joint Venture

3) Of the following expenses, which should Acme Pillow not consider in the calculation for cost of goods sold?
   a. The cost of fabric used in the pillow making process
   b. The cost of freight to ship the feathers to their factory
   c. Salaries for factory employees
   d. Sales commissions paid to an internal sales team

4) Jane bought an old mountain cabin as a second home and began to remodel it. Immediately after she had removed the old appliances and cleaned the cabin, a fire destroyed it. The cost of the cabin was $100,000 (including $10,000 for the land). The fair market value (FMV) of the property before the fire was $120,000 ($105,000 for the building and $15,000 for the land). After the fire, the FMV was $15,000 (value of the land). Jane collected $85,000 from her insurance company. Her casualty loss (before applying the $100 and 10% limits) is:
   a. $0
   b. $20,000
   c. $5,000
   d. $15,000

5) In 2011, your construction company bought and placed in service a dump truck that cost $55,000 and a chain saw that cost $2,000. Section 179 expensing was elected and applied $2,000 to the chain saw and $17,000 to the dump truck for a total of $19,000. What is the depreciable basis in each item for 2011?

a. $2,000 Saw, $38,000 Truck

b. $2,000 Saw, $55,000 Truck

c. $ -0- Saw, $38,000 Truck

d. None of the above

6) In 2001, Sally sold a personal residence on the installment method. She needed cash in 2011, so she sold the note for $7,500 when the balance due to her was $9,000. Her gross profit percentage was 47.5%. How much profit must Sally report on the disposition of the obligation?

a. $2,775

b. $7,500

c. $0

d. $3,225

7) Which of the following statements with respect to the exchange of like-kind property is correct?

a. If there is an exchange of like-kind property in which you also received cash and the exchange results in a loss to you, you are allowed to deduct a loss to the extent of cash received

b. If there is an exchange of like-kind property in which you also give cash and the exchange results in a gain to you, you must report any gain to the extent of the cash given

c. If there is an exchange of like-kind property in which you also receive cash and the exchange results in a gain to you, you do NOT have to report the gain

d. If there is an exchange of like-kind property in which you also give cash and the exchange results in a loss to you, you CANNOT deduct a loss

8) Which of the following transactions is not a transaction that results in a gain or loss subject to Section 1231 treatment?

a. Sales or exchanges of leaseholds

b. Sales or exchanges of cattle and horses

c. The sale of a copyright, literary, musical, or artistic composition that you created

d. Sales or exchanges of unharvested crops sold together with land to the same buyer

For more practice questions, visit fastforwardacademy.com and access our FREE online question bank.

1) **d** A taxpayer with at least two-thirds of gross income from farming who pays the entire tax liability by March 1 following the tax year does not need to make estimated tax payments. Otherwise to avoid penalty, he must make one estimated tax payment by January 15 (following the tax year) equaling the lesser of 66 2/3% of the tax due, or 100% of the prior year tax liability.

2) **c** To file Schedule C the taxpayer must operate a trade or business as a statutory employee, sole proprietor, disregarded entity, or a qualified joint venture.

3) **d** Selling or administrative salaries and office supplies do not directly relate to the cost of the manufactured product and are not part of the cost of goods sold.

4) **d** Adjusted basis $100,000. FMV before fire $120,000 and FMV after fire $15,000. The decrease in FMV is $105,000. Her loss is the smaller of adjusted basis or decrease in FMV, or $100,000 LESS any insurance reimbursements. She was reimbursed $85,000 by her insurance, so her casualty loss before limitations is $15,000.

5) **c** To determine the basis for depreciation, depletion, or amortization, reduce each property by the Section 179 deduction taken.

6) **a** Of the $9,000 still owed to Sally, $4,275 is profit owed to her on the obligation, leaving $4,725 as her basis. She received $7,500 for the note, so she has a profit of $2,775.

7) **d** Taxpayers must recognize the gain up to the amount of money and unlike property received or the amount of realized gain, whichever is less. If the taxpayer realizes a loss on the exchange, no loss is recognized. A taxpayer may recognize a loss only on transfers of unlike property.

8) **c** The sale of a copyright, a literary, musical, or artistic composition, or similar property is not a Section 1231 transaction if your personal efforts (not investment) created the property, or if you acquired the property in a way that entitled you to the basis of the previous owner whose personal efforts created it (for example, if you receive the property as a gift). The sale of such property results in ordinary income and generally is reported in Part II of Form 4797.

10 Deductions

Business Expenses and Deductions · Employee Compensation
SEP IRA · SIMPLE IRA · Qualified Plans

This chapter summarizes IRS Publications 15-A, 15-B, 334, 535, 536, 463, 547, 560 and 571.

Business Expenses and Deductions

Business Start-up and Organizational Costs

Business start-up and organizational costs are generally capital expenditures. However, a taxpayer may elect (on the tax return) to deduct up to $5,000 of business start-up and $5,000 of organizational costs as an expense in the current year. For each category, reduce the deduction by the amount of costs that exceed $50,000. The taxpayer must amortize any remaining costs over a 180-month period, beginning with the initial month of operation.

The amount for start-up expenditures doubled for 2010, due to the *Small Business Jobs Act of 2010*; however, the increased limit of $10,000 for start-up costs was only allowed in 2010. A business using the cash method of accounting can deduct these costs only when paid by the end of the tax year. The business can deduct any cost it could have deducted in an earlier tax year in the year of payment. A business that amortizes these costs must file Form 4562 in the initial year of operation.

- ***Start-up costs*** include any amounts paid or incurred in connection with creating or investigating the creation or acquisition of an active trade or business. Start-up costs do not include deductible interest, taxes, or research and experimental costs. Start-up costs include the following:

  1) Analysis or survey of potential markets, products, labor supply, transportation facilities, etc.
  2) Advertisements for business opening
  3) Salaries and wages for employees who are being trained and their instructors
  4) Travel and necessary costs for securing prospective distributors, suppliers, or customers
  5) Salaries and fees for executives and consultants, or for similar professional services

- ***Organizational costs*** include the costs of creating a corporation or partnership. These costs include temporary directors, organizational meetings, state incorporation, and legal services.

  1) The following items are capital expenses that cannot be amortized:

     A) Costs for issuing and selling stock, securities, or partnership interests, such as commissions, professional fees, and printing costs

     B) Costs associated with the transfer of assets to the business

10.1 On Sept 1, 2011, Manny spent $8,600 in legal fees establishing his new restaurant and $5,000 in advertising for the grand opening. What is his maximum deduction for 2011?

Gifts

A deduction is not available for business gifts made in excess of $25 to a person during the tax year. If a taxpayer gives a gift to a member of a customer's family, the gift is generally considered an indirect gift to the customer. This rule does not apply if taxpayer has a bona fide, independent business connection with that family member and the gift is not intended for the customer's eventual use.

If the taxpayer and the taxpayer's spouse both give gifts, the IRS treats them as one taxpayer. It does not matter whether they have separate businesses, are separately employed, or whether they each have an independent connection with the recipient. If a partnership gives gifts, the IRS treats the partnership and the partners as one taxpayer.

Rental Expenses

Rent is any amount paid for the use of property not owned by the individual. In general, a taxpayer may deduct rent as an expense only if the rent is for the use of property in the taxpayer's business. If the taxpayer has or will receive equity in or title to the property, the rent is not deductible. The taxpayer may not take a rental deduction for unreasonable rent. Ordinarily, the issue of reasonableness arises only if taxpayer and the lessor are related. If an individual rents his home and uses part of it as a place of business, the individual may be able to deduct the rent paid for that part. The taxpayer must meet the requirements for business use of the home. Generally, rent paid because of one's business is deductible in the year paid or accrued. If the taxpayer makes a payment in advance, deduct only the amount that applies to use in the tax year. Deduct the remainder in the period to which it applies.

Expenses on Leased Property

The IRS treats lease payments, including taxes on leased property, as payments of rent. Amortize costs to acquire a lease over the remaining term of the lease. A taxpayer must depreciate permanent improvements to leased property, such as buildings, using the modified accelerated cost recovery system (MACRS) over an appropriate recovery period, not the remaining term of the lease.

Interest Expense

- **Deductible interest** – A taxpayer may generally deduct as a business expense all interest paid or accrued during the tax year on debts related to his business. Interest relates to business if the taxpayer uses the proceeds of the loan for a business expense. It does not matter what type of property secures the loan. A taxpayer may deduct interest on a debt only if all the following requirements are met:

    1) The taxpayer is legally liable for the debt. If liable for part of a business debt, the taxpayer may deduct his share of the total interest paid or accrued.

    2) Both the taxpayer and the lender intend that the taxpayer will repay the debt.

    3) The taxpayer and the lender have a true debtor-creditor relationship.

- **Capitalized interest** – Under the uniform capitalization rules, a taxpayer generally must capitalize interest on debt to produce (construct, build, demolish, install, manufacture, develop, improve, create, raise, or grow) real property or certain tangible personal property. Add the interest (and points) to the basis of the property. Designated property is any of the following:

1) Real property
2) Tangible personal property with a class life of 20 years or more
3) Tangible personal property with an estimated production period of more than two years
4) Tangible personal property with an estimated production period of more than one year if the estimated cost of production is more than $1 million

Insurance Premiums

A deduction may be available for certain premiums paid for insurance related to a business, which includes the following:

- Insurance that covers fire, storm, theft, accident, or similar losses.
- Credit insurance that covers losses from business bad debts.
- Group hospitalization and medical insurance for employees, including long-term care insurance:
  1) If a partnership pays accident and health insurance premiums for its partners, it generally may deduct them as guaranteed payments to partners.
  2) If an S corporation pays accident and health insurance premiums for its more-than-2% shareholder-employees, it generally may deduct them, but it must also include the amount in the shareholder's wages subject to federal income tax withholding.
- Liability insurance.
- Malpractice insurance that covers the taxpayer's personal liability for professional negligence resulting in injury or damage to patients or clients.
- Workers' compensation insurance set by state law that covers any claims for bodily injuries or job-related diseases suffered by employees in the taxpayer's business, regardless of fault:
  1) If a partnership pays workers' compensation premiums for its partners, it generally may deduct them as guaranteed payments to partners.
  2) Workers' compensation premiums paid by S corporation for its more-than-2% shareholder-employees, are generally deductible, but must be included in the shareholder's wages.
- Contributions to a state unemployment insurance fund are deductible as taxes if they are considered taxes under state law.
- Overhead insurance that pays for business overhead expenses incurred during long periods of disability caused by injury or sickness.
- Car and other vehicle insurance that covers vehicles used in business for liability, damages, and other losses. If taxpayer operates a vehicle partly for personal use, deduct only the part of the insurance premium applied to the business use of the vehicle. If using the standard mileage rate to figure car expenses, the taxpayer may <u>not</u> deduct any car insurance premiums.
- Life insurance covering officers and employees if the taxpayer is not a beneficiary under the contract.

- Business interruption insurance for lost profits if the business closes due to a fire or other cause.

A taxpayer may not deduct premiums on the following kinds of insurance:

- Self-insurance reserve funds.
- Premiums for a policy that pays for lost earnings due to sickness or disability.
- Certain life insurance and annuities.
- Insurance to secure a loan. If a taxpayer insures his life or the life of another person with a financial interest in the business to get or protect a business loan, the taxpayer may not deduct the premiums as a business expense. The taxpayer may not deduct the premiums as interest on business loans or as an expense of financing loans. In the event of death, the proceeds of the policy are generally not taxed as income even if the beneficiary uses them to liquidate the debt.

Self-employed Health Insurance Deduction

Premiums paid for medical and dental insurance and qualified long-term care insurance may be deductible provided they are for the taxpayer, his spouse, or his dependents, and the taxpayer is:

- A self-employed individual with a net profit reported on Schedule C Profit or Loss from Business, Schedule C-EZ Net Profit from Business, or Schedule F Profit or Loss from Farming, or
- A partner with net earnings from self-employment reported on Schedule K-1 (Form 1065), or
- A shareholder owning more than 2% of the outstanding stock of an S corporation with wages from the corporation reported on Form W-2, Wage and Tax Statement.

The taxpayer must establish the insurance plan under the taxpayer's business; however, the policy may be either in the name of the business or in the name of the individual.

- **A self-employed** individual filing a Schedule C, C-EZ, or F can have the policy in his name or under the business.
- **Partners** may pay the premiums themselves, or the partnership may pay the premiums and report the premium amounts on Schedule K-1 (Form 1065) as guaranteed payments to be included in the taxpayer's gross income. However, if the policy is in the taxpayer's name and the taxpayer pays the premiums, the partnership must reimburse the taxpayer and report the premium amounts on Schedule K-1 (Form 1065) as guaranteed payments to be included in gross income. Otherwise, the insurance plan is not considered established under the business.
- **More-than-2% shareholders** may pay their own premiums or the SCORP may pay them and report the premium amounts on Form W-2 as wages to be included in taxpayer's gross income. However, if the policy is in the taxpayer's name and he pays the premiums, the SCORP must reimburse the taxpayer and report the amount on Form W-2 as wages included in gross income. Otherwise, the insurance plan is not considered as established under the business.

TIP: Partners and more-than-2% shareholders may be able to amend prior year returns to take any self-employed health insurance deductions allowed under the rules explained above. Shareholders should write "Filed Pursuant to Notice 2008-1" at the top of any amended return.

10.2 Jamie is self-employed and files a Schedule C reporting a loss of $5,000 for the year. She pays health insurance premiums for a policy in her name covering her family. Where does she claim the deduction for her payments?

Travel

An individual is traveling away from home if duties require him to be away from the general area of his tax home for a period substantially longer than an ordinary day's work, and he needs to get sleep or rest to meet the demands of work while away. Generally, a tax home is the entire city or general area where main place of business or work is located, regardless of where the individual maintains a family home. For example, a person lives with family in Florida but works in Boston where he stays in a hotel and eats in restaurants. He returns to Florida every weekend. The taxpayer may not deduct any of the travel, meals, or lodging in Boston because it is his tax home. The travel to the family home in Florida is not for work, so these expenses are also not deductible. If a person regularly works in more than one place, the person's tax home is the general area where main place of business or work is located. Deductible travel expenses while away from home include the costs of the following:

- Travel by airplane, train, bus, or car between home and business destination
- Using personal car while at a business destination
- Fares for taxis or between the airport or train station and the hotel, the hotel and the work location, and from one customer to another, or from one place of business to another
- Meals and lodging
- Tips paid for services related to any of these expenses
- Dry cleaning and laundry
- Business calls while on a business trip. This includes business communications by fax machine or other communication devices.
- Other similar ordinary and necessary expenses related to business travel. These expenses might include transportation to and from a business meal, public stenographer's fees, computer rental fees, and operating and maintaining a house trailer.

In addition to the deductions described below, a taxpayer may deduct 50% of meals when traveling if he must stop for substantial sleep or rest to perform his duties properly while traveling away from home on business. The taxpayer may not deduct expenses for meals that are lavish or extravagant. An expense is not considered lavish or extravagant if it is reasonable based on the facts and circumstances.

- Travel in the United States
    1) Taxpayers may deduct all travel expenses if trip is entirely business related.
    2) If the trip is primarily for business and, while at the business destination, the taxpayer extends his stay for a vacation, makes a personal side trip, or has other personal activities, the taxpayer may deduct only business-related travel expenses.
    3) If the trip is primarily for personal reasons, such as a vacation, the entire cost of the trip is a nondeductible personal expense. However, a taxpayer may deduct any expenses he has while at a destination directly related to business.

- Travel outside the United States

 1) If a taxpayer travels outside the United States and spends the entire time on business activities, he may deduct all of the travel expenses:

 A) Even if he did not spend the entire time on business activities, the trip is considered entirely for business if the taxpayer meets any of the following exceptions:

 (a) Did not have substantial control over arranging the trip

 (b) The taxpayer is outside the United States for a week or less, combining business and non-business activities

 (c) The taxpayer spends less than 25% of the total time the taxpayer was outside the United States on non-business activities

 (d) The taxpayer can establish that a personal vacation is not a major consideration, even if the taxpayer has substantial control over arranging the trip

 2) If the trip is primarily for business but the taxpayer spends time on other activities, he generally may not deduct all of the travel expenses. Only the business portion of the cost of getting to and from the destination is deductible. Individuals must allocate costs between business and other activities to determine the deductible amount.

 3) If the trip is primarily for vacation or for investment purposes, the entire cost of the trip is a non-deductible personal expense. If a taxpayer spends time attending brief professional seminars or a continuing education program, the taxpayer may deduct registration fees and other expenses directly related to business.

Meals and Entertainment

A taxpayer may deduct business-related meals and entertainment expenses incurred for entertaining a client, customer, or employee. To deduct an entertainment-related meal, the taxpayer or the taxpayer's employees must be present when the food or beverages are provided. The deduction for entertainment expenses may be limited. Generally, a taxpayer may deduct 50% of unreimbursed entertainment expenses. Entertainment expenses are deductible only if they are both ordinary and necessary and meet one of the following tests:

- **Directly-related test** – The taxpayer must show all of the following:

 1) The main purpose of the combined business and entertainment is the active conduct of business. Business is generally not considered the main purpose when on hunting or fishing trips, or on yachts or other pleasure boats.

 2) The taxpayer did engage in business with the person during the entertainment period.

 3) There is more than a general expectation of getting income or some other specific business benefit at some future time.

- **Associated test** – Even if the taxpayer's expenses do not meet the directly-related test, they may meet the associated test. The taxpayer must show that the entertainment is as follows:

 1) Associated with the active conduct of the business, and

 2) Directly before or after a substantial business discussion

A taxpayer may <u>not</u> deduct the following expenses:

- **Lavish or extravagant entertainment** – Expenses that are reasonable considering the facts and circumstances will not be disallowed just because they are more than a fixed dollar amount or take place at deluxe restaurants, hotels, nightclubs, or resorts.
- **If a taxpayer rents a private luxury box** for <u>more</u> than one event at the same sports arena, the taxpayer generally may not deduct more than the price of a non-luxury box seat ticket.
- **Membership dues** (including initiation fees) for any club organized for business, pleasure, recreation, or other social purpose.
- **Cost for the use of an entertainment facility** or any property he owns, rents, or uses for entertainment. Examples include a yacht, hunting lodge, fishing camp, swimming pool, tennis court, bowling alley, car, airplane, apartment, hotel suite, or home in a vacation resort.

10.3 Nick is a self-employed mortgage broker. He takes a realtor to an Orlando Magic game. The visit to the show occurred directly after a substantial business discussion. Nick pays a ticket broker $500 for two tickets to game. The face value of each ticket was $200 ($400 total). What is his total deductible expense for both tickets?

Casualty and Theft

If a taxpayer has business or income-producing property, such as rental property, and it is stolen or completely destroyed, the decrease in FMV is <u>not</u> considered. The loss is the taxpayer's adjusted basis in the property minus the salvage value, insurance, and other re-imbursements. There are two methods to deduct a casualty or theft loss of inventory, including items held for sale to customers:

- Deduct the loss through the increase in the cost of goods sold by properly reporting opening and closing inventories. Taxpayers must not claim this loss again as a casualty or theft loss. If a taxpayer takes the loss through the increase in the cost of goods sold, the taxpayer should include any insurance or reimbursement in gross income.
- Deduct the loss separately. If deducted separately, a taxpayer must eliminate the affected inventory items from the cost of goods sold by making a downward adjustment to opening inventory or purchases. The taxpayer must reduce the loss by the reimbursement received and must not include the reimbursement in gross income. If the taxpayer does not receive reimbursement by the end of the year, the taxpayer may not claim a loss to the extent the taxpayer has a reasonable prospect of recovery.

TIP Losses on business property (other than employee property) and income-producing property are <u>not</u> subject to the 2% Misc Itemized Deduction and 10% of AGI limits like personal-use property. Taxpayers generally must deduct a casualty loss in the year it occurs. However, if there is a casualty loss from a federally declared disaster, a taxpayer may choose to deduct that loss on his return or amended return for the tax year immediately <u>preceding</u> the tax year of the disaster. If an individual makes this choice, treat the loss as having occurred in the preceding year. Claiming the loss on the previous year's return may result in a lower tax for that year, often producing or increasing a cash refund.

Bad Debts

If an individual owes a taxpayer money that the taxpayer is unable to collect, then the taxpayer has a bad debt. The taxpayer does not have to wait until a debt is due to determine whether it is worthless. A debt becomes worthless when there is no longer any chance the debtor will pay the amount owed. Generally, a ***business bad debt*** is one that comes from operating a business. A taxpayer may claim a bad debt deduction only if the amount owed to the taxpayer was previously included in gross income. This applies to amounts owed to the taxpayer from all sources of taxable income, including sales, services, rents, and interest. Business bad debts are mainly the result of ***credit sales*** to customers. In the books, record goods that have been sold, but not paid for, and services that have been performed, but not paid for, as either accounts receivable or notes receivable. After a reasonable period, if a taxpayer has tried to collect the amount due but is unable to do so, the uncollectible part becomes a business bad debt.

- A taxpayer who uses the accrual method of accounting should claim a bad debt deduction only if he previously included the entire uncollectible amount in income.
- If a taxpayer uses the cash method of accounting, the taxpayer may not claim a bad debt deduction for amounts owed to him because the amounts were never included in income.
- Taxpayers who claim a deduction for a bad debt and later recover (collect) all or part of it may have to include the recovery in gross income. The amount to include is limited to the amount actually deducted. However, taxpayers can exclude the amount deducted that did not reduce their tax. Report the recovery as "Other income" on the appropriate business form or schedule.

Taxes

The following taxes are deductible:

- **Employment taxes** – A deduction is allowed for FICA and FUTA taxes paid out of company funds as an employer. Deductible taxes also include payments made to a state unemployment compensation fund or to a state disability benefit fund.
- **Self-employment tax** – A self-employed taxpayer can deduct one-half of self-employment tax paid on his personal return.
- **Personal property tax** – Tax imposed by a state or local government on personal property used in a business. Registration fees for the right to use property within a state or local area are deductible.
- **Real estate taxes** – A deduction is allowed for real estate taxes paid on business property. Deductible real estate taxes are any state, local, or foreign taxes on real estate levied for the general public welfare. The taxing authority must base the taxes on the assessed value of the real estate and charge them uniformly against all property under its jurisdiction. Add property assessments for improvements that increase the value of the property assessed to basis. Do not deduct these as taxes. Examples of assessments include roads, sidewalks, water connections, and extending utility service lines to the property.
- **Sales tax** – Sales tax paid on a service or on the purchase or use of property as part of the cost of the service or property. If the service or the cost or use of the property is a deductible business expense, the business can deduct the tax as part of that service or cost. If the property is merchandise bought for resale, the sales tax is part of the cost of the merchandise. If the property is depreciable, add the sales tax to the basis for depreciation.
- **Excise taxes** – A deduction is allowed for excise taxes that are ordinary and necessary expenses of carrying on a business. Taxpayers who owe excise taxes are required to file a quarterly Form 720

Federal Excise Tax Return. The person who receives payment for these items is responsible for collection and payment of the tax. Items subject to excise taxes include:

1) Fuel taxes
2) Environmental taxes
3) Communications and air transportation taxes
4) Manufacturers taxes
5) Retail tax on heavy trucks, trailers, and tractors
6) Ship passenger taxes
7) Foreign insurance taxes
8) Obligations not in registered form

- **Heavy highway use vehicle tax** – The tax applies to highway motor vehicles with a taxable gross weight of 55,000 pounds or more. Vans, pickup trucks, panel trucks, and similar trucks generally are not subject to this tax. The taxpayer who acquires the vehicle for use must report and pay the tax monthly on **Form 2290,** separate from the other excise taxes. A taxpayer may receive a credit or request the suspension of this tax if the vehicle is driven less than 5,000 miles (7,500 if agricultural vehicle) during a one-month tax period.

Miscellaneous Expenses

Business taxpayers may deduct certain expenses that relate directly to the conduct of business as Miscellaneous Expenses. These expenses include the following:

- Advertising
- Expenses for operation of vehicles used in business
- Credit card fees
- Franchise fees
- Internet-related expenses
- Legal and professional fees
- Tax preparation fees
- License and regulatory fees
- Costs of moving machinery
- Penalties paid for late performance or nonperformance of a contract
- Repairs
- Supplies and materials
- Utilities
- Telephone

Nondeductible Business Expenses

Not all business expenses are deductible. The following are examples of nondeductible expenses:

- Anticipated liabilities
- Bribes and kickbacks
- Charitable contributions (except for C corporation, all others claim on personal return)
- Lobbying expenses
- Political contributions
- Penalties or fines for violation of the law
- Demolition expenses
- Club dues and membership fees incurred for any club organized for business, pleasure, recreation, or any other social purpose. Certain exceptions are made for chambers of commerce, boards of trade, business leagues, professional associations, and trade associations.

Employee Compensation

Test for Deducting Pay

The employer may deduct employee pay that is an ordinary and necessary expense, provided it is both reasonable and for services performed. Wages subject to federal employment taxes generally include all pay to an employee for services performed. Payment may be in cash or in other forms. Wages include salaries, vacation pay, bonuses, commissions, and fringe benefits.

Employee Business Expense Reimbursements

A reimbursement or allowance arrangement is a system by which an employer pays the advances, reimbursements, and charges for employees' business expenses. How the employer reports a payment depends on whether the employer has an ***accountable*** or a ***non-accountable plan***. If a single payment includes both wages and an expense reimbursement, the employer must specify the amount of the reimbursement. These rules apply to all ordinary and necessary employee business expenses that would otherwise qualify for a deduction by the employee.

- **Accountable plan** – Amounts paid under an *accountable plan* are not wages and are not subject to the withholding and payment of FICA, FUTA, and income taxes. An *accountable plan* reimbursement or allowance arrangement must require employees to meet all three of the following rules:
    1) They must have paid or incurred deductible expenses while performing services as employees. The reimbursement or advance must be paid for the expense and must not be an amount that would have otherwise been paid by the employee.
    2) They must substantiate these expenses to employer within a reasonable period.
    3) They must return any unsubstantiated expenses within a reasonable period.
- **Non-accountable plan** – Payments to employees for travel and other necessary expenses of the business under a non-accountable plan are wages and are treated as supplemental wages and

subject to the withholding and payment of FICA, FUTA, and income taxes. The payments are treated as paid under a non-accountable plan if:

1) The employee is not required to or does not substantiate expenses to employer with receipts or other documentation,
2) The employer advances an amount to the employee for business expenses, and employee is not required to or does not return in a timely manner any amount not used for business expenses,
3) The employer advances or pays an amount to the employee regardless of whether the employer reasonably expects the employee to incur business expenses related to the business, or
4) The employer pays a reimbursement that he would have otherwise paid as wages.

- **Per diem or other fixed allowance.** An employer may reimburse employees by travel days, miles, or other fixed allowance. In these cases, the employee is considered to have accounted to the employer if the reimbursement does not exceed rates established by the federal government. The standard mileage rate for 2011 is 51 cents per mile (55 1/2 cents after June 30, 2011).

10.4 Kenneth's employer gives him $500 a month ($6,000 for the year) for his business expenses. Kenneth does not have to provide any proof of his expenses to his employer and he can keep any funds that he does not spend. His actual expenses for the year were $1,000 for lodging, $600 for meals while away from home, and $2,000 for entertainment. What reporting is required of Kenneth's employer and what reporting is required of Kenneth?

Wages Not Paid in Money

If in the course of business, an employer pays employees in a medium that is neither cash nor a readily negotiable instrument, such as a check, the employer has paid them "in kind." Payments in kind may be in the form of goods, lodging, food, clothing, or services. Generally, the FMV of such payments at the time that the employer provides them is subject to employment taxes and withholding. If the property is a capital asset, the difference between the FMV and the adjusted basis of the property is taxable income (capital gain) to the business.

Moving Expenses

Reimbursed and employer-paid qualified moving expenses (those that would otherwise be deductible by the employee) paid under an accountable plan are not includible in an employee's income unless the employer has knowledge that the employee deducted the expenses in a prior year. Reimbursed nonqualified moving expenses are includible in income and are subject to employment taxes and withholding. Deductible moving expenses include only the reasonable expenses of the following:

- Moving household goods and personal effects from the former home to the new home
- Traveling (including lodging) from the former home to the new home

Deductible moving expenses do not include any expenses for meals and must meet both the distance test and the time test. To meet the distance test, the new job location must be at least 50 miles farther from the employee's old home than the old job location was. To meet the time test, the employee must work at least 39 weeks during the first 12 months after arriving in the general area of the new job location.

De Minimis Meals

The employer may exclude from wages any meal or meal money provided to an employee if it has so little value (taking into account how frequently the employer provides meals to employees) that accounting for it would be unreasonable or administratively impracticable. The exclusion applies, for example, to the following items:

- Coffee, doughnuts, or soft drinks
- Occasional meals or meal money provided to enable an employee to work overtime (does not apply to meal money figured on the basis of hours worked)
- Occasional parties or picnics for employees and their guests

This exclusion also applies to meals provided at an employer-operated eating facility for employees if the annual revenue from the facility equals or exceeds the direct costs of the facility. If food or beverages furnished to employees qualify as a de minimis benefit, employers may deduct their full cost. The 50% limit on deductions does not apply to de minimis meals.

Meals on Business Premises

The value of meals provided by the employer, furnished on the business premises, for the employer's convenience are not taxable income and are not subject to income tax withholding, FICA, or FUTA taxes. This exclusion does not apply if employees may choose additional pay instead of meals.

- **Food service employees** – Meals furnished to a restaurant or other food service employee during, or immediately before or after, his shift are furnished for employer's convenience.
- **Employees available for emergency calls** – Meals furnished during working hours so an employee will be available for emergency calls during the meal period are furnished for employer's convenience. Employers must have a reasonable expectation for calls to occur.

Lodging on Business Premises

Employers may exclude the value of lodging from wages if it meets the following tests:

- It is furnished on employer's business premises
- It is furnished for employer's convenience
- The employee must accept it as a condition of employment

Different tests may apply to lodging furnished by educational institutions. The exclusion does not apply if employer allows the employee to choose to receive additional pay instead of lodging.

Health Insurance Plans

If the employer pays the cost of an accident or health insurance plan for company employees, including an employee's spouse and dependents, the payments are not wages and are not subject to FICA and FUTA taxes, or federal income tax withholding. Under the recently enacted *Affordable Care Act*, health coverage provided for an employee's children under 27 years of age is now generally tax-free to the employee. Generally, this exclusion also applies to qualified long-term care insurance contracts. However, for income tax withholding, the value of health insurance benefits must be included in the wages of S corporation employees who own more than 2% of the S corporation (2% shareholders). For

FICA and FUTA tax purposes, exclude the health insurance benefits from the wages only for employees and their dependents or for a class or classes of employees and their dependents.

Employer Retirement Plan Contributions

Eligible employer contributions to retirement plans are deductible by the employer and are not gross income for the employee.

Health Savings Accounts and Medical Savings Accounts

Employer contributions to an employee's Health Savings Account (HSA) or Archer medical savings account (MSA) are not subject to FICA or FUTA taxes, or federal income tax withholding if it is reasonable to believe at the time of the contributions that they will be excludable from the income of the employee. To the extent that it is not reasonable to believe that they will be excludable, the contributions are subject to these taxes. Employee contributions to HSAs or MSAs through a payroll deduction plan must be included in wages and are subject to FICA, FUTA, and income tax withholding. However, HSA contributions made under a salary reduction arrangement in a ***Section 125-cafeteria plan*** are not wages and are not subject to employment taxes or withholding.

Medical Care Reimbursements

Generally, medical care reimbursements paid for employees under an employer's self-insured reimbursement plan are not wages and are not subject to employment taxes or withholding.

Fringe Benefits

Employers generally must include fringe benefits in an employee's gross income. The benefits are subject to income tax withholding and employment taxes. Fringe benefits include employer-provided cars or aircraft flights, free or discounted commercial flights, vacations, discounts on property or services, memberships in country clubs or other social clubs, and tickets to entertainment or sporting events. In general, the amount that the employer must include is the amount by which the fair market value of the benefits is more than the sum of what the employee paid for it plus any amount that the law excludes.

Non-taxable Fringe Benefits

The following fringe benefits are not taxable (or are minimally taxable, as noted below):

- Services provided to employees at no additional cost to the employer
- Qualified employee discounts
- Working condition fringes of property or services that the employee could deduct as a business expense if the employee had paid for it. Examples include a company car for business use and subscriptions to business magazines.
- Certain minimal value fringes (including an occasional cab ride when an employee must work overtime, local transportation benefits provided because of unsafe conditions and unusual circumstances, and meals that the employer provides at eating places that the employer runs for the employees if the meals are not furnished at below cost)
- Qualified transportation fringes subject to specified conditions and dollar limitations (including transportation in a commuter highway vehicle, any transit pass, qualified parking, and qualified bicycle commuting reimbursement)

- Qualified moving expense reimbursement
- The use of on-premises athletic facilities, if substantially all of the use is by employees, their spouses, and their dependent children
- A qualified tuition reduction an educational organization provides to employees for education

Awards

An employer may generally deduct amounts paid as awards, whether in cash or property.

- **Achievement awards** – Tangible personal property that meets all the following requirements:
  1) The employer gives the award to an employee for length of service or safety achievement.
  2) The employer gives the award as part of a meaningful presentation.
  3) The employer gives the award under conditions that do not create a significant likelihood of disguised pay.
- **Length-of-service award** – An award where either of the following applies:
  1) The employee receives the award after five years of employment.
  2) The employee did not receive another length-of-service award (other than one of very small value) during the same year or in any of the prior four years.
- **Safety achievement award** – An award for safety achievement will qualify unless:
  1) Given to a manager, administrator, clerical employee, or other professional employee
  2) During the tax year, more than 10% of employees, excluding those listed in (1), have already received a safety achievement award (other than one of very small value)
- The deduction for awards given to any one employee during the tax year is limited to:
  1) $400 for awards that are not qualified plan awards, or
  2) $1,600 for all awards, whether or not qualified plan awards

A qualified plan award is an achievement award given as part of an established written plan or program that does not favor highly compensated employees as to eligibility or benefits. A highly compensated employee for 2011 is an employee who meets either of the following tests:

- The employee was a 5% owner at any time during the year or the preceding year.
- The employee received more than $110,000 in pay for the preceding year.

Domestic Production Activities

Domestic production activities deduction (DPAD) is a deduction under Section 199 directly from income. For 2011, the deduction is equal to **9%** of the lesser of ***qualified production activities income (QPAI)*** or taxable income (AGI for individual taxpayers and shareholders of pass through entities) determined without regard to the deduction. If a taxpayer builds, manufactures, or produces goods in the United States, he may be engaged in domestic production activities Qualified production activities include the following:

- Construction of real property performed in the United States (US)
- Engineering or architectural services performed in the US for construction of real property in the US.
- Any lease, rental, license, sale, exchange, or other disposition of the following:
    1) Tangible personal property, computer software, and sound recordings the taxpayer manufactured, produced, grew, or extracted in whole or in significant part within the US.
    2) Any qualified film the taxpayer produced
    3) Electricity, natural gas, or potable water produced in the United States
- The deduction does not apply to income derived from:
    1) The sale of food and beverages prepared at a retail establishment
    2) Property leased, licensed, or rented for use by any related person
    3) The transmission or distribution of electricity, natural gas, or potable water
    4) The lease, rental, license, sale, exchange, or other disposition of land

What Is QPAI?

Section 199(c)(1) defines QPAI for any taxable year as an amount equal to the excess of domestic production gross receipts over the sum of: (a) the cost of goods sold (CGS) allocable to such receipts; (b) other deductions, expenses, or losses directly allocable to such receipts; and (c) a ratable portion of deductions, expenses, and losses not directly allocable to such receipts or another class of income.

What Are the Limits?

The deduction is limited to 50% of the W-2 wages paid by the employer during the year. This is in addition to the QPAI and net income (or AGI) limitations.

How to Claim the Deduction

Use form 8903 to claim the deduction. A corporation claims the deduction at the entity level. The deduction for the qualified production activities of a partnership or S corporation is taken at the partner or shareholder level. For simplification purposes, the partnership or S corporation can calculate the QPAI at the entity level and report pertinent information to the shareholder on Schedule K-1. Each partner or shareholder must compute its deduction separately using form 8903.

SEP IRA

Simplified Employee Pensions (SEP) provide a simplified method for employers to contribute to a retirement plan for themselves and employees. Under a SEP, the employer can contribute to a traditional individual retirement arrangement (called a SEP-IRA) set up by or for each eligible employee. A SEP cannot be a Roth IRA. A SEP-IRA is one that the employee owns and controls; the employer contributes to the financial institution that maintains the SEP-IRA.

Establishing a SEP Plan

Employers can establish a SEP for any year as late as the due date (including extensions) of the income tax return for that year.

How Contributions Are Made

Employees cannot contribute to a SEP IRA (other than SAR SEP, which was discontinued in 1997). Annual employer contributions are not mandatory. If contributing, the employer must base all contributions on a written allocation formula and must not discriminate in favor of highly compensated employees. When the employer contributes, the employer must contribute to the SEP-IRAs of all participants who actually performed personal services during the year for which the contributions are made, including employees who die or terminate employment before contributions are made. Contributions are made as a percentage of each employee's compensation. The percentage must be the same for all employees.

Annual Contribution Limit

The SEP rules permit employers to contribute a limited amount of money each year to each employee's SEP-IRA. The self-employed taxpayer can contribute to a SEP-IRA established on his behalf. Contributions must be in the form of money (cash, check, or money order), not property.

Contributions made by employer for 2011 to a common-law employee's SEP-IRA cannot exceed the lower of 25% of the employee's compensation or $49,000. Compensation generally does not include the employer's contributions to the SEP.

- **Compensation** – Compensation for plan allocations is the pay a participant received from the employer for personal services for a year. Compensation includes all of the following payments:
  1) Wages and salaries
  2) Fees for professional services
  3) Other amounts received (cash or noncash) for personal services actually rendered by an employee, including, but not limited to commissions, tips, fringe benefits, and bonuses
- **Compensation for the self-employed** – A self-employed taxpayer must make a special computation to determine compensation for purposes of retirement plan contributions and deductions for his own account. Compensation is net earnings from self-employment, plus the following:
  1) The deduction for self-employment tax
  2) The deduction for contributions on own behalf to the plan

Deduction Limits

The amount employers can deduct for contributions to a SEP-IRA is limited to the annual contribution limit, per participant. Those who are self-employed must make a special computation to determine contributions for their own accounts. When figuring the deduction made to one's own SEP-IRA, compensation is net earnings from self-employment, which takes into account:

- The deduction for self-employment tax, and
- The deduction for contributions to one's own SEP-IRA

The deduction for contributions to the SEP-IRA and net earnings depend on each other. For this reason, a self-employed individual determines the deduction for contributions to his SEP-IRA indirectly by reducing the contribution rate called for in the plan.

Peter is a sole proprietor with $100,000 net income on his Schedule C. He took a deduction for self-employment tax on Form 1040 of $7,650. Net earnings from self-employment equal $92,350. The contribution rate for his SEP plan for employees is 25%. The formula to determine his contribution percentage is *rate*/(1+*rate*) or .25/1.25 =.20. His SEP contribution is $18,470 ($92,350 x 20%).

Employer/Employee Contribution Limits

An employer cannot consider the part of an employee's compensation above the *annual compensation limit* ($245,000) when figuring the contribution limit for an employee. However, $49,000 is the maximum contribution for an eligible employee. Excess contributions are included in the employee's income for the year and are treated as contributions by the employee to his SEP-IRA. SEP contributions are not included on an employee's Form W-2 unless contributions were made under a salary reduction arrangement. Additionally, if the employer maintains another ***defined contribution*** plan for employees, the ***annual additions*** to an account are limited to the lesser of $49,000 or 100% of the participant's compensation. When figuring this limit, the employer must combine contributions to <u>all</u> defined contribution plans. Because a SEP is considered a defined contribution plan for this limit, employer contributions to a SEP must be added to employer contributions to other defined contribution plans. Contributions are 100% immediately vested to the employee.

SIMPLE IRA

Generally, an employer with <u>100 or fewer</u> employees making at least $5,000 in compensation last year can set up a ***Savings Incentive Match Plan for Employees (SIMPLE)***. The employer <u>cannot</u> maintain another qualified plan unless the other plan is for collective bargaining (union) employees. Under a SIMPLE plan, <u>employees</u> can choose to make <u>salary reduction</u> contributions rather than receiving these amounts as part of their regular pay. In addition, the <u>employer</u> will contribute either matching <u>or</u> non-elective contributions.

In order to avoid additional tax, the participant must maintain a SIMPLE IRA for at least two years from the date of initial contribution. If a withdrawal, rollover distribution, or transfer from a SIMPLE IRA does not satisfy the 2-year rule, and is otherwise an early distribution, the additional tax imposed because of the early distribution increases from 10% to 25% of the amount distributed.

The two types of SIMPLE plans are the SIMPLE IRA plan and the SIMPLE 401(k) plan. A SIMPLE plan cannot be a Roth IRA. Contribution methods and limits of a SIMPLE IRA and SIMPLE 401(k) are the same. Unlike the IRA version, the SIMPLE 401(k) is a ***qualified plan*** and is subject to those rules (under certain conditions, a SIMPLE 401(k) plan is not subject to the nondiscrimination and top-heavy rules).

Establishing a SIMPLE Plan

An employer can set up a SIMPLE IRA plan effective on any date from January 1 through October 1 of a year, provided the employer did not previously maintain a SIMPLE IRA plan. A new employer that comes into existence after October 1 may set up a SIMPLE IRA plan as soon as administratively feasible after the business comes into existence. If the employer previously maintained a SIMPLE IRA plan, he can establish a SIMPLE IRA plan effective only on January 1 of a year.

Contribution Deadline

The employer must make the salary reduction contributions to the SIMPLE IRA within 30 days after the end of the month in which the amounts would otherwise have been payable to the employee in cash. Matching contributions or non-elective contributions are due by the due date (including extensions) for filing the employer's federal income tax return for the year. Certain plans subject to Department of Labor rules may have an earlier due date for salary reduction contributions.

Employer/Employee Contribution Limits

- **Salary reduction contributions** – Employees may contribute to the SIMPLE IRA through salary reductions up to $11,500 for 2011. These contributions must be expressed as a percentage of the employee's compensation unless the employer permits the employee to express them as a specific dollar amount. Employers cannot place restrictions on the contribution amount (such as limiting the contribution percentage), except to comply with the $11,500 limit. The maximum percentage an employee may contribute is 100% of his compensation up to the dollar limit.

- **Catch-up contribution** – A plan can permit participants who are age 50 or older at the end of the calendar year to make catch-up contributions in addition to elective deferrals and SIMPLE plan salary reduction contributions.

    1) The catch-up contribution limitation for SIMPLE plans remains $2,500 for 2011.

    2) The catch-up contribution limitation for defined contribution plans other than SIMPLE plans is $5,500 in 2011.

- The employer must also contribute, using one of two methods:

    1) **Elective contributions** – The employer must match employee contributions, dollar for dollar, up to a maximum of 3% of compensation. If the matching contribution is less than 3%, the percentage must be at least 1%. The employer must notify the employees of the lower match within a reasonable period before the 60-day election period for the calendar year. Employers cannot choose a percentage less than 3% for more than two years during the five-year period that ends with (and includes) the year for which the choice is effective, or

    2) **Non-elective contributions** – The employer must make mandatory 2% contributions based on compensation for all eligible employees, regardless of whether or not the employee chooses to make salary reduction contributions.

An employer deducts contributions for employees its tax return, and employees can exclude these contributions from their gross income. However, salary reduction contributions are subject to FICA and federal unemployment (FUTA) taxes. Matching and non-elective contributions are not subject to these taxes. Contributions are not subject to federal income tax withholding.

TIP Sole proprietors and partners cannot deduct contributions made to a retirement plan for themselves as a business expense, only those made for their common-law employees. Sole proprietors and partners deduct contributions for themselves on Form 1040.

Qualified Plans

A ***qualified plan*** is a retirement plan that offers a tax-favored way to save for retirement. Employers may deduct contributions made to the plan for employees. Earnings on these contributions are generally tax free until distributed at retirement. Profit sharing, money purchase, and defined benefit plans are qualified plans. A 401(k) plan is also a qualified plan. The qualified plan rules are more complex than the SEP plan and SIMPLE plan rules. However, there are advantages to qualified plans, such as increased flexibility in designing plans and increased contribution and deduction limits in some cases. There are two basic kinds of qualified plans, ***defined contribution*** plans and ***defined benefit*** plans, and different rules apply to each. An employer can have more than one qualified plan, but contributions to all plans must not total more than the overall limits.

Defined Contribution Plan

A defined contribution plan has an individual account for each participant in the plan. It provides benefits largely based on the amount contributed to that participant's account. Any income, expense, gain, loss, and forfeiture of other accounts that may be allocated to an account also affect benefits. A defined contribution plan can be either ***a profit-sharing plan*** or a ***money purchase pension plan***.

Defined Benefit Plan

A defined benefit plan is any plan that is not a defined contribution plan. Contributions to a defined benefit plan are based on what is needed to provide definitely determinable benefits to plan participants. Actuarial assumptions and computations are required to figure these contributions. Generally, continuing professional help is necessary to have a defined benefit plan.

Establishing a Plan

To take a deduction for contributions for a tax year, the plan must be set up (adopted) by the last day of that year (December 31 for calendar year employers).

Contributions

Employer contributions generally fund a qualified plan. However, employees participating in the plan may be permitted to contribute, and the employer may be permitted to contribute on its own behalf. The employer may make deductible contributions for a tax year up to the due date of its tax return (plus extensions) for that year.

Limits on Contributions and Benefits

The plan must provide that contributions or benefits cannot exceed certain limits. The limits differ depending on whether a plan is a defined contribution plan or a defined benefit plan.

- **Defined benefit plan** – For 2011, the annual benefit for a participant under a defined benefit plan cannot exceed the lesser of the following amounts:

    1) 100% of the participant's average compensation for his highest three consecutive calendar years

    2) $195,000

- **Defined contribution plan** – For 2011, a defined contribution plan's annual contributions and other additions (excluding earnings) to the account of a participant cannot exceed the lesser of the following amounts:

    1) 100% of the participant's compensation

    2) $49,000

Employer Deduction Limits

Employers can usually deduct, subject to limits, contributions made to a qualified plan, including those made for their own retirements. The contributions (and earnings and gains on them) are generally tax free until distributed by the plan. The deduction limit for employer contributions to a qualified plan depends on the kind of plan the employer has.

- **Defined contribution plans** – The deduction for contributions to a defined contribution plan cannot be more than 25% of the compensation paid (or accrued) during the year to eligible employees participating in the plan. The following rules apply:

  1) Elective deferrals (discussed later) are not subject to the limit.

  2) Compensation includes elective deferrals.

  3) The maximum compensation taken into account for each employee in 2011 is $245,000.

- **Defined benefit plans** – The deduction for contributions to a defined benefit plan is based on actuarial assumptions and computations. An actuary must figure the deduction limit.

401(k) Plan Elective Deferrals

A qualified plan can include a cash or deferred arrangement under which a participant can choose to have the employer contribute part of his before-tax compensation to the plan rather than receive the compensation in cash. A plan with this type of arrangement is a ***401(k) plan***. This contribution is an ***elective deferral*** because participants choose (elect) to defer receipt of the money.

The plan <u>cannot</u> require, as a condition of participation, that an employee complete <u>more than one</u> year of service. There is a limit on the amount an employee can defer each year under these plans. The plan must provide that employees cannot defer more than the limit that applies for a particular year. For 2011, the basic limit on elective deferrals is **$16,500**, plus the catch-up contribution amount if the employee is old than age 50. This limit applies to all salary reduction contributions and elective deferrals. If, considering the plan in conjunction with other plans, the employee has exceeded the deferral limit, include the difference in gross income.

Employer contributions to a 401(k) plan are generally deductible by the employer for the year the employer contributes to the plan. Matching or non-elective contributions made to the plan are also deductible by the employer in the year of contribution. The employees' elective deferrals other than designated Roth contributions are not taxed until distributed from the plan. Elective deferrals are included in wages for FICA and federal unemployment (FUTA) tax. Employers report the total amount of elective deferrals to employees on Form W-2.

Distributions

Generally, an employer cannot make distributions until one of the following occurs:

- The employee retires, dies, becomes disabled, or otherwise severs employment.
- The plan ends, and the employer does not establish or continue another defined contribution plan.
- In the case of a 401(k) plan that is part of a profit-sharing plan, the employee reaches age 59.5 or suffers financial hardship.
- The employee becomes eligible for a qualified reservist distribution.

Rollovers

Distributions from a qualified plan minus a prorated part of any cost basis are subject to income tax in the year they are distributed. Since most recipients have no cost basis, a distribution is taxable. An exception is a distribution that is properly rolled over. If, during a year, a qualified plan pays to a participant one or more eligible rollover distributions that are reasonably expected to total $200 or more, the payor must withhold 20% of each distribution for federal income tax. If the participant chooses to have the plan pay it directly to an IRA or another eligible retirement plan (a direct rollover), no withholding is required.

Tax on Early Distributions

If a distribution is made to an employee under the plan before he reaches age 59.5, the employee may have to pay a 10% additional tax on the distribution. This tax applies to the amount received that the employee must include in income. The 10% tax will not apply if distributions before age 59.5 are made in any of the following circumstances:

- Made to a beneficiary (or to the estate of the employee) on or after the death of the employee
- Made due to the employee having a qualifying disability
- Made as part of a ***series of substantially equal periodic payments*** **(SOSEPP under IRS Rule 72t)** beginning after separation from service and made at least annually for the life or life expectancy of the employee or the joint lives or life expectancies of the employee and his designated beneficiary. (Payments, except in the case of death or disability, must continue for at least five years or until the employee reaches age 59.5, whichever is longer.)
- Made to an employee after separation from service if the separation occurred during or after the calendar year in which the employee reached age 55
- Made to an alternate payee under a QDRO
- Made to an employee for medical care up to the amount allowable as a medical expense deduction (determined without regard to whether the employee itemizes deductions)
- Timely made to reduce excess contributions under a 401(k) plan
- Timely made to reduce excess employee or matching employer contributions
- Timely made to reduce excess elective deferrals
- Made because of an IRS levy on the plan
- Made as a qualified reservist distribution

Tax on Prohibited Transaction

The initial tax on a prohibited transaction is 15% of the amount involved for each year (or part of a year) in the taxable period. If the person does not correct the transaction within the taxable period, the IRS will impose an additional tax of 100% of the amount involved.

10.5 Peter is deciding between a SIMPLE IRA and a SEP IRA for his business. He is 30 years old and expects his Schedule C to reflect $30,000 in net income for 2011. Of the two plans, which would provide him with the largest maximum deduction in 2011?

Table 10-1. Key Retirement Plan Rules for 2011

Type of Plan	Last Date for Contribution	Maximum Contribution	Maximum Deduction	When to Set Up Plan
SEP	Due date of employer's return (including extensions)	Smaller of $49,000 or 25% of participant's compensation	25% of all participants' compensation	Any time up to the due date of employer's return (including extensions)
SIMPLE IRA and SIMPLE 401(k)	**Salary reduction contributions:** 30 days after the end of the month for which the contributions are to be made **Matching or nonelective contributions:** Due date of employer's return (including extensions)	**Employee contribution:** Salary reduction contribution up to $11,500, $14,000 if age 50 or older **Employer contribution:** *Either* dollar-for-dollar matching contributions, up to 3% of employee's compensation, *or* fixed non-elective contributions of 2% of compensation	Same as maximum contribution	Any time between 1/1 and 10/1 of the calendar year For a new employer coming into existence after 10/1, as soon as administratively feasible
Qualified Plan: Defined Contribution Plan	**Elective deferral:** Due date of employee's return (including extensions) **Employer contribution:** Money Purchase or Profit-Sharing: Due date of employer's return (including extensions)	**Employee contribution:** Elective deferral up to $16,500, $22,000 if age 50 or older **Employer contribution:** Money Purchase: Smaller of $49,000 or 100% of participant's compensation Profit-Sharing: Smaller of $49,000 or 100% of participant's compensation.	25% of all participants' compensation, plus amount of elective deferrals made	By the end of the tax year
Qualified Plan: Defined Benefit Plan	Contributions must be paid in quarterly installments depending on the plan year, due 15 days after the end of each quarter.	Amount needed to provide an annual benefit no larger than the smaller of $195,000 or 100% of the participant's average compensation for his highest three consecutive calendar years	Based on actuarial assumptions and computations	By the end of the tax year

Tax Return Preparer Competency Exam – Chapter 10 Quiz

Circle the letter next to the best answer. Remember to read the question carefully.

1) John, a self-employed taxpayer, has a SEP plan for his business. He has three eligible employees, Sara (age 35), Joseph (age 37), and Jean (age 45), who have worked for him for the past 10 years. For the year 2011, Sara earned $15,000, Joseph earned $25,000, and Jean earned $30,000. He wants to elect the 25% contribution rate so he can put as much as possible in for himself. If he elects 25%, how much must he contribute to the plan for his employees?

   a. $0.

   b. $2,100.

   c. $17,500.

   d. $40,000.

2) Your employee, Jane Wood (age 37), earned $145,000 and elected to defer 10% of her salary. You make a 2% non-elective contribution. The total contribution that may be made for Jane under a SIMPLE IRA plan is:

   a. $17,400

   b. $ 14,500

   c. $ 2,900

   d. $ 14,400

3) Mike is self-employed. He is a calendar year taxpayer. If he wants to set up a SEP plan for his business for the year 2011, he must do so by (including extensions):

   a. December 31, 2011.

   b. January 31, 2012.

   c. April 15, 2012.

   d. October 15, 2012.

4) Which of the following costs qualify as business "start-up costs"?

   a. Deductible interest.

   b. State and local taxes.

   c. A survey of potential markets.

   d. Research and experimental costs.

5) Which of the following taxpayers could be considered to be self-employed for the purposes of claiming the self-employed health insurance deduction?

a. A sole proprietor of a home improvement business.

b. A general partner in a law firm.

c. A salaried employee of an S corporation who owns 50% of the corporation.

d. All of the above.

6) Which of the following fringe benefits for meals is subject to the 50% deduction limit?

a. Meals furnished to your employees at the work site when you operate a restaurant

b. Meals furnished to your employees as part of the expense of a company picnic

c. Meals furnished to your employees at your place of business when more than half of these employees are provided the meals for your convenience

d. Meals furnished to a customer during a business discussion

7) When an employer reimburses an employee for meals under an accountable plan while the employee is away from home, the employer must:

a. Include 50% of the cost of meals as income to the employee.

b. Do nothing.

c. Deduct only 50% of the reimbursement on his/her tax return.

d. Add 100% of the meals as income to the employee.

8) What is an eligible individual taxpayer's Domestic Production Activities Deduction (DPAD) for 2011?

a. 9% of his qualified production activities income (QPAI)

b. 9% of his AGI, figured without the DPAD

c. The smaller of A or B

d. The larger of A or B

Tax Return Preparer Competency Exam – Chapter 10 Quiz Rationale

For more practice questions, visit fastforwardacademy.com and access our FREE online question bank.

1) **c** Contributions you make for 2011 to a common-law employee's SEP-IRA cannot exceed the lesser of 25% of the employee's compensation or $49,000. Compensation generally does not include your contributions to the SEP. The SEP plan document will specify how the employer determines contributions and how it will allocate them to participants. The total allowed for all employees is $17,500 or 25% of total salary.

2) **d** Employees may contribute 100% of salary to a SIMPLE IRA through salary reductions up to $11,500 for 2011. Instead of matching contributions, the employer can choose to make non-elective contributions of 2% of compensation on behalf of each eligible employee who has at least $5,000 (or some lower amount you select) of compensation for the year.

3) **d** A SEP must be established by the due date (including extensions) of the business tax return for the year.

4) **c** Start-up costs include any amounts paid or incurred in connection with creating or investigating the creation or acquisition of an active trade or business. Start-up costs do <u>not</u> include deductible interest, taxes, or research and experimental costs.

5) **d** The self-employed health insurance deduction permits eligible taxpayers to deduct premiums paid for medical and dental insurance and qualified long-term care insurance for himself, his spouse, and his dependents. Eligible taxpayers include: a self-employed individual (with a net profit reported on Schedule C (Form 1040), Schedule C-EZ (Form 1040), or Schedule F (Form 1040); a partner with net earnings from self-employment reported on Schedule K-1 (Form 1065); and a shareholder owning more than 2% of the outstanding stock of an S corporation with wages from the corporation reported on Form W-2, Wage and Tax Statement.

6) **d** If food or beverages furnished to employees qualify as a de minimis benefit, employers may deduct their full cost. The 50% limit on deductions for the cost of meals does not apply. A meal with a customer is not a fringe benefit and is subject to the 50% limitation.

7) **c** Amounts paid under an accountable plan are <u>not wages</u> and are not subject to the withholding and payment of income, Social Security, Medicare, and federal unemployment (FUTA) taxes. Generally, the amount you can deduct for meals and entertainment is subject to a 50% limit.

8) **c** A taxpayer's DPAD is generally 9% of the smaller of his qualified production activities income (QPAI) or his AGI. But, the DPAD generally cannot be more than 50% of the wages he paid to his employees who worked in the qualifying business.

11 Practice Before the IRS

Director of the OPR · Return Preparer Office · Practice before the IRS · Preparer Considerations · Continuing Professional Education · Duties and Restrictions · Sanctions and Penalties · Preparer Penalties

This chapter relates to *Practice before the IRS* as explained in IRS Circular 230 and Publication 947.

Director of the Office of Professional Responsibility

Appointed by the Secretary of the Treasury, the duties of the Director of the ***Office of Professional Responsibility*** **(OPR)** include the following:

- Acting on applications for enrollment to practice before the IRS
- Inquiries on matters under the Director's jurisdiction
- Institutes' disciplinary proceedings related to practitioners

IRS Return Preparer Office

The IRS ***Return Preparer Office*** **(RPO)** is responsible for implementing the new requirements and oversight of the IRS return preparer program. It will work in partnership with the Office of Professional Responsibility, which is responsible for the enforcement of Circular 230 conduct issues.

Practice before the IRS

Definition of Practice before the IRS

Practice before the IRS comprehends all matters connected with a presentation to the IRS relating to a taxpayer's rights, privileges, or liabilities under laws or regulations administered by the IRS. Such presentations include but are not limited to the following:

- Preparing documents (this includes preparing a tax return)
- Filing documents
- Corresponding and communicating with the IRS
- Representing a taxpayer at conferences, hearings, or meetings with the IRS
- Rendering written advice with respect to any entity, transaction, plan, or arrangement

TIP: Certain tasks, which anyone may perform, do not constitute practice before the IRS. These tasks include appearing as a witness for a taxpayer before the IRS, or furnishing information at the request of the IRS.

Who May Practice

Any of the following individuals may practice before the IRS, with the assumption that they are not currently under suspension or disbarred:

- **Attorneys** – Any attorney who is a member in good standing of the bar of the highest court of any state, possession, territory, commonwealth, or the District of Columbia
- **Certified public accountants (CPAs)** – Any CPA who is duly qualified to practice as a CPA in any state, possession, territory, commonwealth, or the District of Columbia
- **Enrolled agents** – Any enrolled agent in active status
- **Enrolled retirement plan agents** – Any enrolled retirement plan agent in active status
- **Enrolled actuaries** – Any individual enrolled as an actuary by the Joint Board for the Enrollment of Actuaries
- **Registered Tax Return Preparers** – Practice is limited to preparing and signing tax returns and claims for refund, and other documents for submission to the Internal Revenue Service.

Practice for *enrolled retirement plan agents* and *enrolled actuaries* is limited to certain Internal Revenue Code sections that relate to their area of expertise, principally those governing retirement plans.

11.1 Peter is a tax preparer who for compensation prepares and files tax returns for individuals in his home town. Is filing a 1040 tax return considered "practice" before the IRS?

Form 2848 Power of Attorney and Declaration of Representative

Form 2848 appoints a representative admitted to practice before the IRS to act on a taxpayer's behalf. Specific authorization on the form is necessary to authorize:

- A ***durable power of attorney***; otherwise, the powers terminate if a taxpayer becomes incapacitated or incompetent.
- Signing the return for a taxpayer, if permitted.
- Receive a refund check. If a representative is to receive a refund check on a taxpayer's behalf, it must specifically authorize this in the power of attorney. However, those permitted to practice before the IRS may not endorse or otherwise cash a refund check.
- Substitution or delegation of authority under the power of attorney to another recognized representative.
    1) Under a substitution, the IRS recognizes only the newly recognized representative as the taxpayer's representative.
    2) Under a delegation, the IRS recognizes both representatives as authorized to represent the taxpayer.
- Disclosure of returns to a third party. A representative may not execute consents that will allow the IRS to disclose tax return or return information to a third party unless this authority is specifically delegated to the representative.

The IRS will accept a **non-IRS power of attorney**, other than Form 2848. To be valid, the practitioner must sign a ***Declaration of Representative***, and the taxpayer must provide the following information:

- Name and mailing address
- Social Security number and/or employer identification number
- Employee plan number, if applicable
- The name and mailing address of the representative
- The types of tax involved
- The federal tax form number
- The specific year(s) or period(s) involved
- For estate tax matters, the decedent's date of death
- A clear expression of intention concerning the scope of authority granted to a representative
- Signature and date

TIP A newly filed power of attorney concerning the same matter will revoke a previously filed power of attorney. A copy of the previously executed power of attorney sent to the IRS with the word "REVOKE" written across the top will serve to revoke an existing power of attorney. If a representative wants to withdraw from representation, he may perform the same action.

Central Authorization File

The IRS has a centralized computer database system called the ***centralized authorization file*** (CAF) system. It contains information on the authority of taxpayer representatives and those with ***Tax Information Authorization (TIA)***. The TIA allows a third party to receive or inspect written and/or oral tax account information, subject to limitations. Individuals may represent themselves before the IRS or grant another the legal authority to represent them with a power of attorney. Entry of ***Form 2848, Power of Attorney and Declaration of Representative*** on the CAF system enables IRS personnel who do not have a copy of the power of attorney to verify the authority of a representative by accessing the CAF. It also enables automatic mailing of notices and other IRS communications to the representative.

Third Party Designee

The IRS does not honor Form 2848 for any purpose other than representation before the IRS. A taxpayer can authorize the IRS to discuss his tax return with a preparer, a friend, family member, or any other person through a "checkbox authorization" indicating the ***Third party designee*** directly on the tax return and providing the information required. In doing so, the taxpayer authorizes the following:

- The IRS to call the designee to answer any questions that arise during the processing of the return
- The designee to:
    1) Give information that is missing from the return to the IRS
    2) Call the IRS about the processing of the return or the status of a refund or payments
    3) Receive copies of notices or transcripts related to the return, upon request

4) Respond to certain IRS notices about math errors, offsets, and return preparation

The authorization automatically ends no later than the due date (without any extensions) for filing the tax return for the following year. The CAF does not record information about third party designees.

Tax Information Authorization, Form 8821

A power of attorney is not necessary to authorize the IRS to discuss and provide specific confidential tax return information to anyone designated with a Tax Information Authorization (TIA). There are two methods to grant the authorization–***Form 8821*** or ***Oral Tax Information Authorization*** (verbal equivalent of Form 8821). However, the TIA is strictly a disclosure authorization. A taxpayer may <u>not</u> use this form to designate an individual as a representative. The authorization remains in effect until a taxpayer revokes or the appointee withdraws. Form 8821 does not revoke existing authority under a power of attorney, as Forms 2848 and Form 8821 do not affect each other in any way.

11.2 Diego is a registered tax return preparer. His client Tom asks Diego to communicate with the IRS regarding a tax return Diego prepared in 2008. That return lists Diego as the Third Party Designee. Tom's current year tax return also lists Diego as the Third Party Designee. Will Diego need additional authorization on Form 8821 to receive information regarding the 2008 return?

Preparer Considerations

Registered Tax Return Preparers

Beginning in 2011 all paid tax return preparers (including attorneys, CPAs, and enrolled agents) must have a ***Preparer Tax Identification Number (PTIN)*** before preparing any federal tax returns. A PTIN is a number issued by the IRS to paid tax return preparers. It is the tax preparer's identification number and, when applicable, must be placed in the paid preparer section of a tax return. Any individual who, for compensation, prepares all or substantially all of a tax return or claim for refund–including making determinations that affect tax liability–needs a PTIN. A candidate must have a PTIN to schedule an exam. Upon receipt of the PTIN, the candidate may schedule an exam using his online PTIN account.

New regulations require all paid tax return preparers—other than certain exempt individuals—to register for a PTIN, pass a competency exam, and complete <u>15 hours</u> of annual continuing education. These ***registered tax return preparers*** need to follow the rules in Circular 230, but are not enrolled to practice before the IRS.

The IRS makes an exception in ***Notice 2011-6*** for certain non-signing preparers who are at least 18 years old and under the supervision of a ***Circular 230 practitioner*** such as a CPA, attorney, or enrolled agent. A supervised non-signing preparer may obtain a PTIN and receive compensation to prepare, or assist in the preparation of, a tax return or claim for refund. Individuals who obtain a PTIN under this provision will not be subject to a competency examination or continuing education requirements. These individuals may not sign any tax return they prepare for compensation, represent taxpayers before the IRS in any capacity, or represent to the IRS, their clients, or the public that they are a registered tax return preparer or a Circular 230 practitioner. The supervising practitioner must sign the return.

A Circular 230 practitioner such as an attorney, CPA, or enrolled agent *"enrolled to practice before the IRS"* is exempt from the new testing and continuing education requirements.

- A Registered Tax Return Preparer's ability to practice is generally limited to examinations with respect to a return that he has prepared if he signed the tax return or claim for refund for the taxable year or period under examination. He may represent taxpayers <u>only</u> before customer service representatives, or similar officers and employees of the Internal Revenue Service (including the Taxpayer Advocate Service), revenue agents, and examination officers. Do not confuse *examination officers* with *revenue officers*, who are highly skilled employees of the IRS Collection Division.

- A Registered Tax Return Preparer may not sign documents (other certain tax returns or claims for refund) for a taxpayer and may only represent taxpayers in limited situations. A Registered Tax Return Preparer **<u>may not</u>**:

  1) Represent a taxpayer before other offices of the IRS, such as <u>Collection</u> or <u>Appeals</u>
  2) Execute closing agreements
  3) Extend the statutory period for tax assessments or collection of tax
  4) Execute waivers
  5) Execute claims for refund
  6) Receive refund checks

11.3 Roberta prepares tax returns for compensation. She is not a Circular 230 practitioner, nor does one supervise her. What amount of continuing education should she plan to take annually?

Other Un-enrolled Individuals

Because of their special relationship with a taxpayer, the following un-enrolled individuals may represent the specified taxpayers before the IRS, provided they present satisfactory identification and proof of authority to represent the taxpayer:

- ***Individuals*** may represent themselves and members of their immediate family. Immediate family means a spouse, child, parent, brother, or sister of the individual.
- An ***officer*** of a corporation may represent the corporation.
- A ***general partner*** may represent the partnership before the IRS.
- A regular full-time ***employee*** may represent his employer.
- A ***fiduciary*** (trustee, executor, administrator, receiver, or guardian) stands in the position of a taxpayer and acts as the taxpayer, not as a representative.

Any individual may represent an individual or entity, located outside the United States, before personnel of the IRS when such representation takes place outside the United States.

Those Who May Not Practice

In general, individuals who are not eligible or who have lost the privilege may not practice before the IRS. Corporations, associations, partnerships, and other non-individuals are not eligible to practice before the IRS.

Designation as a Registered Tax Return Preparer

The Commissioner, or delegate, may designate an individual eighteen years of age or older as a Registered Tax Return Preparer upon demonstration of competence in tax matters by passing a written examination administered by the IRS. The IRS ***Return Preparer Office (RPO)*** administers the oversight program for the nation's federal tax professionals, including Registered Tax Return Preparers. This is different from the "enrollment" status received by practitioners such as enrolled agents. The practice of enrolled agents is not limited.

Individuals placed in inactive status and individuals ineligible to practice before the Internal Revenue Service may not state or imply that they are eligible to practice before the Internal Revenue Service, or use the terms enrolled agent, enrolled retirement plan agent, or registered tax return preparer, the designations "EA" or "RTRP" or other form of reference to eligibility to practice before the IRS.

Table 11-1 Preparer Requirements.

Category	**PTIN**	**Tax Compliance Check**	**Background Check**	**IRS Test**	**Continuing Education**
Attorneys	Yes	Yes	Pending	No	No
CPAs	Yes	Yes	Pending	No	No
Enrolled Agents	Yes	Yes	Pending	Yes (EA Exam)	72 hours every 3 years
Registered Tax Return Preparers	**Yes**	**Yes**	**Pending**	**Yes (RTRP test)**	**15 hours a year**
Supervised Preparers	Yes	Yes	Pending	No	No
Non-1040 Preparers	Yes	Yes	Pending	No	No

Supervised Preparers are those who do not sign returns and who are employed by attorney, CPA or EA firms and are supervised by an attorney, CPA or EA. Non-1040 preparers are those who do not prepare any Form 1040 series returns. Form 1040-PR and 1040-SS are not considered Form 1040 series returns for this purpose.

Continuing Professional Education

Registered tax return preparers must renew their preparer tax identification number (PTIN) and their status as a registered tax return preparer as prescribed by the Internal Revenue Service (details unavailable at this time). Certain requirements are necessary in order to continue enrollment. These include, but are not limited to, ongoing professional education and the avoidance of actions that can subject a practitioner to censure, suspension, or disbarment.

A Registered Tax Return Preparer must complete a minimum of **15 hours** of continuing education credit for 2012, including two hours of ethics or professional conduct, three hours of Federal tax law updates, and 10 hours of Federal tax law topics, during each registration year. This is true even for those who have not completed the exam requirement.

To qualify for continuing education credit for a registered tax return preparer, a course of learning must be a qualifying continuing education program designed to enhance professional knowledge in Federal taxation or Federal tax related matters (programs comprised of current subject matter in Federal taxation or Federal tax related matters, including accounting, tax return preparation software, taxation, or ethics); and be a qualifying continuing education program consistent with the Internal Revenue Code and effective tax administration.

- All continuing education programs are measured in terms of ***contact hours***. A contact hour is 50 minutes of continuous participation in a program. The IRS only grants credit for a full contact hour, i.e., 50 minutes or multiples thereof.

- Qualifying CPE programs must meet certain standards. A qualified sponsor must run all CPE programs. They must require attendance and issue a certificate of attendance. The instructor's background, experience, education, and training should be appropriate for the subject matter. The course must provide a written outline, textbook, or suitable electronic educational materials. Self-study courses (including online, correspondence, and taped program courses) meet this standard if they require registration by the participant, provide a means of measuring completion such as a written test, provide a certification of successful completion of said test, and provide a written outline, textbook, or acceptable electronic substitutes.

- Keep records of completed CPE for **four years** following the date of renewal

---

TIP This course qualifies for 10-hours of Federal tax law! To receive a certificate for 10-hours of credit, you must pass a 50 question test online at http://fastforwardacademy.com. The test is available automatically in the CPE dashboard for those who purchase this course on our website.

Duties and Restrictions

Duties

Practitioners must promptly submit records or information requested by officers or employees of the IRS. When the Office of Professional Responsibility requests information concerning possible violations of the regulations by other parties, the practitioner must provide the information and be prepared to testify in disbarment or suspension proceedings. The IRS may exempt a practitioner from these rules if the information requested is privileged or the request is of doubtful legality. When making this determination, the practitioner must be acting in good faith and on reasonable grounds.

Contingent Fees

A contingent fee is one that is based on whether or not a position taken on a return avoids challenge by the IRS. A practitioner may not charge a contingent fee for services in connection with any matter before the IRS, except:

- Services related to an IRS examination or challenge of:

  1) An original tax return, or

  2) An amended tax return filed within 120 days of a taxpayer receiving a notice of examination

- For services rendered in connection with a claim for credit or refund filed solely in connection with the determination of statutory interest or penalties assessed by the IRS.

- Services connected to a judicial proceeding

Confidentiality Privilege

A practitioner must, on a proper and lawful request by a duly authorized officer or employee of the Internal Revenue Service, promptly submit records or information in any matter before the Internal Revenue Service unless the practitioner believes in good faith and on reasonable grounds that the records or information are privileged. The confidentiality protection of certain communications between a taxpayer and an attorney (privileged communications) applies to similar communications between a taxpayer and any federally authorized tax practitioner.

- One may not invoke this confidentiality privilege in any administrative proceeding with an agency other than the IRS.
- The protection of this privilege applies only to tax advice given to the taxpayer by any individual who is a federally authorized tax practitioner. The confidentiality protection applies to communications that would be considered privileged if they were between the taxpayer and an attorney and that relate to:
    1) Noncriminal tax matters before the IRS, or
    2) Noncriminal tax proceedings brought in federal court by or against the United States.
- This protection does not apply to any written communications between a federally authorized tax practitioner and certain representatives or employees of a corporation nor does it apply if the communication promotes a tax shelter to a corporation.

Client Omissions – Duty to Advise

A practitioner generally may rely in good faith on information furnished by the client. The practitioner may not, however, ignore the implications of information furnished and must make reasonable inquiries if it appears to be incorrect or inconsistent. A practitioner who is aware the client has not complied with the rules and regulations of the IRS, or knows of any error or omission, must promptly <u>advise</u> the <u>client</u> concerning the existence of the error or omission and of the consequences of allowing them to remain uncorrected. If not corrected, the practitioner <u>cannot</u> sign the return. A practitioner may not advise a client to take a frivolous position on a return.

Advertising and Solicitation

The practitioner may advertise using any method(s) he chooses. A practitioner may not make any advertising statement that is in any way false, fraudulent, coercive, misleading, or deceptive or that violates any state, federal, or other applicable rule. A practitioner may not use the word "certified" or otherwise imply an employment relationship with the IRS. If the practitioner publishes a schedule of fees, he must adhere to the schedule for at least 30 days from the last date of publication. Such a schedule must include fixed fees for specific routine services, hourly rates, range of fees for particular services and any fees charged for an initial consultation.

TIP

Examples of acceptable descriptions for enrolled agents are "enrolled to practice before the IRS," "admitted to practice before the IRS" or "enrolled to represent taxpayers before the IRS." An example of an acceptable description for registered tax return preparers is "designated as a registered tax return preparer by the Internal Revenue Service."

Diligence as to Accuracy

A practitioner must exercise due diligence in preparing, approving, and filing tax returns and all other documents, as well as any oral statements relating to IRS or Treasury Department matters. The practitioner must use the same diligence in determining the correctness of oral or written statements made to clients with reference to any matter administered by the Internal Revenue Service. A practitioner will be presumed to have exercised due diligence if the practitioner relies on the work product of another person and the practitioner used reasonable care in engaging, supervising, training, and evaluating the person.

Conflict of Interest

A conflict of interest exists if the representation of one client is directly adverse to another client or if there is a significant risk that the representation of one or more clients will be materially limited by the practitioner's responsibilities to another client, to a former client or a third person, or by a personal interest of the practitioner. Practitioners may not represent a client if such representation causes or appears to cause a conflict of interest unless:

- The practitioner reasonably believes that he will be able to provide competent and diligent representation to each affected client,
- The representation is not prohibited by law, and
- Each affected client waives the conflict of interest <u>in writing</u> at the time the practitioner knows of the existence of the conflict of interest. The confirmation may be made within a reasonable period of time, but in no event later than 30 days after the practitioner becomes aware of the conflict.

Refund Check Negotiation

A practitioner who prepares tax returns may <u>not</u> endorse or otherwise negotiate any check issued to a client by the government in respect of a federal tax liability.

Performance as a Notary

A practitioner who is a notary public and has an interest in a matter before the IRS may <u>not</u> engage in any notary activities related to that matter.

Practice of Law

Nothing in the regulations in this part may be construed as authorizing those who are not members of the bar to practice law.

Best Practices for Tax Advisors

Practitioners should provide clients with the highest quality representation concerning federal tax issues by adhering to best practices in providing advice and in preparing or assisting in the preparation of a submission to the Internal Revenue Service. Best practices include the following:

- Communicating clearly with the client regarding the terms of the engagement
- Establishing the facts, determining which facts are relevant, evaluating the reasonableness of any assumptions or representations, relating the applicable law to the relevant facts, and arriving at a conclusion supported by the law and the facts. The practitioner generally may rely in good faith without verification upon information furnished by the client. The practitioner may not, however,

ignore the implications of information furnished to, or actually known by, the practitioner, and must make reasonable inquiries if the information as furnished appears to be incorrect, inconsistent with an important fact or another factual assumption, or incomplete.

- Advising the client regarding the import of the conclusions reached, including, for example, whether a taxpayer may avoid accuracy-related penalties under the Internal Revenue Code if a taxpayer acts in reliance on the advice
- Acting fairly and with integrity in practice before the Internal Revenue Service

Recordkeeping

In general, practitioners must keep records for a period of three years. They must:

- Keep records of completed CPE for four years following the date of renewal of enrollment
- Keep written consents due to conflicts of interest for at least 36 months from the date of the conclusion of the representation of the affected clients
- Maintain copies of any direct mail, Internet, or radio/television advertising for at least 36 months from date of last publication or transmission
- The preparer must either retain a copy of the return, or as an alternative, a list showing the name, taxpayer identification number, type of return, and tax year for each return prepared. The records must available for inspection for three years following the close of the return period in which the return is presented to the taxpayer for signature (or the date the return becomes due for an extended return). A "return period" is the 12-month period beginning on July 1 of each year.

11.4 Lucy prepares a Form 1040 tax return for the calendar year 2011. The return is extended to October 15, 2012 and is presented to her client for signature on October 1, 2012. On what date is she no longer required to maintain a copy of that return in her records?

Sanctions and Penalties

The Secretary of the Treasury, or delegate, after notice and an opportunity for a proceeding, may censure, suspend, or disbar any practitioner from practice before the Internal Revenue Service if the practitioner is shown to be incompetent or disreputable, fails to comply with the prohibited conduct standards of §10.52 (not best practices), or with intent to defraud, willfully and knowingly misleads or threatens a client or prospective client. Censure is a public reprimand.

A practitioner may face a monetary penalty if engaging in conduct subject to sanction. The amount of the penalty shall not exceed the gross income derived (or to be derived) from the conduct giving rise to the penalty. The Secretary of the Treasury, or delegate, may impose a monetary penalty on an employer, firm, or entity if it knew, or reasonably should have known of such conduct of a preparer acting on its behalf. Any monetary penalty imposed on an employer, firm or other entity may be in addition to or in lieu of penalties imposed on the practitioner.

Incompetence and Disreputable Conduct

Incompetence and disreputable conduct for which the IRS may sanction a practitioner includes, but is not limited, to the following:

- Conviction of any criminal offense under the Federal tax laws
- Conviction of any criminal offense involving dishonesty or breach of trust
- Conviction of any felony under federal or state law for which the conduct involved renders the practitioner unfit to practice before the Internal Revenue Service
- Giving false or misleading information, or participating in any way in the giving of false or misleading information to the Department of the Treasury or any officer or employee thereof, or to any tribunal authorized to pass upon federal tax matters in connection with any matter pending or likely to be pending before them
- Solicitation of employment as prohibited under §10.30, the use of false or misleading representations with intent to deceive a client or prospective client in order to procure employment, or intimating that the practitioner is able to improperly obtain special consideration or action from the IRS or any officer or employee thereof
- Willfully failing to make a federal tax return in violation of the federal tax laws, or willfully evading, attempting to evade, or participating in any way in evading or attempting to evade any assessment or payment of any federal tax
- Willfully assisting, counseling, or encouraging a client or prospective client in violating, or suggesting to a client or prospective client to violate, any Federal tax law, or knowingly counseling or suggesting to a client or prospective client an illegal plan to evade federal taxes
- Misappropriation of, or failure to properly or promptly remit funds received from a client for the purpose of payment of taxes or other obligations due the United States
- Directly or indirectly attempting to influence, or offering or agreeing to attempt to influence, the official action of any officer or employee of the IRS by the use of threats, false accusations, duress, or coercion by the offer of any special inducement or promise of an advantage or by the bestowing of any gift, favor, or item of value
- Disbarment or suspension from practice as an attorney, certified public accountant, public accountant, or actuary by any duly constituted authority of any state, territory, or possession of the United States, including a commonwealth, the District of Columbia, any federal court of record, or any federal agency, body, or board
- Knowingly aiding and abetting another person to practice before the Internal Revenue Service during a period of suspension, disbarment, or ineligibility of such other person
- Contemptuous conduct in connection with practice before the IRS, including the use of abusive language, making false accusations or statements, knowing them to be false, or circulating or publishing malicious or libelous matter
- Giving a false opinion, knowingly, recklessly, or through gross incompetence, including an opinion that is intentionally or recklessly misleading, or engaging in a pattern of providing incompetent opinions on questions arising under the federal tax laws
- Willfully failing to sign a tax return prepared by the practitioner when federal tax laws require the signature, unless the failure is due to reasonable cause and not due to willful neglect
- Willfully disclosing or otherwise using a tax return or tax return information in a manner not authorized by the Internal Revenue Code, contrary to the order of a court of competent jurisdiction,

or contrary to the order of an administrative law judge in a proceeding instituted under the Circular 230 instructions for sanction proceedings

Preparer Penalties

Return preparers are responsible for taking a reasonable position on a tax return. To be reasonable, there must be ***substantial authority*** for the position, or in the case of a disclosed position, a ***reasonable basis*** for the treatment of such item on the return. The return cannot contain ***frivolous positions***, which have no basis for validity in existing law or which have been deemed frivolous by the U.S. Tax Court or other federal court. The IRS may assess penalties within three years after the taxpayer files the return. No proceeding in court without assessment for the collection of such tax shall begin after the expiration of such period. There is no statute of limitations for fraudulent returns.

The substantial authority standard is an objective standard involving an analysis of the law and application of the law to relevant facts. It is less stringent than the ***more likely than not*** standard (the standard that is met when there is a greater than 50% likelihood of the position being upheld), but more stringent than the reasonable basis standard. There is substantial authority for the tax treatment of an item only if the weight of the authorities supporting the treatment is substantial in relation to the weight of authorities supporting contrary treatment. All authorities relevant to the tax treatment of an item, including the authorities contrary to the treatment, are taken into account in determining whether substantial authority exists. The weight of authorities is determined in light of the pertinent facts and circumstances.

Reasonable basis is a relatively high standard of tax reporting that is significantly higher than not frivolous or not patently improper. The reasonable basis standard is not satisfied by a return position that is merely arguable. If a return position is reasonably based on one or more of the authorities set forth in §1.6662–4(d)(3)(iii) (taking into account the relevance and persuasiveness of the authorities, and subsequent developments), the return position will generally satisfy the reasonable basis standard even though it may not satisfy the substantial authority standard.

A ***tax shelter***, for purposes of the substantial understatement portion of the accuracy-related penalty, is a partnership or other entity, plan, or arrangement, with a significant purpose to avoid or evade federal income tax. Tax shelters have a higher standard and must have a confidence level of at least *more likely than not* (greater than 50% likelihood) that one or more significant tax issues would be resolved in the taxpayer's favor.

Taxpayers and tax return preparers who wish to avoid certain penalties can use Form 8275, Form 8275-R, or Rev. Proc. 2008-14 to disclose items or positions—except those taken contrary to a regulation—that are not otherwise adequately disclosed on a tax return. The form is filed in order to avoid the portions of the accuracy-related penalty due to disregard of rules or to a substantial understatement of income tax for non-tax shelter items if the return position has a reasonable basis. It also is used for disclosures relating to preparer penalties for understatements due to unreasonable positions or disregard of rules.

The portion of the accuracy-related penalty attributable to the following types of misconduct cannot be avoided by disclosure on Form 8275:

- Negligence
- Disregard of regulations

- Any substantial understatement of income tax on a tax shelter item
- Any substantial valuation misstatement under chapter one of the Internal Revenue Code
- Any substantial overstatement of pension liabilities
- Any substantial estate or gift tax valuation understatements

Understatement of Liability §6694

Preparer penalties are applicable in the following circumstances:

- **Unreasonable positions** – A penalty of $1,000 or 50% of preparer's fee, whichever is greater.
  1) A position lacking substantial authority is unreasonable if the preparer knew (or should have known) of the position, and
     A) For undisclosed positions – The position does not have substantial authority.
     B) For disclosed positions – The position does not have a reasonable basis.
     C) For tax shelters – There was not a reasonable belief that the position would *more likely than not* be sustained on its merits.
  2) If a return preparer understates tax liability on a return, the IRS will not impose a penalty if the preparer shows that there is reasonable cause and the tax return preparer acted in good faith.
- **Willful or reckless conduct** – A penalty of $5,000 or 50% of preparer's fee, whichever is greater.
  1) Willful or reckless conduct is conduct by the tax return preparer that is a willful attempt in any manner to understate the liability for tax on the return or claim, or a reckless or intentional disregard of rules or regulations.
  2) The amount of any penalty payable for willful misconduct is reduced by any penalty for an unreasonable position.

Failures under §6695

Any tax return preparer who fails to take certain actions may be assessed other penalties with respect to the preparation of tax returns for other persons.

- Penalty of **$50** for each occurrence up to a maximum of **$25,000/year** unless it is shown that such failure is due to reasonable cause and not willful neglect:
  1) **§6695(a) Failure to furnish copy of return to taxpayer** – The tax preparer must furnish a completed copy of the return or claim for refund to the taxpayer no later than the time it is presented for the taxpayer's signature.
  2) **§6695(b) Failure to sign return** – The tax preparer must sign a tax return or claim for refund if the tax preparer has primary responsibility for the overall substantive accuracy of the preparation of the tax return or claim for refund.
  3) **§6695(c) Failure to furnish identifying number** – A tax return preparer must obtain and exclusively use a PTIN, rather than a social security number (SSN), as the identifying number to be included with the tax return preparer's signature on a tax return or claim for refund.

4) **§6695(d) Failure to retain copy or list** – A tax return preparer must keep a copy of the tax return, or retain, on a list, the name and taxpayer identification number of the taxpayer for whom the return was prepared. The records must be available for inspection for the 3-year period following the close of the return period during which the return or claim for refund was presented for signature to the taxpayer.

5) **§6695(e) Failure to file correct information returns** – Each person who employs (or engages) one or more income tax return preparers to prepare any return of tax is responsible for retaining a record of the name, taxpayer identification number, and principal place of work during the return period of each income tax return preparer employed (or engaged) by the person at any time during that period. The record must be available for inspection upon request by the district director for the 3-year period following the close of the return period.

- **§6695(f) Negotiation of check** – Any tax return preparer who endorses or otherwise negotiates (directly or through an agent) any check made in respect of the taxes imposed by this title, which is issued to a taxpayer, shall pay a penalty of **$500** with respect to each check. This does not apply with respect to the deposit by a bank of the full amount of the check in the taxpayer's account for the benefit of the taxpayer.

- **§6695(g) Failure to be diligent in determining eligibility for earned income credit** – Any return preparer who fails to comply with due diligence requirements imposed to determining eligibility for, or the amount of, the credit allowable shall pay a penalty of **$500** for each failure. Those who prepare Earned Income Tax Credit (EITC) claims must not only ask all the questions required on ***Form 8867***, Paid Preparers' Earned Income Credit Checklist, but must also ask additional questions when information seems incorrect, inconsistent or incomplete. In addition, the preparer must verify identity, prepare an EIC computational checklist (Form 8867 or equivalent), and meet a recordkeeping requirement (keep form 8867 and the EIC worksheet (or equivalents) for 3 years after the June 30th following the date the return or claim was presented for signature).

11.5 Michelle prepares a Form 1040 tax return for the calendar year 2011. Her client Tammy claims the Earned Income Credit, using her brother's child to qualify. Tammy told Michelle the child was hers, and Michelle had no reason to doubt her client. Michelle completed the EIC checklist and worksheet before submitting the return, but was unable to locate the file when the IRS made the request. What penalty, if any, is Michelle liable to pay?

Safeguarding Taxpayer Information

Tax return preparers must obtain consent to use tax return information before tax return information is used and before returns are provided to the taxpayer for signature. Internal Revenue Code §7216 is a criminal provision enacted by the U.S. Congress in 1971 that prohibits preparers of tax returns from knowingly or recklessly disclosing or using tax return information. A convicted preparer may be fined not more than $1,000 or imprisoned not more than one year or both, for each violation.

Internal Revenue Code §6713 imposes a civil penalty of $250 on any person who is engaged in the business of preparing, or providing services in connection with the preparation of returns of tax, or any person who for compensation prepares a return for another person, and who:

- Discloses any information furnished to him for, or in connection with, the preparation of any such return, or

- Uses any such information for any purpose other than to prepare, or assist in preparing, any such return. Imposition of the penalty under Internal Revenue Code §6713 does not require that the disclosure be knowing or reckless as it does under Internal Revenue Code §7216.

Generally, unless otherwise specified, a written consent is effective for a period of one year from the date the taxpayer signs the consent. Disclosing tax return information to another tax preparer within the United States that is assisting in the preparation of the return generally does not require the consent of the taxpayer.

Payment

The tax preparer has 30 days to pay the penalty upon receipt of a demand for payment from the IRS. The preparer may elect to pay at least 15% of the amount of the penalty and file a claim for refund. If the claim for refund is denied (or six months have passed), the preparer has 30 more days to begin a proceeding in the appropriate U.S. district court for determination of liability.

Tax Return Preparer Competency Exam – Chapter 11 Quiz

Circle the letter next to the best answer. Remember to read the question carefully.

1) A Registered Tax Return Preparer generally must complete continuing education credits for renewed enrollment. Which of the following describes the credit requirements?

   a. A minimum of 10 hours must be completed in each year, with 5 hours of ethics

   b. A minimum of 24 hours must be completed in each year of an enrollment cycle

   c. A minimum of 20 hours must be completed, overall, for the entire enrollment cycle

   d. A minimum of 15 hours must be completed during each registration year

2) John Bright recently passed the IRS tax preparer competency exam. He wants to advertise for his business. Which of the following presentations will not violate the Circular 230 rules for advertising?

   a. John Bright, enrolled to practice before the Internal Revenue Service

   b. John Bright, Certified Registered Tax Return Preparer

   c. John Bright, designated as a registered tax return preparer by the Internal Revenue Service

   d. John Bright, admitted to practice before the Internal Revenue Service

3) The Director of Practice has documentation that a tax preparer has violated the law or regulations governing practice before the IRS. He may:

   a. Reprimand such person.

   b. Institute proceedings for disbarment.

   c. Institute proceedings for suspension.

   d. All of the above.

4) A tax preparer can recommend a position on the client's tax return as long as the position is:

   a. Reasonable.

   b. Not frivolous.

   c. Adequately disclosed.

   d. All of the above.

5) Which of the following statements is correct with respect to the limited practice of a registered tax return preparer:

a. A registered tax return preparer may represent the taxpayer for any year the taxpayer provides authorization, whether or not the preparer prepared the return in question.

b. A registered tax return preparer is only permitted to represent taxpayers before the examination and collection functions of the Internal Revenue Service.

c. If authorized by the taxpayer, a registered tax return preparer can sign consents to extend the statutory period for assessment or collection of tax.

d. A registered tax return preparer cannot receive refund checks.

6) Tiki is designated as a Registered Tax Return Preparer. His client requests his written advice on structuring assets within a corporation in order to reduce his taxes. Can Tiki provide this advice to his client?

a. No, his ability to practice is limited.

b. Yes, if the advice is disclosed on the return

c. Yes, because he is a registered tax return preparer

d. Yes, but only if he is experienced in that area

7) What is the penalty when a preparer fails to sign a form 1040 tax return due to reasonable cause?

a. $0

b. $50 for each occurrence

c. $50 for the first offense, and $250 for each additional failure

d. $100

8) Michael is designated as a registered tax return preparer by the IRS. He has a signed Form 2848 power of attorney for his client Armando, covering his 2011 tax return that Michael prepared. Michael did not preparer any other returns for Armando. Which of the following acts is Michael unable to perform?

a. Represent Armando during an appeal regarding his 2010 tax return

b. Discus Armando's 2011 return with the Taxpayer Advocate Service

c. Represent Armando during an examination of his 2011 return

d. Receive confidential information regarding Armando's 2011 tax return

9) For what purpose does a taxpayer use Form 8821, tax information authorization?

a. Appoint a third party designee

b. Revoke existing authority under a power of attorney

c. Designate an individual as a representative

d. Authorize the IRS to discuss and provide specific confidential tax return information to anyone designated

10) The Central Authorization File does not reflect which of the following authorizations?

a. Third party designee

b. Power of attorney

c. Tax information authorization

d. Oral tax information authorization

11) The new regulations for paid tax return preparers require all of the following, except:

a. Registration on the PTIN system

b. Competency testing

c. 15 hours of annual continuing education

d. Enrollment to practice before the IRS

Tax Return Preparer Competency Exam – Chapter 11 Quiz Rationale

For more practice questions, visit fastforwardacademy.com and access our FREE online question bank.

1) **d** A minimum of 15 hours of continuing education credit including two hours of ethics or professional conduct, three hours of Federal tax law updates, and 10 hours of Federal tax law topics, must be completed during each registration year.

2) **c** The use of the word "certified" is expressly forbidden in Section 10.30(a)(1) of Circular 230. An example of an acceptable description for registered tax return preparers is "designated as a registered tax return preparer by the Internal Revenue Service."

3) **d** The Secretary of the Treasury, or delegate, after notice and an opportunity for a proceeding, may censure, suspend, or disbar any practitioner from practice before the Internal Revenue Service if the practitioner is shown to be incompetent or disreputable, fails to comply with any regulation under the prohibited conduct standards of §10.52, or with intent to defraud, willfully and knowingly misleads or threatens a client or prospective client. Censure is a public reprimand.

4) **d** The practitioner cannot recommend frivolous or unreasonable positions to a client, and the practitioner must adequately advise the client as to the likelihood of the position being sustained and the basis upon which it is being made.

5) **d** A registered tax return preparer's ability to practice is generally limited to examinations with respect to a return he prepares. He may represent taxpayers only before customer service representatives, revenue agents, and examination officers. He cannot appear before collections or appeals, execute waivers, or receive refund checks.

6) **a** A registered tax return preparer's authorization to practice does not include the authority to provide tax advice to a client or another person except as necessary to prepare a tax return, claim for refund, or other document intended to be submitted to the Internal Revenue Service.

7) **a** The penalty is <u>$50</u> for each occurrence up to a maximum of <u>$25,000/year</u> unless it is shown that such failure is due to reasonable cause and not willful neglect.

8) **a** The ability to practice has limits for Registered Tax Return Preparers. One may not represent a taxpayer before certain offices of the IRS, such as Collection or Appeals, or regarding a return that he did not sign as the preparer.

9) **d** A third party designee is appointed by checking a box on a specific tax return. The authorization is specific to the tax return upon which it appears. Form 8821 authorizes any individual, corporation, firm, organization, or partnership the taxpayer designates to inspect and/or receive confidential information in any office of the IRS for the type of tax and the years or periods listed. Form 2848, Power of Attorney and Declaration of Representative designates a taxpayer's representative.

10) **a** Currently, the Third Party Designee (checkbox authorization) is not recorded on the CAF. Instead, during return processing, the authorization is recorded directly onto the account of the taxpayer.

11) **d** Circular 230 limits the practice of those "designated as" registered tax return preparers. Practice before the IRS comprehends all matters connected with a presentation to the IRS relating to a taxpayer's rights, privileges, or liabilities under laws or regulations administered by the IRS. Attorneys, CPAs, and Enrolled Agents are "enrolled" or "admitted" to practice without restriction.

Quick Quiz Answer Key

1.1 The last day Joe can file a claim for refund is April 15, 2015, three years after the date for filing his return. The IRS treats payments or returns made before the due date–without regard to extensions–as received on the due date.

1.2 The year Jill earns the right to the income is 2011. Under the accrual method, she must recognize the income in 2011.

1.3 She cannot file 1040-EZ because she is too old. In terms of simplicity, Form 1040A would be the next choice; however, this is a trick question. None of her social security is subject to tax. She is not required to file an income tax return because she does not have taxable income and does not need to file a claim for refund.

1.4 Jasmine has taxable income over $100,000 so she must use Form 1040.

1.5 Yes. The year of death is the last year to file a joint return.

2.1 Randy has to pay both income tax and self-employment tax on his salary, but only self-employment tax for the housing allowance. For income tax purposes, he only reports his salary, as housing allowance is not subject to income tax.

2.2 Divide the discount by the months remaining before maturity. Multiply this by the number of months in the calculation year. $150 / 60 x 6 = $15.

2.3 She must include all the dividends in gross income; however, a taxpayer in the 15% tax bracket pays no taxes on qualified dividends or capital gains.

2.4 She uses the property more than 10% of the time and must allocate expenses between rental and personal use. If 80% of the use is rented out at fair market rental rates, she can deduct 80% of the expenses from her rental income. Total expense of $3,000 x 80% = $2,400. Gross rental income of $10,000 – $2,400 of allowable expenses = $7,600 net rental income.

2.5 Her municipal bond interest is not subject to federal income tax; however, tax-free interest is part of provisional income. Provisional income is $55,000 and is $30,000 well above the upper base amount for her filing status. The maximum amount of benefits subject to tax is 85%, which makes her AGI $8,500.

3.1 His total basis is $38,240. Basis includes the purchase price plus the tax paid, reduced by depreciation.

3.2 $0. The amount of the assessment increases the basis of her property.

3.3 The dual basis rules apply since Jennifer received the gift when it was valued at less than her mother's basis. Jennifer recognizes neither gain nor loss under these rules because the selling price is between the FMV at the time of the gift and her mother's basis.

3.4 Louie has a $250,000 long-term loss. Basis steps-up at his father's death. Louie uses the property for investment purposes, which is important since no deduction is allowed on personal use property.

3.5 Sheila has a net long-term gain of $100. ($200 net LTCG - $100 net STCL)

4.1 They must recognize the entire gain of $575,000, as the summer home is not a main home for a period of 24 months in the 5-year period leading up to the sale.

4.2 Sales price of $340,000 less adjusted basis of $230,000 leaves net gain $110,000. She cannot exclude the portion of gain attributed to depreciation. Report the $20,000 of claimed depreciation as an unrecaptured Section 1250 gain. Therefore, the correct amount to exclude is $90,000. The rule for nonqualified use does not apply because it does not include any portion of the 5-year period ending on the date of the sale that is after the last date she uses the property as a main home.

4.3 She can exclude 2/3 of her interest or $4,000 from income. ($20,000 qualified expenses / $30,000 total proceeds = 66.667%)

4.4 $0. A beneficiary may exclude life insurance proceeds from income.

4.5 He can exclude the entire $80,000 from his U.S. income because his tax home is in Brazil, and he meets the physical presence test.

5.1 In general, a person under age 70.5 with taxable compensation can contribute to an IRA. Compensation for IRA purposes includes only Benjamin's wages of $800.

5.2 $11,000. Mary can contribute $6,000 and Gary can contribute $5,000.

5.3 He did not rollover the money within 60 days. His penalty $225. Since he uses the money for unreimbursed medical expenses, he may exclude the portion he pays for expenses that exceed 7.5% of his AGI. The exclusion is $2,750. He must pay the 10% penalty on the remaining $2,250.

5.4 He cannot deduct any of his expenses. John meets all of the tests to deduct his moving expenses, except the distance test. His new office must be at least 60 miles away from his former home (50+10).

5.5 He can exclude only $1,200 of monthly expenses. Alimony does not include child support, payments to maintain his property, or the use of his property.

6.1 Jill qualifies as a dependent on her parent's return. She can claim a standard deduction of $5,700 equal to her earned income for the year + $300 (but not more than the regular standard deduction amount).

6.2 She can consider her husband's expenses since they are married at the time of payment. She can only deduct the portion exceeding 7.5% of AGI. The allowable deduction is $1,250. Insurance premiums paid with pre-tax dollars from a cafeteria plan are not income to the employee, so no deduction is allowed on Schedule A. In general, an employee contribution for health insurance is deducted from wages on an after-tax basis except for certain plans established under Section 125.

6.3 Neither may claim a deduction. Marcus is not legally obligated to make the payment, and his mother did not make the payment. A deduction could be possible for his mother if he makes a direct gift to her, and she later makes the tax payment.

6.4 $300. The gift to his neighbor is not a charitable deduction, as the neighbor is not a qualifying charitable organization.

6.5 $0. Even if she pays the ticket, it would not qualify as a deduction. A taxpayer may not deduct fines or penalties. Certain legal fees are deductible (e.g., those related to doing or keeping a job, or producing or collecting taxable income). In this case, the legal fees are a personal expense, which is nondeductible.

7.1 Increase his taxable income by adjustment items to arrive at AMTI ($137,300 + $11,600 deduction + $25,900 exemptions = $174,800). AMTI exceeds $150,000 so his exemption reduces to $66,387 ($72,450 - $6,063). His tentative minimum tax is $28,187 ($108,413 x 26%). His AMT liability is $1,499 ($28,187 - $26,688).

7.2 His tax cannot be below the tentative minimum tax, so he can only claim a credit of $1,500 for prior year's minimum tax paid. He can carry the rest forward.

7.3 Neither. A return is not necessary since her interest is below $950, the standard deduction amount for a dependent. If her income exceeds $1,900 the "kiddie tax" would apply, subjecting the excess income to tax at the parent's rate.

7.4 Meg's nanny is considered a household employee. Meg must pay Social Security and Medicare taxes. Total Social Security and Medicare taxes are 13.3% of wages. Meg may withhold (5.65% or $113) from the nanny's wages. Meg is required to remit the entire 13.3% (which is $266) regardless of whether or not she withholds it from the nanny's pay. Household employers do not benefit from withholding rates under the HIRE Act.

7.5 No. He can report the 10% penalty directly on Form 1040.

7.6 Yes. A taxpayer requesting a complete waiver can elect to have the IRS calculate the penalty, while a taxpayer requesting a partial waiver must calculate the penalty on Form 2210.

7.7 No. The question does not indicate that the cost of care allows Camilla to work or look for a job.

7.8 Since this is a foreign adoption, he cannot claim the credit until 2012–the year the adoption becomes final.

7.9 Since law school is a graduate program, only the lifetime learning credit applies. Her credit is $2,000.

7.10 Jake satisfies the relationship, age and residency test for both Gloria and her mother, so Gloria can choose to claim her son for the EIC or let her mom claim the EIC.

8.1 She should receive a 1099-INT from her broker, a W-2 from her employer, and a Form 1099-MISC reporting compensation for services. The bank does not report interest payments less than $10 on form 1099-MISC.

8.2 David should maintain his records indefinitely, as there is no limit to the period of limitations. The IRS period for assessment does not start until a taxpayer files his return. For this reason, a taxpayer may benefit by filing a return–even if owing no tax.

8.3 $135. She files her return more than 60 days late. The minimum failure to file penalty is $135, or 100% of the tax due, whichever is less. Since she paid her tax on time, the penalty is $135.

8.4 No. Juanita is required to obtain Form 1099-R prior to electronically filing the return. She is also required to keep copies of Forms W-2, W-2G and 1099-R.

8.5 A taxpayer uses his own PIN with the self-select PIN method. If he enters it directly into the electronic return record, the preparer does not need Form 8879. Form 8879 is necessary only when a preparer enters the taxpayer PIN.

9.1 No. Each must file a separate schedule C.

9.2 Total cost of $200,000 includes materials and factory labor. Only 10% of inventory sold, so COGS is $20,000.

9.3 A cow not "used in the business" is not a capital asset. He must use Schedule F to figure his net profit or loss from regular farming operations. The gain on the sale is ordinary income.

9.4 She actively participates and can deduct $20,000 against ordinary income. The $25,000 special allowance is limited to 50% of the difference between $150,000 and MAGI ($150,000 - $110,000 x 50% = $20,000)

9.5 Certain items stated separately on Schedule K-1 reflect a distributive share of certain income or deduction items. These items are not calculated at the entity level and do not factor into "ordinary business income." Donna reports the gain as "long-term capital gain" on Schedule D as income distributed by the entity retains the same character in her hands.

10.1 His total deduction is $10,000. He expenses all $5,000 of the advertising as a start-up cost. He expenses $5,000 of organizational costs leaving $3,600 to amortize over 180 months. Amortization for 2011 is $80 ($3,600 x 4/180).

10.2 The deduction for self-employed health insurance is only available to a taxpayer filing Schedule C if the business has a net profit. Jamie cannot claim the deduction on Form 1040 as an adjustment to gross income. She may be able to deduct her premiums as a medical expense on Schedule A.

10.3 The entertainment meets the directly related test (directly before or after a substantial business discussion), so the cost is a business expense. The deduction is limited to $200, which is the face value of the tickets $400 subject to the 50% limit on entertainment expenses.

10.4 The payments made to Kenneth are considered made under a nonaccountable plan. His employer must report the payments as wages. However, Kenneth can claim his actual expenses on Form 2106, Employee Business Expense.

10.5 A self-employed taxpayer may deduct SIMPLE IRA elective deferrals to his own account equal to the smaller of two amounts– 100% of net earnings from self-employment or $11,500. In addition, he may contribute a matching contribution of an additional three percent of net earnings from self-employment. Net earnings from self-employment (after adjusting for 1/2 SE tax) equals $27,881 ($30,000 - $2,119). While the maximum contribution limits for a SEP IRA could be higher, Peter does not have enough income to benefit. The maximum SIMPLE IRA contribution is $12,336 ($11,500 + $836). The maximum SEP contribution is $5,576 ($27,881 x 20%).

11.1 Yes. In Circular 230 (effective August 2011), the final regulations clarify that either preparing or filing a document is practice before the IRS.

11.2 Yes. The authorization granted in 2008 ends April 15, 2009. A Third Party Designee is only valid for the return on which it appears. Tom should authorize Diego with–***Form 8821*** or ***Oral Tax Information Authorization***.

11.3 Roberta is a "registered tax return preparer" and must satisfy 15 hours of CPE each year.

11.4 July 1, 2016. An extension was obtained and the return became due on Oct 15, 2012. The applicable return period ends June 30, 2013. She must keep the records through June 30, 2016.

11.5 Michelle satisfied her due diligence requirements with the exception of maintaining the required records. As a result, she did not comply with all the due diligence requirements and may have to pay a $100 penalty.

Appendix

☐ CORRECTED (if checked)

RECIPIENT'S/LENDER'S name, address, and telephone number		* **Caution:** *The amount shown may not be fully deductible by you. Limits based on the loan amount and the cost and value of the secured property may apply. Also, you may only deduct interest to the extent it was incurred by you, actually paid by you, and not reimbursed by another person.*	OMB No. 1545-0901 **2011** Form **1098**	**Mortgage Interest Statement**
RECIPIENT'S federal identification no.	PAYER'S social security number	**1** Mortgage interest received from payer(s)/borrower(s)* $		**Copy B** **For Payer/Borrower** The information in boxes 1, 2, 3, and 4 is important tax information and is being furnished to the Internal Revenue Service. If you are required to file a return, a negligence penalty or other sanction may be imposed on you if the IRS determines that an underpayment of tax results because you overstated a deduction for this mortgage interest or for these points or because you did not report this refund of interest on your return.
PAYER'S/BORROWER'S name		**2** Points paid on purchase of principal residence $		
Street address (including apt. no.)		**3** Refund of overpaid interest $		
City, state, and ZIP code		**4** Mortgage insurance premiums $		
Account number (see instructions)		**5**		

Form **1098** (keep for your records) Department of the Treasury - Internal Revenue Service

Instructions for Payer/Borrower

A person (including a financial institution, a governmental unit, and a cooperative housing corporation) who is engaged in a trade or business and, in the course of such trade or business, received from you at least $600 of mortgage interest (including certain points) on any one mortgage in the calendar year must furnish this statement to you.

If you received this statement as the payer of record on a mortgage on which there are other borrowers, furnish each of the other borrowers with information about the proper distribution of amounts reported on this form. Each borrower is entitled to deduct only the amount he or she paid and points paid by the seller that represent his or her share of the amount allowable as a deduction. Each borrower may have to include in income a share of any amount reported in box 3.

If your mortgage payments were subsidized by a government agency, you may not be able to deduct the amount of the subsidy. See the instructions for Form 1040, Schedule A, C, or E for how to report the mortgage interest. Also, for more information, see Pub. 936 and Pub. 535.

Account number. May show an account or other unique number the lender has assigned to distinguish your account.

Box 1. Shows the mortgage interest received during the year. This amount includes interest on any obligation secured by real property, including a home equity, line of credit, or credit card loan. This amount does not include points, government subsidy payments, or seller payments on a "buy-down" mortgage. Such amounts are deductible by you only in certain circumstances. **Caution:** *If you prepaid interest in 2011 that accrued in full by January 15, 2012, this prepaid interest may be included in box 1. However, you cannot deduct the prepaid amount in 2011 even though it may be included in box 1.* If you hold a mortgage credit certificate and can claim the mortgage interest credit, see Form 8396. If the interest was paid on a mortgage, home equity, line of credit, or credit card loan secured by your personal residence, you may be subject to a deduction limitation.

Box 2. Not all points are reportable to you. Box 2 shows points you or the seller paid this year for the purchase of your principal residence that are required to be reported to you. Generally, these points are fully deductible in the year paid, but you must subtract seller-paid points from the basis of your residence. Other points not reported in box 2 may also be deductible. See Pub. 936 to figure the amount you can deduct.

Box 3. Do not deduct this amount. It is a refund (or credit) for overpayment(s) of interest you made in a prior year or years. If you itemized deductions in the year(s) you paid the interest, you may have to include part or all of the box 3 amount on the "Other income" line of your 2011 Form 1040. No adjustment to your prior year(s) tax return(s) is necessary. For more information, see Pub. 936 and *Itemized Deduction Recoveries* in Pub. 525.

Box 4. Shows mortgage insurance premiums which may qualify to be treated as deductible mortgage interest. See the Schedule A (Form 1040) instructions.

Box 5. The interest recipient may use this box to give you other information, such as the address of the property that secures the debt, real estate taxes, or insurance paid from escrow.

☐ CORRECTED (if checked)

RECIPIENT'S/LENDER'S name, address, and telephone number			OMB No. 1545-1576 **2011** Form **1098-E**	**Student Loan Interest Statement**
RECIPIENT'S federal identification no.	BORROWER'S social security number	**1** Student loan interest received by lender $		**Copy B** **For Borrower** This is important tax information and is being furnished to the Internal Revenue Service. If you are required to file a return, a negligence penalty or other sanction may be imposed on you if the IRS determines that an underpayment of tax results because you overstated a deduction for student loan interest.
BORROWER'S name Street address (including apt. no.) City, state, and ZIP code				
Account number (see instructions)		**2** If checked, box 1 does **not** include loan origination fees and/or capitalized interest for loans made before September 1, 2004 . . ☐		

Form **1098-E** (keep for your records) Department of the Treasury - Internal Revenue Service

Instructions for Borrower

A person (including a financial institution, a governmental unit, and an educational institution) that receives interest payments of $600 or more during the year on one or more qualified student loans must furnish this statement to you.

You may be able to deduct student loan interest that you actually paid in 2011 on your income tax return. However, you may not be able to deduct the full amount of interest reported on this statement. Do not contact the recipient/lender for explanations of the requirements for (and how to figure) any allowable deduction for the interest paid. Instead, for more information, see Pub. 970, Tax Benefits for Education, and the Student Loan Interest Deduction Worksheet in your Form 1040 or 1040A instructions.

Account number. May show an account or other unique number the lender assigned to distinguish your account.

Box 1. Shows the interest received by the lender during the year on one or more student loans made to you. For loans made on or after September 1, 2004, box 1 must include loan origination fees and capitalized interest received in 2011. If your loan was made before September 1, 2004, you may be able to deduct loan origination fees and capitalized interest not reported in box 1.

Box 2. If checked, indicates that loan origination fees and/or capitalized interest are **not** included in box 1 for loans made before September 1, 2004. See Pub. 970 for how to figure any deductible loan origination fees or capitalized interest.

☐ CORRECTED

FILER'S name, street address, city, state, ZIP code, and telephone number		1 Payments received for qualified tuition and related expenses $	OMB No. 1545-1574 **2011** Form **1098-T**	**Tuition Statement**
		2 Amounts billed for qualified tuition and related expenses $		
FILER'S federal identification no.	STUDENT'S social security number	3 If this box is checked, your educational institution has changed its reporting method for 2011 ☐		**Copy B** **For Student**
STUDENT'S name		4 Adjustments made for a prior year $	5 Scholarships or grants $	This is important tax information and is being furnished to the Internal Revenue Service.
Street address (including apt. no.)		6 Adjustments to scholarships or grants for a prior year $	7 Checked if the amount in box 1 or 2 includes amounts for an academic period beginning January - March 2012 ► ☐	
City, state, and ZIP code				
Service Provider/Acct. No. (see instr.)	8 Checked if at least half-time student ☐	9 Checked if a graduate student ☐	10 Ins. contract reimb./refund $	

Form **1098-T** (keep for your records) Department of the Treasury - Internal Revenue Service

Instructions for Student

An eligible educational institution, such as a college or university in which you are enrolled, and an insurer who makes reimbursements or refunds of qualified tuition and related expenses to you must furnish this statement to you. You, or the person who can claim you as a dependent, may be able to claim an education credit on Form 1040 or 1040A for the qualified tuition and related expenses that were actually paid in 2011. To see if you qualify for the credit, see Pub. 970, Tax Benefits for Education; Form 8863, Education Credits; and the Form 1040 or 1040A instructions.

Institutions may report either payments received in box 1 or amounts billed in box 2. The amount shown in box 1 or 2 may represent an amount other than the amount actually paid in 2011. Your institution must include its name, address, and information contact telephone number on this statement. It may also include contact information for a service provider. Although the service provider may be able to answer certain questions about the statement, do not contact them or the filer for explanations of the requirements for (and how to figure) any education credit that you may claim.

Account number. May show an account or other unique number the filer assigned to distinguish your account.

Box 1. Shows the total payments received from any source for qualified tuition and related expenses less any related reimbursements or refunds.

Box 2. Shows the total amounts billed for qualified tuition and related expenses less any related reductions in charges.

Box 3. Shows whether your institution changed its method of reporting for 2011. It has changed its method of reporting if the method (payments received or amounts billed) used for 2011 is different than the reporting method used for 2010. You should be aware of this change in figuring your education credits. The credits are allowable only for amounts actually paid during the year and not amounts reported as billed, but not paid, during the year.

Box 4. Shows any adjustment made for a prior year for qualified tuition and related expenses that were reported on a prior year Form 1098-T. This amount may reduce any allowable education credit that you claimed for the prior year. See "recapture" in the index to Pub. 970 to report a reduction in your education credit or tuition and fees deduction.

Box 5. Shows the total of all scholarships or grants administered and processed by the eligible educational institution. The amount of scholarships or grants for the calendar year (including those not reported by the institution) may reduce the amount of the education credit you claim for the year.

Box 6. Shows adjustments to scholarships or grants for a prior year. This amount may affect the amount of any allowable tuition and fees deduction or education credit that you claimed for the prior year. You may have to file an amended income tax return (Form 1040X) for the prior year.

Box 7. Shows whether the amount in box 1 or 2 includes amounts for an academic period beginning January-March 2012. See Pub. 970 for how to report these amounts.

Box 8. Shows whether you are considered to be carrying at least one-half the normal full-time workload for your course of study at the reporting institution. If you are at least a half-time student for at least one academic period that begins during the year, you meet one of the requirements for the American Opportunity credit. You do not have to meet the workload requirement to qualify for the lifetime learning credit.

Box 9. Shows whether you are considered to be enrolled in a program leading to a graduate degree, graduate-level certificate, or other recognized graduate-level educational credential. If you are enrolled in a graduate program, you are not eligible for the American Opportunity credit, but you may qualify for the lifetime learning credit.

Box 10. Shows the total amount of reimbursements or refunds of qualified tuition and related expenses made by an insurer. The amount of reimbursements or refunds for the calendar year may reduce the amount of any education credit you can claim for the year.

☐ CORRECTED (if checked)

PAYER'S name, street address, city, state, ZIP code, and telephone no.	1a Date of sale or exchange	OMB No. 1545-0715	Proceeds From Broker and Barter Exchange Transactions
	1b CUSIP no.	2010 Form 1099-B	
	2 Stocks, bonds, etc. $	Reported to IRS ☐ Gross proceeds ☐ Gross proceeds less commissions and option premiums	
PAYER'S federal identification number / RECIPIENT'S identification number	3 Bartering $	4 Federal income tax withheld $	
RECIPIENT'S name	5 No. of shares exchanged	6 Classes of stock exchanged	**Copy B For Recipient** This is important tax information and is being furnished to the Internal Revenue Service. If you are required to file a return, a negligence penalty or other sanction may be imposed on you if this income is taxable and the IRS determines that it has not been reported.
Street address (including apt. no.)	7 Description		
City, state, and ZIP code	8 Profit or (loss) realized in 2010 $	9 Unrealized profit or (loss) on open contracts—12/31/2009 $	
CORPORATION'S name	10 Unrealized profit or (loss) on open contracts–12/31/2010 $	11 Aggregate profit or (loss) $	
Account number (see instructions)	12 If the box is checked, the recipient cannot take a loss on their tax return based on the amount in box 2 . . ☐		

Form **1099-B** (keep for your records) Department of the Treasury - Internal Revenue Service

Instructions for Recipient

Brokers and barter exchanges must report proceeds from transactions to you and the IRS on Form 1099-B. Reporting is also required when your broker knows or has reason to know that a corporation in which you own stock has had a change in control or a substantial change in capital structure. You may be required to recognize gain from the receipt of cash, stock, or other property that was exchanged for the corporation's stock. If your broker reported this type of transaction to you, the corporation is identified in the box below your name and address on Form 1099-B.

Recipient's identification number. For your protection, this form may show only the last four digits of your social security number (SSN), individual taxpayer identification number (ITIN), or adoption taxpayer identification number (ATIN). However, the issuer has reported your complete identification number to the IRS and, where applicable, to state and/or local governments.

Account number. May show an account or other unique number the payer assigned to distinguish your account.

Box 1a. Shows the trade date of the transaction. For aggregate reporting, no entry will be present.

Box 1b. For broker transactions, may show the CUSIP (Committee on Uniform Security Identification Procedures) number of the item reported.

Box 2. Shows the aggregate cash proceeds from transactions involving stocks, bonds, other debt obligations, commodities, or forward contracts. May show the proceeds from the disposition of your interest(s) in a widely held fixed investment trust. May also show the aggregate amount of cash and the fair market value of any stock or other property received in a change in control or substantial change in capital structure arising from the corporate transfer of property to a foreign corporation. Losses on forward contracts are shown in parentheses. This box does not include proceeds from regulated futures contracts. The broker must indicate whether gross proceeds or gross proceeds less commissions and option premiums were reported to the IRS. Report this amount on Schedule D (Form 1040), Capital Gains and Losses. But, for changes in control or substantial changes in capital structure, see box 12.

Box 3. Shows the cash you received, the fair market value of any property or services you received, and/or the fair market value of any trade credits or scrip credited to your account by a barter exchange. See Pub. 525, Taxable and Nontaxable Income, for information on how to report this income.

Box 4. Shows backup withholding. Generally, a payer must backup withhold at a 28% rate if you did not furnish your taxpayer identification number to the payer. See Form W-9, Request for Taxpayer Identification Number and Certification, for information on backup withholding. Include this amount on your income tax return as tax withheld.

Box 5. Shows the number of shares of the corporation's stock that you held which were exchanged in the change in control or substantial change in capital structure.

Box 6. Shows the class or classes of the corporation's stock that were exchanged in the change in control or substantial change in capital structure.

Box 7. Shows a brief description of the item or service for which the proceeds or bartering income is being reported. For regulated futures contracts and forward contracts, "RFC" or other appropriate description may be shown.

Regulated Futures Contracts:

Box 8. Shows the profit or (loss) realized on regulated futures or foreign currency contracts closed during 2010.

Box 9. Shows any year-end adjustment to the profit or (loss) shown in box 8 due to open contracts on December 31, 2009.

Box 10. Shows the unrealized profit or (loss) on open contracts held in your account on December 31, 2010. These are considered sold as of that date. This will become an adjustment reported in box 9 in 2011.

Box 11. Boxes 8, 9, and 10 are all used to figure the aggregate profit or (loss) on regulated futures or foreign currency contracts for the year. Include this amount on your 2010 Form 6781.

Box 12. If checked, you cannot take a loss on your tax return based on gross proceeds from an acquisition of control or substantial change in capital structure reported in box 2. Do not report this loss on Schedule D (Form 1040). The broker should advise you of any losses on a separate statement.

☐ CORRECTED (if checked)

CREDITOR'S name, street address, city, state, ZIP code, and telephone no.	1 Date canceled	OMB No. 1545-1424	Cancellation of Debt
	2 Amount of debt canceled $	2011	
	3 Interest if included in box 2 $	Form **1099-C**	
CREDITOR'S federal identification number | DEBTOR'S identification number	4 Debt description		**Copy B** **For Debtor** This is important tax information and is being furnished to the Internal Revenue Service. If you are required to file a return, a negligence penalty or other sanction may be imposed on you if taxable income results from this transaction and the IRS determines that it has not been reported.
DEBTOR'S name			
Street address (including apt. no.)	5 If checked, the debtor was personally liable for repayment of the debt . . . . ▶ ☐		
City, state, and ZIP code			
Account number (see instructions)	6 Bankruptcy (if checked) ☐	7 Fair market value of property $	

Form **1099-C** (keep for your records) Department of the Treasury - Internal Revenue Service

Instructions for Debtor

If a Federal Government agency, certain agencies connected with the Federal Government, financial institution, credit union, or an organization having a significant trade or business of lending money (such as a finance or credit card company) cancels or forgives a debt you owe of $600 or more, this form must be provided to you. Generally, if you are an individual, you must include all canceled amounts, even if less than $600, on the "Other income" line of Form 1040. If you are a corporation, partnership, or other entity, report the canceled debt on your tax return. See the tax return instructions.

However, some canceled debts are not includible, or fully includible, in your income, such as certain student loans, certain debts reduced by the seller after purchase, qualified farm debt, qualified real property business debt, qualified principal residence debt, or debts canceled in bankruptcy. See Pub. 4681. Do not report a canceled debt as income if you did not deduct it but would have been able to do so on your tax return if you had paid it. Also, do not include canceled debts in your income to the extent you were insolvent immediately before the cancellation of the debt. If you exclude a canceled debt from your income, file Form 982.

Account number. May show an account or other unique number the creditor assigned to distinguish your account.

Box 1. Shows the date the debt was canceled.

Box 2. Shows the amount of debt canceled. **Note:** If you do not agree with this amount, contact your creditor.

Box 3. Shows interest if included in the canceled debt in box 2. See Pub. 4681 to see if you must include the interest in gross income.

Box 4. Shows a description of the debt. If box 7 is completed, box 4 shows a description of the property.

Box 5. Shows whether you were personally liable for repayment of the debt when the debt was created or, if modified, at the time of the last modification. See Pub. 4681 for reporting instructions.

Box 6. If the box is marked, the creditor has indicated the debt was canceled in a bankruptcy proceeding.

Box 7. If, in the same calendar year, a foreclosure or abandonment of property occurred in connection with the cancellation of the debt, the fair market value (FMV) of the property will be shown, or you will receive a separate Form 1099-A. Generally, the gross foreclosure bid price is considered to be the FMV. For an abandonment or voluntary conveyance in lieu of foreclosure, the FMV is generally the appraised value of the property. You may have income or loss because of the acquisition or abandonment. See Pub. 4681 for information about foreclosures and abandonments. If the property was your main home, see Pub. 523 to figure any taxable gain or ordinary income.

☐ CORRECTED (if checked)

PAYER'S name, street address, city, state, ZIP code, and telephone no.		1a Total ordinary dividends $	OMB No. 1545-0110 **2011** Form **1099-DIV**	**Dividends and Distributions**
		1b Qualified dividends $		
		2a Total capital gain distr. $	2b Unrecap. Sec. 1250 gain $	**Copy B** **For Recipient**
PAYER'S federal identification number	RECIPIENT'S identification number	2c Section 1202 gain $	2d Collectibles (28%) gain $	
RECIPIENT'S name		3 Nondividend distributions $	**4 Federal income tax withheld** $	This is important tax information and is being furnished to the Internal Revenue Service. If you are required to file a return, a negligence penalty or other sanction may be imposed on you if this income is taxable and the IRS determines that it has not been reported.
			5 Investment expenses $	
Street address (including apt. no.)		6 Foreign tax paid $	7 Foreign country or U.S. possession	
City, state, and ZIP code		8 Cash liquidation distributions $	9 Noncash liquidation distributions $	
Account number (see instructions)				

Form **1099-DIV** (keep for your records) Department of the Treasury - Internal Revenue Service

Instructions for Recipient

Account number. May show an account or other unique number the payer assigned to distinguish your account.

Box 1a. Shows total ordinary dividends that are taxable. Include this amount on line 9a of Form 1040 or 1040A. Also, report it on Schedule B (Form 1040 or 1040A), if required.

The amount shown may be dividends a corporation paid directly to you as a participant (or beneficiary of a participant) in an employee stock ownership plan (ESOP). Report it as a dividend on your Form 1040/1040A but treat it as a plan distribution, not as investment income, for any other purpose.

Box 1b. Shows the portion of the amount in box 1a that may be eligible for the 15% or zero capital gains rates. See Form 1040/1040A instructions for how to determine this amount. Report the eligible amount on line 9b, Form 1040 or 1040A.

Box 2a. Shows total capital gain distributions from a regulated investment company or real estate investment trust. Report the amounts shown in box 2a on Schedule D (Form 1040), line 13. But, if no amount is shown in boxes 2c–2d and your only capital gains and losses are capital gain distributions, you may be able to report the amounts shown in box 2a on line 13 of Form 1040 (line 10 of Form 1040A) rather than Schedule D. See the Form 1040/1040A instructions.

Box 2b. Shows the portion of the amount in box 2a that is unrecaptured section 1250 gain from certain depreciable real property. Report this amount on the Unrecaptured Section 1250 Gain Worksheet–Line 19 in the Schedule D instructions (Form 1040).

Box 2c. Shows the portion of the amount in box 2a that is section 1202 gain from certain small business stock that may be subject to a 50% exclusion and certain empowerment zone business stock that may be subject to a 60% exclusion. See the Schedule D (Form 1040) instructions.

Box 2d. Shows 28% rate gain from sales or exchanges of collectibles. If required, use this amount when completing the 28% Rate Gain Worksheet–Line 18 in the instructions for Schedule D (Form 1040).

Box 3. Shows the part of the distribution that is nontaxable because it is a return of your cost (or other basis). You must reduce your cost (or other basis) by this amount for figuring gain or loss when you sell your stock. But if you get back all your cost (or other basis), report future distributions as capital gains. See Pub. 550, Investment Income and Expenses.

Box 4. Shows backup withholding. A payer must backup withhold on certain payments if you did not give your taxpayer identification number to the payer. See Form W-9, Request for Taxpayer Identification Number and Certification, for information on backup withholding. Include this amount on your income tax return as tax withheld.

Box 5. Shows your share of expenses of a nonpublicly offered regulated investment company, generally a nonpublicly offered mutual fund. If you file Form 1040, you may deduct these expenses on the "Other expenses" line on Schedule A (Form 1040) subject to the 2% limit. This amount is included in box 1a.

Box 6. Shows the foreign tax that you may be able to claim as a deduction or a credit on Form 1040. See the Form 1040 instructions.

Box 7. This box should be left blank if a regulated investment company reported the foreign tax shown in box 6.

Boxes 8 and 9. Shows cash and noncash liquidation distributions.

Nominees. If this form includes amounts belonging to another person, you are considered a nominee recipient. You must file Form 1099-DIV with the IRS for each of the other owners to show their share of the income, and you must furnish a Form 1099-DIV to each. A husband or wife is not required to file a nominee return to show amounts owned by the other. See the 2011 General Instructions for Certain Information Returns.

☐ CORRECTED (if checked)

PAYER'S name, street address, city, state, ZIP code, and telephone no.		1 Unemployment compensation $	OMB No. 1545-0120 **2011** Form **1099-G**	**Certain Government Payments**
		2 State or local income tax refunds, credits, or offsets $		
PAYER'S federal identification number	RECIPIENT'S identification number	3 Box 2 amount is for tax year	4 Federal income tax withheld $	**Copy B** **For Recipient**
RECIPIENT'S name		5 ATAA/RTAA payments $	6 Taxable grants $	This is important tax information and is being furnished to the Internal Revenue Service. If you are required to file a return, a negligence penalty or other sanction may be imposed on you if this income is taxable and the IRS determines that it has not been reported.
Street address (including apt. no.)		7 Agriculture payments $	8 If checked, box 2 is trade or business income ▶ ☐	
City, state, and ZIP code		9 Market gain $		
Account number (see instructions)		10a State / 10b State identification no.	11 State income tax withheld $	

Form **1099-G** (keep for your records) Department of the Treasury - Internal Revenue Service

Instructions for Recipient

Account number. May show an account or other unique number the payer has assigned to distinguish your account.

Box 1. Shows the total unemployment compensation paid to you this year. Combine the box 1 amounts from all Forms 1099-G and report the total as income on the unemployment compensation line of your tax return. Except as explained below, this is your taxable amount. If you are married filing jointly, each spouse must figure his or her taxable amount separately. If you expect to receive these benefits in the future, you can ask the payer to withhold federal income tax from each payment. Or, you can make estimated tax payments. For details, see Form 1040-ES. If you made contributions to a governmental unemployment compensation program or to a governmental paid family leave program and received a payment from that program, the payer must issue a separate Form 1099-G to report this amount to you. If you itemize deductions, you may deduct your contributions on Schedule A (Form 1040) as taxes paid. If you do not itemize, you only need to include in income the amount that is in excess of your contributions.

Box 2. Shows refunds, credits, or offsets of state or local income tax you received. It may be taxable to you if you deducted the state or local income tax paid on Schedule A (Form 1040). Even if you did not receive the amount shown, for example, because it was credited to your state or local estimated tax, it is still taxable if it was deducted. If you received interest on this amount, you should receive Form 1099-INT for the interest. However, the payer may include interest of less than $600 in the blank box next to Box 9 on Form 1099-G. Regardless of whether the interest is reported to you, report it as interest income on your tax return. See your tax return instructions.

Box 3. Identifies the tax year for which the box 2 refunds, credits, or offsets shown were made. If there is no entry in this box, the refund is for 2010 taxes.

Box 4. Shows backup withholding or withholding you requested on unemployment compensation, Commodity Credit Corporation (CCC) loans, or certain crop disaster payments. Generally, a payer must backup withhold on certain payments if you did not give your taxpayer identification number to the payer. See Form W-9 for information on backup withholding. Include this amount on your income tax return as tax withheld.

Box 5. Shows alternative trade adjustment assistance (ATAA) and/or reemployment trade adjustment assistance (RTAA) payments you received. Include on Form 1040 on the "Other income" line. See the Form 1040 instructions.

Box 6. Shows taxable grants you received from a federal, state, or local government.

Box 7. Shows your taxable Department of Agriculture payments. If the payer shown is anyone other than the Department of Agriculture, it means the payer has received a payment, as a nominee, that is taxable to you. This may represent the entire agricultural subsidy payment received on your behalf by the nominee, or it may be your pro rata share of the original payment. See Pub. 225 and the Instructions for Schedule F (Form 1040) for information about where to report this income. Partnerships, see Form 8825 for how to report.

Box 8. If this box is checked, the amount in box 2 is attributable to an income tax that applies exclusively to income from a trade or business and is not a tax of general application. If taxable, report the amount in box 2 on Schedule C or F (Form 1040), as appropriate.

Box 9. Shows market gain on CCC loans whether repaid using cash or CCC certificates. See the Instructions for Schedule F (Form 1040).

Boxes 10a–11. State income tax withheld reporting boxes.

☐ CORRECTED (if checked)

PAYER'S name, street address, city, state, ZIP code, and telephone no.		Payer's RTN (optional)	OMB No. 1545-0112	
		1 Interest income $	2011	**Interest Income**
		2 Early withdrawal penalty $	Form **1099-INT**	
PAYER'S federal identification number	RECIPIENT'S identification number	3 Interest on U.S. Savings Bonds and Treas. obligations $		**Copy B For Recipient**
RECIPIENT'S name		4 Federal income tax withheld $	5 Investment expenses $	This is important tax information and is being furnished to the Internal Revenue Service. If you are required to file a return, a negligence penalty or other sanction may be imposed on you if this income is taxable and the IRS determines that it has not been reported.
Street address (including apt. no.)		6 Foreign tax paid $	7 Foreign country or U.S. possession	
City, state, and ZIP code		8 Tax-exempt interest $	9 Specified private activity bond interest $	
Account number (see instructions)		10 Tax-exempt bond CUSIP no. (see instructions)		

Form **1099-INT** (keep for your records) Department of the Treasury - Internal Revenue Service

Instructions for Recipient

Account number. May show an account or other unique number the payer assigned to distinguish your account.

Box 1. Shows taxable interest paid to you during the calendar year by the payer. This does not include interest shown in box 3. May also show the total amount of the credits from clean renewable energy bonds, Gulf tax credit bonds, qualified forestry conservation bonds, new clean renewable energy bonds, qualified energy conservation bonds, qualified zone academy bonds, Midwestern tax credit bonds, qualified school construction bonds, and build America bonds that must be included in your interest income. These amounts were treated as paid to you during 2011 on the credit allowance dates (March 15, June 15, September 15, and December 15). For more information, see Form 8912, Credit to Holders of Tax Credit Bonds.

Box 2. Shows interest or principal forfeited because of early withdrawal of time savings. You may deduct this amount to figure your adjusted gross income on your income tax return. See the instructions for Form 1040 to see where to take the deduction.

Box 3. Shows interest on U.S. Savings Bonds, Treasury bills, Treasury bonds, and Treasury notes. This may or may not all be taxable. See Pub. 550. This interest is exempt from state and local income taxes. This interest is not included in box 1.

Box 4. Shows backup withholding. Generally, a payer must backup withhold if you did not furnish your taxpayer identification number (TIN) or you did not furnish the correct TIN to the payer. See Form W-9. Include this amount on your income tax return as tax withheld.

Box 5. Any amount shown is your share of investment expenses of a single-class REMIC. If you file Form 1040, you may deduct these expenses on the "Other expenses" line of Schedule A (Form 1040) subject to the 2% limit. This amount is included in box 1.

Box 6. Shows foreign tax paid. You may be able to claim this tax as a deduction or a credit on your Form 1040. See your Form 1040 instructions.

Box 8. Shows tax-exempt interest, including exempt-interest dividends from a mutual fund or other regulated investment company, paid to you during the calendar year by the payer. Report this amount on line 8b of Form 1040 or Form 1040A. This amount may be subject to backup withholding. See box 4.

Box 9. Shows tax-exempt interest subject to the alternative minimum tax. This amount is included in box 8. See the Instructions for Form 6251.

Box 10. Shows CUSIP number(s) for tax-exempt bond(s) on which tax-exempt interest was paid to you during the calendar year and reported in box 8. If blank, no CUSIP number was issued for the bond(s).

Nominees. If this form includes amounts belonging to another person(s), you are considered a nominee recipient. Complete a Form 1099-INT for each of the other owners showing the income allocable to each. File Copy A of the form with the IRS. Furnish Copy B to each owner. List yourself as the "payer" and the other owner(s) as the "recipient." File Form(s) 1099-INT with Form 1096 with the Internal Revenue Service Center for your area. On Form 1096 list yourself as the "filer." A husband or wife is not required to file a nominee return to show amounts owned by the other.

☐ CORRECTED (if checked)

PAYER'S name, street address, city, state, ZIP code, and telephone no.		1 Original issue discount for 2011* $	OMB No. 1545-0117 **2011** Form **1099-OID**	**Original Issue Discount**
		2 Other periodic interest $		
PAYER'S federal identification number	RECIPIENT'S identification number	3 Early withdrawal penalty $	**4 Federal income tax withheld** $	**Copy B For Recipient**
RECIPIENT'S name		5 Description		This is important tax information and is being furnished to the Internal Revenue Service. If you are required to file a return, a negligence penalty or other sanction may be imposed on you if this income is taxable and the IRS determines that it has not been reported.
Street address (including apt. no.)		6 Original issue discount on U.S. Treasury obligations* $		
City, state, and ZIP code		7 Investment expenses $		
Account number (see instructions)		* This may not be the correct figure to report on your income tax return. See instructions on the back.		

Form **1099-OID** (keep for your records) Department of the Treasury - Internal Revenue Service

Instructions for Recipient

Original issue discount (OID) is the excess of an obligation's stated redemption price at maturity over its issue price (acquisition price for a stripped bond or coupon). OID is taxable as interest over the life of the obligation. If you are the holder of an OID obligation, generally you must include an amount of OID in your gross income each year you hold the obligation. Obligations that may have OID include a bond, debenture, note, certificate, or other evidence of indebtedness having a term of more than 1 year. For example, the OID rules may apply to certificates of deposit (CDs), time deposits, bonus savings plans, and other deposit arrangements, especially if the payment of interest is deferred until maturity. In addition, the OID rules apply to Treasury inflation-protected securities. See Pub. 550, Investment Income and Expenses, for more information.

If, as the record holder, you receive Form 1099-OID showing amounts belonging to another person, you are considered a nominee recipient. Complete a Form 1099-OID for each of the other owners showing the amounts allocable to each. File Copy A of the form with the IRS. Furnish Copy B to each owner. List yourself as the "payer" and the other owner as the "recipient." File Form(s) 1099-OID with Form 1096, Annual Summary and Transmittal of U.S. Information Returns, with the Internal Revenue Service Center for your area. On Form 1096, list yourself as the "filer." A husband or wife is not required to file a nominee return to show amounts owned by the other. If you bought or sold an obligation during the year and you are not a nominee, you are not required to issue or file Form 1099-OID showing the OID or stated interest allocable to the seller/buyer of the obligation.

Account number. May show an account or other unique number the payer assigned to distinguish your account.

Box 1. Shows the OID on the obligation for the part of the year you owned it. Report the amount in box 1 as interest income on your income tax return. However, depending on the type of debt instrument, the issue or acquisition date, and other factors (for example, if you paid acquisition or bond premium, or the obligation is a stripped bond or coupon), you may have to figure the correct amount of OID to report on your return. See Pub. 1212, Guide to Original Issue Discount (OID) Instruments, for details on how to figure the correct OID.

Box 2. Shows other interest on this obligation for the year, which is an amount separate from the OID. If you held the obligation the entire year, report this amount as interest income on your tax return. If you disposed of the obligation or acquired it from another holder during the year, see Pub. 550 for reporting instructions. If there is an amount in both boxes 2 and 6, the amount in box 2 is interest on a U.S. Treasury obligation and is exempt from state and local income taxes.

Box 3. Shows interest or principal forfeited if you withdrew the money before the maturity date of the obligation, such as from a CD. You may deduct this amount to figure your adjusted gross income on your income tax return. See the instructions for Form 1040 to see where to take the deduction.

Box 4. Shows backup withholding. Generally, a payer must backup withhold if you did not furnish your taxpayer identification number (TIN) or you did not furnish the correct TIN to the payer. See Form W-9, Request for Taxpayer Identification Number and Certification, for information on backup withholding. Include this amount on your income tax return as tax withheld.

Box 5. Shows the identification number (CUSIP number) or description of the obligation. The description may include the stock exchange, issuer, coupon rate, and year of maturity.

Box 6. Shows OID on a U.S. Treasury obligation for the part of the year you owned it. Report this amount as interest income on your federal income tax return, and see Pub. 1212 to figure any appropriate adjustments to this amount. This OID is exempt from state and local income taxes and is not included in box 1.

Box 7. Any amount shown is your share of investment expenses of a single-class REMIC. If you file Form 1040, you may deduct these expenses on the "Other expenses" line of Schedule A (Form 1040) subject to the 2% limit. This amount is included in box 2.

☐ CORRECTED (if checked)

PAYER'S name, street address, city, state, ZIP code, and telephone no.		1 Rents $	OMB No. 1545-0115	Miscellaneous Income
		2 Royalties $	2011 Form 1099-MISC	
		3 Other income $	4 Federal income tax withheld $	Copy B For Recipient
PAYER'S federal identification number	RECIPIENT'S identification number	5 Fishing boat proceeds $	6 Medical and health care payments $	
RECIPIENT'S name		7 Nonemployee compensation $	8 Substitute payments in lieu of dividends or interest $	This is important tax information and is being furnished to the Internal Revenue Service. If you are required to file a return, a negligence penalty or other sanction may be imposed on you if this income is taxable and the IRS determines that it has not been reported.
Street address (including apt. no.)		9 Payer made direct sales of $5,000 or more of consumer products to a buyer (recipient) for resale ► ☐	10 Crop insurance proceeds $	
City, state, and ZIP code		11	12	
Account number (see instructions)		13 Excess golden parachute payments $	14 Gross proceeds paid to an attorney $	
15a Section 409A deferrals $	15b Section 409A income $	16 State tax withheld $ $	17 State/Payer's state no.	18 State income $ $

Form **1099-MISC** (keep for your records) Department of the Treasury - Internal Revenue Service

Instructions for Recipient

Account number. May show an account or other unique number the payer assigned to distinguish your account.

Amounts shown may be subject to self-employment (SE) tax. If your net income from self-employment is $400 or more, you must file a return and compute your SE tax on Schedule SE (Form 1040). See Pub. 334 for more information. If no income or social security and Medicare taxes were withheld and you are still receiving these payments, see Form 1040-ES. Individuals must report these amounts as explained in the box 7 instructions on this page. Corporations, fiduciaries, or partnerships must report the amounts on the proper line of their tax returns.

Form 1099-MISC incorrect? If this form is incorrect or has been issued in error, contact the payer. If you cannot get this form corrected, attach an explanation to your tax return and report your income correctly.

Boxes 1 and 2. Report rents from real estate on Schedule E (Form 1040). However, report rents on Schedule C (Form 1040) if you provided significant services to the tenant, sold real estate as a business, or rented personal property as a business. Report royalties from oil, gas, or mineral properties, copyrights, and patents on Schedule E (Form 1040). However, report payments for a working interest as explained in the box 7 instructions. For royalties on timber, coal, and iron ore, see Pub. 544.

Box 3. Generally, report this amount on the "Other income" line of Form 1040 and identify the payment. The amount shown may be payments received as the beneficiary of a deceased employee, prizes, awards, taxable damages, Indian gaming profits, or other taxable income. See Pub. 525. If it is trade or business income, report this amount on Schedule C or F (Form 1040).

Box 4. Shows backup withholding or withholding on Indian gaming profits. Generally, a payer must backup withhold if you did not furnish your taxpayer identification number. See Form W-9 and Pub. 505 for more information. Report this amount on your income tax return as tax withheld.

Box 5. An amount in this box means the fishing boat operator considers you self-employed. Report this amount on Schedule C (Form 1040). See Pub. 334.

Box 6. For individuals, report on Schedule C (Form 1040).

Box 7. Shows nonemployee compensation. If you are in the trade or business of catching fish, box 7 may show cash you received for the sale of fish. If the amount in this box is SE income, report it on Schedule C or F (Form 1040), and complete Schedule SE (Form 1040). You received this form instead of Form W-2 because the payer did not consider you an employee and did not withhold income tax or social security and Medicare tax. If you believe you are an employee and cannot get the payer to correct this form, report the amount from box 7 on Form 1040, line 7 (or Form 1040NR, line 8). You must also complete Form 8919 and attach it to your return. If you are not an employee but the amount in this box is not SE income (for example, it is income from a sporadic activity or a hobby) report it on Form 1040, line 21 (or Form 1040NR, line 21).

Box 8. Shows substitute payments in lieu of dividends or tax-exempt interest received by your broker on your behalf as a result of a loan of your securities. Report on the "Other income" line of Form 1040.

Box 9. If checked, $5,000 or more of sales of consumer products was paid to you on a buy-sell, deposit-commission, or other basis. A dollar amount does not have to be shown. Generally, report any income from your sale of these products on Schedule C (Form 1040).

Box 10. Report this amount on Schedule F (Form 1040).

Box 13. Shows your total compensation of excess golden parachute payments subject to a 20% excise tax. See the Form 1040 instructions for where to report.

Box 14. Shows gross proceeds paid to an attorney in connection with legal services. Report only the taxable part as income on your return.

Box 15a. May show current year deferrals as a nonemployee under a nonqualified deferred compensation (NQDC) plan that is subject to the requirements of section 409A, plus any earnings on current and prior year deferrals.

Box 15b. Shows income as a nonemployee under an NQDC plan that does not meet the requirements of section 409A. This amount is also included in box 7 as nonemployee compensation. Any amount included in box 15a that is currently taxable is also included in this box. This income is also subject to a substantial additional tax to be reported on Form 1040. See "Total Tax" in the Form 1040 instructions.

Boxes 16–18. Shows state or local income tax withheld from the payments.

☐ CORRECTED (if checked)

PAYER'S name, address, ZIP code, federal identification number, and telephone number	1 Gross winnings	2 Federal income tax withheld	OMB No. 1545-0238 **2011** **Form W-2G** **Certain Gambling Winnings**
	3 Type of wager	4 Date won	
	5 Transaction	6 Race	
	7 Winnings from identical wagers	8 Cashier	
WINNER'S name, address (including apt. no.), and ZIP code	9 Winner's taxpayer identification no.	10 Window	This is important tax information and is being furnished to the Internal Revenue Service. If you are required to file a return, a negligence penalty or other sanction may be imposed on you if this income is taxable and the IRS determines that it has not been reported.
	11 First I.D.	12 Second I.D.	
	13 State/Payer's state identification no.	14 State income tax withheld	
Under penalties of perjury, I declare that, to the best of my knowledge and belief, the name, address, and taxpayer identification number that I have furnished correctly identify me as the recipient of this payment and any payments from identical wagers, and that no other person is entitled to any part of these payments. **Signature ▶** **Date ▶**			**Copy C** **For Winner's Records**

Form **W-2G** Department of the Treasury - Internal Revenue Service

Instructions to Winner

Box 1. The payer must furnish a Form W-2G to you if you receive:

1. $1,200 or more in gambling winnings from bingo or slot machines;
2. $1,500 or more in proceeds (the amount of winnings minus the amount of the wager) from keno;
3. More than $5,000 in winnings (reduced by the wager or buy-in) from a poker tournament;
4. $600 or more in gambling winnings (except winnings from bingo, keno, slot machines, and poker tournaments) and the payout is at least 300 times the amount of the wager; or
5. Any other gambling winnings subject to federal income tax withholding.

Generally, report all gambling winnings on the "Other income" line of Form 1040. You can deduct gambling losses as an itemized deduction, but you cannot deduct more than your winnings. Keep an accurate record of your winnings and losses, and be able to prove those amounts with receipts, tickets, statements, or similar items that you have saved. For additional information, see Pub. 529, Miscellaneous Deductions, and Pub. 525, Taxable and Nontaxable Income.

Box 2. Any federal income tax withheld on these winnings is shown in this box. Federal income tax must be withheld on certain winnings less the wager.

Certain winnings that are not subject to regular gambling withholding may be subject to backup withholding if you did not provide your federal identification number to the payer.

Include the amount shown in box 2 on your Form 1040 as federal income tax withheld. See Pub. 505, Tax Withholding and Estimated Tax, for additional information.

Signature. You must sign Form W-2G if you are the only person entitled to the winnings and the winnings are subject to regular gambling withholding. Return the signed form to the payer, who will give you your copies.

Other winners. Prepare Form 5754, Statement by Person(s) Receiving Gambling Winnings, if another person is entitled to any part of these winnings. Give Form 5754 to the payer, who will use Form 5754 to prepare Form W-2G for each person listed as a winner.

	a Employee's social security number	OMB No. 1545-0008	Safe, accurate, FAST! Use IRS e-file	Visit the IRS website at www.irs.gov/efile
b Employer identification number (EIN)			1 Wages, tips, other compensation	2 Federal income tax withheld
c Employer's name, address, and ZIP code			3 Social security wages	4 Social security tax withheld
			5 Medicare wages and tips	6 Medicare tax withheld
			7 Social security tips	8 Allocated tips
d Control number			9	10 Dependent care benefits
e Employee's first name and initial	Last name	Suff.	11 Nonqualified plans	12a See instructions for box 12 Code
			13 Statutory employee ☐ Retirement plan ☐ Third-party sick pay ☐	12b Code
			14 Other	12c Code
				12d Code
f Employee's address and ZIP code				

15 State	Employer's state ID number	16 State wages, tips, etc.	17 State income tax	18 Local wages, tips, etc.	19 Local income tax	20 Locality name

Form **W-2** **Wage and Tax Statement** **2011**

Department of the Treasury—Internal Revenue Service

Copy B—To Be Filed With Employee's FEDERAL Tax Return.
This information is being furnished to the Internal Revenue Service.

Instructions for Employee (Also see *Notice to Employee,* on the back of Copy B.)

Box 1. Enter this amount on the wages line of your tax return.

Box 2. Enter this amount on the federal income tax withheld line of your tax return.

Box 8. This amount is **not** included in boxes 1, 3, 5, or 7. For information on how to report tips on your tax return, see your Form 1040 instructions.

Unless you have records that show you did not receive the amount reported in box 8 as allocated tips, you must file Form 4137, Social Security and Medicare Tax on Unreported Tip Income, with your income tax return to report the allocated tip amount. On Form 4137 you will figure the social security and Medicare tax owed on the allocated tips shown on your Form(s) W-2 that you must report as income and on other tips you did not report to your employer. By filing Form 4137, your social security tips will be credited to your social security record (used to figure your benefits).

Box 10. This amount is the total dependent care benefits that your employer paid to you or incurred on your behalf (including amounts from a section 125 (cafeteria) plan). Any amount over $5,000 is also included in box 1. Complete Form 2441, Child and Dependent Care Expenses, to compute any taxable and nontaxable amounts.

Box 11. This amount is (a) reported in box 1 if it is a distribution made to you from a nonqualified deferred compensation or nongovernmental section 457(b) plan or (b) included in box 3 and/or 5 if it is a prior year deferral under a nonqualified or section 457(b) plan that became taxable for social security and Medicare taxes this year because there is no longer a substantial risk of forfeiture of your right to the deferred amount.

Box 12. The following list explains the codes shown in box 12. You may need this information to complete your tax return. Elective deferrals (codes D, E, F, and S) and designated Roth contributions (codes AA, BB, and EE) under all plans are generally limited to a total of $16,500 ($11,500 if you only have SIMPLE plans; $19,500 for section 403(b) plans if you qualify for the 15-year rule explained in Pub. 571). Deferrals under code G are limited to $16,500. Deferrals under code H are limited to $7,000.

However, if you were at least age 50 in 2011, your employer may have allowed an additional deferral of up to $5,500 ($2,500 for section 401(k)(11) and 408(p) SIMPLE plans). This additional deferral amount is not subject to the overall limit on elective deferrals. For code G, the limit on elective deferrals may be higher for the last 3 years before you reach retirement age. Contact your plan administrator for more information. Amounts in excess of the overall elective deferral limit must be included in income. See the "Wages, Salaries, Tips, etc." line instructions for Form 1040.

Note. If a year follows code D through H, S, Y, AA, BB, or EE, you made a make-up pension contribution for a prior year(s) when you were in military service. To figure whether you made excess deferrals, consider these amounts for the year shown, not the current year. If no year is shown, the contributions are for the current year.

A—Uncollected social security or RRTA tax on tips. Include this tax on Form 1040. See "Total Tax" in the Form 1040 instructions.

B—Uncollected Medicare tax on tips. Include this tax on Form 1040. See "Total Tax" in the Form 1040 instructions.

C—Taxable cost of group-term life insurance over $50,000 (included in boxes 1, 3 (up to social security wage base), and 5)

D—Elective deferrals to a section 401(k) cash or deferred arrangement. Also includes deferrals under a SIMPLE retirement account that is part of a section 401(k) arrangement.

E—Elective deferrals under a section 403(b) salary reduction agreement

(continued on back of Copy 2)

Instructions for Employee *(continued from back of Copy C)*

F—Elective deferrals under a section 408(k)(6) salary reduction SEP

G—Elective deferrals and employer contributions (including nonelective deferrals) to a section 457(b) deferred compensation plan

H—Elective deferrals to a section 501(c)(18)(D) tax-exempt organization plan. See "Adjusted Gross Income" in the Form 1040 instructions for how to deduct.

J—Nontaxable sick pay (information only, not included in boxes 1, 3, or 5)

K—20% excise tax on excess golden parachute payments. See "Total Tax" in the Form 1040 instructions.

L—Substantiated employee business expense reimbursements (nontaxable)

M—Uncollected social security or RRTA tax on taxable cost of group-term life insurance over $50,000 (former employees only). See "Total Tax" in the Form 1040 instructions.

N—Uncollected Medicare tax on taxable cost of group-term life insurance over $50,000 (former employees only). See "Total Tax" in the Form 1040 instructions.

P—Excludable moving expense reimbursements paid directly to employee (not included in boxes 1, 3, or 5)

Q—Nontaxable combat pay. See the instructions for Form 1040 or Form 1040A for details on reporting this amount.

R—Employer contributions to your Archer MSA. Report on Form 8853, Archer MSAs and Long-Term Care Insurance Contracts.

S—Employee salary reduction contributions under a section 408(p) SIMPLE (not included in box 1)

T—Adoption benefits (not included in box 1). Complete Form 8839, Qualified Adoption Expenses, to compute any taxable and nontaxable amounts.

V—Income from exercise of nonstatutory stock option(s) (included in boxes 1, 3 (up to social security wage base), and 5). See Pub. 525 and instructions for Schedule D (Form 1040) for reporting requirements.

W—Employer contributions (including amounts the employee elected to contribute using a section 125 (cafeteria) plan) to your health savings account. Report on Form 8889, Health Savings Accounts (HSAs).

Y—Deferrals under a section 409A nonqualified deferred compensation plan

Z—Income under section 409A on a nonqualified deferred compensation plan. This amount is also included in box 1. It is subject to an additional 20% tax plus interest. See "Total Tax" in the Form 1040 instructions.

AA—Designated Roth contributions under a section 401(k) plan

BB—Designated Roth contributions under a section 403(b) plan

DD—Cost of employer-sponsored health coverage. **The amount reported with Code DD is not taxable.**

EE—Designated Roth contributions under a governmental section 457(b) plan. This amount does not apply to contributions under a tax-exempt organization section 457(b) plan.

Box 13. If the "Retirement plan" box is checked, special limits may apply to the amount of traditional IRA contributions you may deduct.

Note. Keep **Copy C** of Form W-2 for at least 3 years after the due date for filing your income tax return. However, to help **protect your social security benefits,** keep Copy C until you begin receiving social security benefits, just in case there is a question about your work record and/or earnings in a particular year. Compare the Social Security wages and the Medicare wages to the information shown on your annual (for workers over 25) Social Security Statement.

CPSIA information can be obtained at www.ICGtesting.com
Printed in the USA
LVOW031052220412

278546LV00004B/2/P

9 780983 279457